The Alliance of Iron and Wheat
in the Third French Republic, 1860–1914

Augustin Pouyer-Quertier, with symbols of industry and agriculture.
From a statue in Rouen.

HERMAN LEBOVICS

The Alliance
of Iron and Wheat
in the Third French Republic
1860–1914

Origins of the New Conservatism

Louisiana State University Press
Baton Rouge and London

Designer: Laura Roubique Gleason
Typeface: Palatino
Typesetter: The Composing Room of Michigan, Inc.
Printer: Thomson-Shore, Inc.
Binder: John H. Dekker & Sons, Inc.

10 9 8 7 6 5 4 3 2 1

Louisiana State University Press gratefully acknowledges support for publication of this book which has been provided by the History Department and the Division of Social and Behavioral Sciences of the State University of New York at Stony Brook.

LIBRARY OF CONGRESS CATALOGING-IN-PUBLICATION DATA

Lebovics, Herman.
  The alliance of iron and wheat in the Third French
Republic, 1860–1914.

Bibliography: p.
  Includes index.
  1. France—Economic policy.   2. France—Social policy.
3. France—Politics and government—1870–1940.
4. France—Politics and government—1852–1870.
5. France—History—Third Republic, 1870–1940.
6. Conservatism—France—History.   I. Title.
HC276.L354 1988   338.944   87-21386
ISBN 0-8071-3150-6

For Aldona

Contents

Acknowledgments

In the course of writing this book I have benefited greatly from the encouragement and advice of friends and colleagues. I wish to thank all of them for their friendly and improving criticism, while freeing each of them from responsibility for the ideas and arguments that follow. Special thanks go to Richard Kuisel, Konrad Bieber, Clara Lida, Judith Wishnia, Barbara Weinstein, Arno Mayer, Philip Nord, Bernard Scholl, Nicholas Papayanis, Sanford Elwitt, and Brigitte Howard.

I also owe a debt to the helpful people at the Frank Melville, Jr., Memorial Library at the State University of New York at Stony Brook, as well as the staffs of the Bibliothèque Nationale and the Archives Nationales in Paris and the Internationaal Instituut voor Sociale Geschiedenis in Amsterdam. I wish to thank both Joel Rosenthal and Egon Neuberger for their generous support of this study. Thanks also to Homer Neal, Jr., for plotting the graphs, to Barbara Beresford for her good will and accuracy in the course of typing the manuscript, and Lucie Quirk for helping me get it on diskettes.

Finally, I wish to express my gratitude to my wife Aldona for her encouragement, support, loyalty, and good will in the course of my writing of this book.

The Alliance of Iron and Wheat
in the Third French Republic, 1860–1914

Preface

In the two decades after 1950, with the beginnings of France's revolution of modern development, an epoch of French history came to a close. At midcentury French business leaders, moderate politicians, and key civil servants began to steer France out of a century-old tradition of socially conservative economic policy—what in France was known as Malthusianism—and into the mainstream of international capitalist development. As it has unfolded in the last decades, the venture has had impressively stabilizing consequences for French society, chief of which has been the destruction of any remaining hope that an industrial working class would free France from capitalism by revolutionary means.

Now that the era that began with the Paris Commune and ended with the explosion of discontent of peasants and the independent middle class in the 1950s has drawn to a close, we are in a position to look back upon it and to judge its achievements, as well as what was prevented from happening. Contemporary governments must, willy nilly, gamble on achieving social peace and stability by means of holding out the possibility of more for all in society. But what can political leaders *in extremis* do when, as in the case of the Opportunist republicans who led France in the last decades of the nineteenth century, economic growth might be destabilizing and, at the moment, elusive? The new leaders of the Third Republic initiated a policy of securing social peace by means of isolating and limiting the growth of the dangerous classes, which they identified as industrial workers and radicalized peasants, while they benefited the conservative classes of protectionist industrialists and growers. Later, Radical politicians would add artisans, small shopkeepers, and members of the liberal professions to the socially conservative alliance. "One could re-analyze the vast majority of state interventions [beginning with the period of the Opportunist republican ascendancy]

1

as a consequence of this initial decision," Simon Nora, onetime head of the Ecole Nationale d'Administration, has written. However, as Nora also points out, the reasoning informing the praxis was never verbalized.[1]

It would make the historian's task much easier if changes in a society's organization of public authority and the new principles that underpin that authority always arrived heralded in the manifestos and rhetorical flourishes of intellectuals. That would make this investigation into the origins of a new French conservatism in the last decades of the nineteenth century much simpler. However, the literary articulation of a formal ideology by intellectuals is not necessarily the litmus test for the emergence of a new approach to public order.[2] Rather, we should look to the efforts of social groups to shore up, or reconstitute, sheltering institutions and practices and at the efforts of their organic intellectuals—to use Antonio Gramsci's apt words—to render articulate the values implicit in the measures taken.[3] A study of the stabilization of the Third Republic merits this approach.

In the 1890s France acquired a new conservative order that successfully countered pressures from the agents of social disharmony until at least the mid-1930s. The main ideological texts of this new conservatism were writings Jules Méline published in the years after the fall of his ministry and the end of his career in the Chamber of Deputies. In the preface to Francis Laur's book on monopolies, *Monopoly: Cartels and Industrial Pools in Germany* (1903), and in his *Return*

---

1. Simon Nora, "Servir l'État. Entretien avec Marcel Gauchet," *Le Débat*, XL (1986), 91.

2. See most recently the excellent historiographical discussion that affirms this point in Geoff Eley, "What Produces Fascism: Preindustrial Traditions or a Crisis of the Capitalist State," *Politics and Society*, XII (1983), 53–82, especially 75–76.

3. On our tendency to inflate the ideological content of conservative movements at the expense of institutional analyses of what they sought to protect, see Hans-Gerd Schumann, "The Problem of Conservatism: Some Notes on Methodology," *Journal of Contemporary History*, XIII (1978), 803–17, and Shearer Davis Bowman, "Antebellum Planters and *Vormärz* Junkers in Comparative Perspective," *American Historical Review*, LXXXV (1980), 779–808. On the gap between language and the social as deepened in the analyses of structuralism and poststructuralism see the critique by Perry Anderson, *In the Track of Historical Materialism* (Chicago, 1984), 32–55. Also insightful in this context is Dominick LaCapra's distinction between a "work" and a "document," in his "Rethinking Intellectual History and Reading Texts," in Dominick LaCapra and Steven Kaplan (eds.), *Modern European Intellectual History: Reappraisals and New Perspectives* (Ithaca, N.Y., 1982), 47–85.

to the Land (1905), Méline wrote of reversing the flight of people from the land and championed the peasant syndicates (the collaboration to foil the forces of the market place) as models for French industrial cartels and syndicates. He was understandably silent, however, on the manner of, and on his role in, mediating the social coalition of the new republican conservatism.[4] We will learn more of his activities in coalition-building in the course of this study. Whether intellectuals are present or not at the birth, however, new conservatisms are born when hitherto distant or even antagonistic members of social elites of breeding, education, or wealth must negotiate a new sociopolitical coalition for ruling society in the face of felt challenges to the social peace that protects them all.

René Rémond's influential study of the history of French conservatism, *La Droite en France*, discusses three historic streams of French conservative thought and loyalties. The first took its doctrines from the *Ultras* of the Restoration. It held sway on the French Right until 1830. Its proponents were counterrevolutionary, landed, and Legitimist. However, the king had to be Bourbon, and God, or at least the Church, had to bless his authority. What was once an unsystematized tradition was now articulated into a philosophy. After 1830 a second variety of conservatism, Orleanist in loyalty, came to the fore. Orleanists could accept both constitutional monarchy and market capitalism. More worldly and flexible than the *Ultra* soldiers and country squires, they could work with liberal bourgeois in government; their names often appear in the annals of French finance. The third tradition on the Right articulated various elements of belief into a framework of nationalism. The first important example of this kind, Rémond suggests, was the Bonapartism of Napoleon III.[5]

Rémond weaves his history of the varieties of the French Right around these three archetypes. Although Rémond is too good a historian to use the models in a reductionist fashion, they nevertheless prevent him from focusing upon the birth of a republican conservatism in the years of the Great Depression. For after undertak-

4. Jules Méline, Preface to Francis Laur, *L'Accaparement: les cartels et syndicats en Allemagne* (2nd ed.; 2 vols.; Paris, 1903), II ; Méline, *Retour à la terre* (Paris, 1905).

5. René Rémond, *La Droite en France* (Paris, 1954). The most recent edition, the fourth, is entitled *Les Droites en France* (Paris, 1982). The English translation, *The Right Wing in France from 1815 to de Gaulle*, trans. by James M. Laux (Philadelphia, 1969) is based on the third French edition. The changes from edition to edition are primarily updates in the sections on contemporary conservative trends.

3

ing a chronological treatment for the years from 1815 to 1879, his account jumps to 1899. He presents no sustained analysis of the shaping of the conservative republic in the 1880s and early 1890s. Wedded to his three streams of the Right, and perhaps overly impressed with the importance of the tiny Paris-based *ligues* of far-Right nationalist intellectuals, Rémond fails to perceive the emergence of a more solid, if less sensationalist, republican conservatism. The new republican conservatism that took shape in those years, or more precisely, the conservative coalition that formed to fight off the economic and social dangers of depression, foreign competition, and threatening upheaval, is the subject of this study.

A second related theme that I shall develop is that of the second founding of the Republic in the course of the late 1880s and 1890s. In 1875 republicans hurriedly formulated laws to serve as the constitutional basis for a republic that owed its existence more to the failure of the monarchists to consolidate their power than to republican stratagems. In the 1870s and early 1880s Léon Gambetta dominated the republican party, working to forge the provincial middle and upper bourgeoisie into a ruling stratum and to win the peasants to his Republic. Yet the republican victory remained precarious. At the end of the 1880s the new order was turned against itself by the supporters of General Georges Boulanger, who shamelessly manipulated the general's candidacy for multiple seats in the Chamber of Deputies from all over the country and nearly discredited the still fragile parliamentary system. The intensification of the economic depression provided both the need and the opportunity for the final establishment of a neoconservative hegemony.

Although we cannot find the manifestations of this newly ascendant coalition—the new practices, the new affinities, the new spirit—in manifestos or theoretical tracts, we can bring to light the values and identify the interests of republican conservatism embedded in the testimony of representatives of industry before parliamentary commissions of inquiry, in passages in addresses at businessmen's meetings, in speeches made at meetings of growers, and even in the debates and orations pronounced in the Chamber of Deputies and the Senate. We will examine the response to certain pressing questions touching upon the welfare of mineowners, iron manufacturers, cotton millowners, sugar refiners, and great landowners. What caused the current depression of prices and sales that wheat growers and industrialists suffered? What produced economic downturns? What was the best means of self-protection against depression? What might be done to pacify the growing numbers of industrial workers who struck, or supported syndicalist organizations, or voted for socialist candidates for municipal and parliamentary seats? How could the rural exodus be stemmed, and what would be its consequences if not halted? What benefits might derive from the colonial empire? Could the Bank of France or any bank aid business or agriculture to recover from the depression? Conversely, of what value was the conservative republic to the enterprise of the bankers? The answers that industrialists and growers gave to these questions in speeches and in policies reveal the shape of the new conservatism.

A third and last inquiry will focus on the social functions of French commercial policy. In the report of the parliamentary committee especially created to frame a proposal for an omnibus tariff for France in 1891 (a report released at the peak of the uproar over the Fourmies Massacre, the greatest industrial bloodletting of the Third Republic), the chairman, republican deputy Jules Méline, offered his sociopolitical assessment of the importance of the new duties he and his committee were proposing to the Chamber of Deputies. He wrote,

> What we have to defend by means of the tariffs is labor, that is, the jobs and the bread of our workers. Our industrialists have cut their operating costs to the bone. Only the compression [*sic*] of the work force remains: upon its shoulders would fall fatally the inadequacies of our new economic regime. It cannot enter anyone's head further to reduce the pay of our workers, which in certain branches of production is already manifestly inadequate. On the contrary, we have to bend all our efforts to raising wages. To do this, we have to maintain the prices of our products at a profitable level by thwarting the excessive inroads of foreign competition. That is how customs duties are linked to the social question itself in its most acute form.[6]

But what is the evidence for these connections, and what theoretical guides make sense of the evidence? Rather than analyzing grand philosophical doctrines like Léon Bourgeois' *Solidarité* (the concrete influence of which was at best uncertain), we will piece

6. Jules Méline, "Rapport général fait au nom de la commission des douanes," May 12–13, 1891. I have followed, with some modification, the translation of David Thomson (ed.), *France: Empire and Republic, 1850–1940* (New York, 1968), 150–51.

together from the utterances of growers, business leaders, and their spokesmen a pattern of questions and solutions to pressing economic and social problems weighing on the early Third Republic. We shall deal here with practical men, who, as the American saying goes, had to meet a payroll. With them we will have to follow the international prices of cotton thread, pig-iron ingots, and bushels of wheat. We will see them trying to keep their enterprises afloat during hard times while attempting to appease or co-opt their restive workers. We will observe the aristocrats of the Société des Agriculteurs de France agonizing over the sinking value of their land, the decline of their land rents, their shrinking labor force, and the erosion of their influence in the countryside. At the same time, we will observe their nonaristocratic confreres among the republicans trying to restore rural solvency, credit, and stability. Finally, in the absence of any great rallying point—dynastic or constitutional—we will observe these men of order drawn from all camps cement a basis for common action in the 1890s around the needs for tariff protection.

I wish to renew a fruitful tradition of analysis promoted by the German economist of the years of the Weimar Republic, Rudolf Goldscheid, who sought to understand the interplay of state fiscal and budgetary policy with the array of class power in the society. He labeled his work social economics (*Sozialökonomik*).[7] Here we are mainly interested in state commercial policy, in particular, the so-

7. See Goldscheid's *Steuerwendung und Interessenpolitik* (Munich, 1928); *Staatssozialismus oder Staatskapitalismus: Ein finanzsoziologischer Beitrag zur Lösung des Staatsschuldenproblems* (Vienna, 1917); and *Staat, öffentlicher Haushalt und Gesellschaft: Wesen und Aufgaben der Finanzwirtschaft vom Standpunkt der Soziologie* (Tübingen, 1926). Goldscheid was especially interested in the role of war and of military budgets in determining the total pattern of state income and expenditure, and the social implications of that process. He influenced an early work of Joseph Schumpeter; *Die Krise des Steuerstaats* (Leipzig, 1918). Peter Christian Witt, *Das Finanzpolitik des Deutschen Reiches von 1903 bis 1913* (Lübeck, 1970), especially 63–74 on the German tariff of 1902, represents the modern tradition in Germany. In the United States, James O'Connor has been one of the most creative practitioners of *Sozialökonomik*. His *The Fiscal Crisis of the State* (New York, 1973) analyzes how the social peace-keeping functions of the state— the police, welfare, aid to the unemployed, and social security measures—have created an intolerable fiscal burden on private investment. See also his *Accumulation Crisis* (New York, 1984). Although the foci of these works are primarily on state fiscal policy, their approaches and insights have helped me focus my own analyses of the social and political uses of the commercial policy of the Third Republic.

ciopolitical implications of tariffs. Like Goldscheid, I seek to treat no group—not even the most blatantly self-seeking ones—in isolation from the strata with which it conflicts and/or cooperates to make history. Even measures as technical and, alas, sometimes as dry as French tariffs have a social history. In the Third Republic, for example, they served as poles of accumulation of political power.

Although I will have much to say about the concerns of the workers, I am not writing working-class history. Nor is this a history of the French countryside. Least of all is my concern business history. These three currents of investigation—especially in the momentarily anthropological garbs of the first two and the managerial emphasis of the last—present their subjects in a one-sided fashion.

In what follows I wish to offer a history that communicates both a sense of the complex connectedness and conflicts of a multiclass society within the larger European order. This study will be a constitutional history, therefore, in the broadest and most classical sense: it will ask how and why the Third Republic was refounded as a conservative state at a time of the founding of other new conservative polities in Europe.

This reconsideration of the early history of the Third Republic will seek not so much to refute the brilliant analysis of Third Republic France as a stalemated society offered by Stanley Hoffmann some twenty years ago as to transcend it. Doubtless, as Michel Crozier argued in support of Hoffmann, there arose in late-nineteenth-century France a *société bloquée*; certainly, as both men agreed, the working class was frozen out of public life.[8]

However, this study will trace the origins of French *immobilisme* not to the cumulative effects of *positions acquises*, as Hoffmann believed, nor to bureaucratic rigidities, as Crozier viewed it, but rather to the consequences of the deliberate efforts of Opportunist republicans and former monarchists to craft a conservative coalition to defend rank, wealth, and aristocratic family heritage at a major turning point in the history of the society. For what made that conjuncture so fraught with danger for those who possessed and those who would lead was the simultaneous convergence of two threats to their power. The first arose from the long-term depression that,

8. Stanley Hoffmann, "Paradoxes of the French Political Community," in Hoffmann, *et al.* (eds.), *In Search of France* (New York, 1963), 1–117; Michel Crozier, *La Société bloquée* (Paris, 1970).

having darkened economic life throughout the 1880s, worsened at the start of the new decade, compounding the stresses caused by already sinking profits and ruinous foreign competition. The second, which contemporaries dubbed euphemistically the social question, emerged in its modern form of organized and militant industrial workers pressing for immediate economic demands and long-term social transformations that their depression-struck employers could not meet. The new industrial working class of the provinces was not numerous, but it was powerful enough in textiles, metalworking, and mining to make employers dread its growing militancy and seek remedies against it. A corollary of worker awakening in the depression years was the continuing flight from the land and the rekindling of peasant radicalism in the southern and central parts of the country.

The Hoffmann-Crozier thesis tells us nothing of the role of either depression or socioeconomic pressure from below in the formation of the republican order. It defines political power in France negatively, as that which remains of state authority after interest groups have staked their claims, rather than as the possession of a newly formed bloc dedicated to creating a conservative republic. Finally, it tends to depict France and the maladies of French society in the late nineteenth century as unique, eschewing a comparative perspective. Neither depression nor an awakening working class and peasantry were unique to late-nineteenth-century France. Nor was neoconservative coalition building needed only in France; *trasformismo* in Italy and *Sammlungspolitik* in Germany represented parallel efforts to rule new states in new ways.

The republican conservatives built so well, indeed, that the levers of government could be left in the hands of the petite bourgeoisie. For when around the turn of the century they had completed their work of framing out the conservative edifice, the Opportunist architects and their allies among the agricultural notables passed on the governance of the Republic to others. The initial ruling coalition crafted in the late 1880s and early 1890s dissolved, its work accomplished and its ideological contents transfused into the greater society. But they left structures of social order and structures of mind that ensured that Radical politicians would perpetrate no mischief upon the social hierarchy or the economic constitution, however self-indulgently they harassed the Church. The moment of the Dreyfus affair marked the passing of government authority to the

Radicals, but it did not seriously injure the newly created republican conservatism.[9] That would remain standing for decades to come.

In reassessing the origins of republican conservatism in the early decades of the Third Republic, I wish to direct scholarly attention more toward questions of long-term social power than have the plethora of works on authors of the radical Right and groupuscules of the Third Republic. The social order that new republican conservatives projected triumphed and endured, however short-lived were the party coalitions of the 1890s. Except for a brief moment under German tutelage, the far Right had no role in the constitution or governing of French society.

In French politics following World War II, the leaders of the radical Right have played the role of channelizing the *ressentiments* of social groups who viewed themselves as vulnerable or betrayed, as in the case of Poujadism and the current Le Pen phenomenon. Like the malaria that lives in the bodies of tropical populations in non-epidemic forms, strains of fascism will continue to be present in western societies such as France. But the radical Right will multiply to critical strength only when the health of moderate conservatism begins to fail and a Left can present itself as a serious alternative. It does not appear that such a crisis of conservatism is occurring in contemporary France. The special purgatory reserved for historians seeking to understand the exercise of great social and political power lies not in puzzling out the often pedestrian semiology of that power as it is manifested in everyday life, nor in having to research the development of marginal if often flamboyantly led groups of Right radicals, but in having to study the ideas of those cautious bureaucrats, prosaic businessmen, and posturing politicians who make up the collective brain of the modern established Right.

---

9. As the perspicacious Antonio Gramsci put it with more lucidity than translated literary elegance, "Elements of the dominant social bloc itself thwarted the Caesarism of the most reactionary part of the same bloc" (*Selections from the Prison Notebooks*, ed. and trans. Quinton Hoare and Geoffrey Nowell Smith (New York, 1971), 223). The distinction between ruling power and governing authority I owe to Nicos Poulantzas, *Political Power and Social Classes* (London, 1978), 173–80. His works obliged me to think or to rethink analyses of much that I had taken for gospel or for granted. I regret his loss greatly.

Introduction

Unfinished Business

On Saturday, March 16, 1867, at the start of the lunch hour, hundreds of factory hands left their workplaces to rampage through the streets of Roubaix. These were not angry artisans attacking rival methods of fabrication; they were mill workers attacking particularly hated employers. Groups of workers entered the mills and smashed looms, cut drive belts, and shredded woven cloth. The family-owned textile firms of Grimonprez, Henri Roussel, Delattre, Dillies, Desrousseaux, François Roussel, and P. Scamp suffered attacks. The demonstrators set fire to the factories of Henri Roussel and Desrousseaux. Mobs of angry workers damaged Delattre's residence, and forcing entry into Scamp's great house, they wrecked it. Such was the response in one town to the attempts of employers to make the textile workers pay for the current commercial depression by ordering them to work two looms simultaneously—a radical increase in work—and by stiffening the fines for tardiness and faulty work. Labor peace was only restored under the surveillance of the troops that, on the advice of the chief of police, the prefect had summoned that evening. After desultory negotiations and further sporadic walkouts, the majority of workers returned to their looms six days later defeated and, for the moment, tamed.[1]

The shaken industrialists impaneled a committee to investigate the causes of the labor riot. Chaired by the distinguished textile

---

1. Claude Fohlen, "Crise textile et troubles sociaux: le Nord à la fin du Second Empire," *Revue du Nord*, XXXV (April-June, 1953), 116–123. See the account of this same Saturday's events in William M. Reddy, *The Rise of Market Culture: The French Textile Trade and French Society, 1750–1900* (Cambridge, England, 1984), 248–50. Reddy offers this as a case study in his reinterpretation of French labor radicalism as a nonaccommodation, indeed rejection, of the "rules of the market game" (p. 252).

manufacturer Louis Motte-Bossuet, the committee presented the industrialists' understanding of the deeper causes behind the events of March 16. To justify the speedups that had touched off the labor explosion they blamed the great pressures that foreign competition had brought upon them. Ironically, they also complained about the extra financial burden they had to bear because of the "costly installation of the garrison as a consequence of the troubles." [2] *Le Propagateur du Nord*, voice of the industrialists of the region, echoed the conclusions of the report by blaming the current commercial crisis and the workings of free trade for the labor troubles in Roubaix. [3]

The Roubaix riot was just the beginning of a wave of strikes and labor actions. During that same March the cloth dyers of Amiens walked off their workplaces in a dispute over pay and the length of the pieces they had to dye. In 1868 laborers in workshops and factories in Alsace, Cambrai, Vienne (the weavers in April, the key spinners in December) struck against the textile manufacturers. These strikes exacerbated the difficult situation of the manufacturers, who were already deeply wounded by the depression in sales and the great swings in prices. [4] The explosion of strikes in the Nord, Normandy, and even hitherto conservative Alsace—leading at times to troops shooting demonstrating strikers, as in la Ricamerie and Aubin—continued until the outbreak of the war with Prussia in July, 1870. [5]

But a pattern of cooperation between owners and workers against the imperial government and its free trade policies also obtained. The industrial centers of the Nord and Normandy were paradigmatic in this respect, too. When in 1868 Napoleon III toured the depression-struck Nord, he had been greeted by delegations of workers petitioning him to abandon the policy of commercial free

2. See the committee's report on what it termed "the riot of March 16" in Motte-Bossut, *et al.*, *Rapport sur l'émeute du 16 mars 1867 à Roubaix à M. Masson, Préfet du Nord à Lille* (N.p., n.d.).

3. Claude Fohlen, *L'Industrie textile au temps du Second Empire* (Paris, 1965), 415. Fohlen dismisses this explanation as hypocrisy or at least obtuseness. For the next three decades, however, the industrialists blamed their problems with labor on the pressures from foreign competition and pressured their workers for concessions to justify their position by pointing to the special problems posed by foreign competition.

4. *Ibid.*, 417.

5. See the excellent short study by Fernand L'Huillier, *La Lutte ouvrière à la fin du Second Empire* (Paris, 1957).

11

trade initiated in 1860 by the trade treaty with Britain, and confirmed and extended in similar treaties with other nations. In the fall of 1869 he sent his secretary-general of the Ministry of Industry and Commerce, Jules Ozenne, to gather more data on the distress in the Nord. The emperor's representative was ushered into great meetings and rallies of both employers and workers organized around calls for the repudiation of the policy of free trade.

On November 6, 4,000 workers gathered at the Halle aux Sucres in Lille to protest the current economic hardships. They elected Jules Brame, a cotton manufacturer and deputy from the Nord, their honorary president. On the ninth, 2,000 workmen and representatives of the owners of the textile mills of Lille, Roubaix, Tourcoing, and Cambrai gathered again in Lille to protest the recent conclusion of additional free trade treaties. The rioters of 1867 were making common cause with their employers two years deeper into the crisis. Why should they not, many workers reasoned. "All we want," a member of a workers' delegation announced to the prefect at the time of the Roubaix workers' riot, "is work."[6]

In Normandy, too, reduced orders had shaken owners of shipyards, foundries, railway construction shops, mechanical engineering firms, and cotton mills. Their employees were driven to defensive strikes as the owners tried by various means to transfer the losses resulting from the depression to their shoulders.[7] In October, 1869, the Rouennais cotton millowner who had served as minister of finance in 1871 and 1872 (and in that capacity had negotiated the financial terms of the peace with Prussia), Augustin Pouyer-Quertier, called together a number of industrialist friends—including several who claimed to be representing their workers as well as themselves—to form the Comité pour la Défense de l'Industrie Nationale. To communicate the concerns of the industries of Normandy, Pouyer-Quertier scheduled a meeting of the new organization with six of the deputies of the region. As the discussions held in Rouen began, on October 10, 1869, a deputation of textile workers arrived at the door to tender a petition they claimed bore names of nine thousand workers "demanding the repudiation of the treaties of commerce." They were ushered into the room. The assembled workers and owners then voted a common resolution endorsing the sentiments of the petition.[8]

6. Fohlen, *L'Industrie textile*, 414.
7. L'Huillier, *La Lutte ouvrière*, 56.
8. Fohlen, "Crise textile," 122; Fohlen, *L'Industrie textile*, 429–32.

The *Journal des économistes* in December, 1869, carried a short statement of the views of the organized workers of Rouen on the issue of free trade versus protection. It had been authored by Rouennais typographer Emile Aubry, known to many workers, owners, and police alike as a militant working-class radical and one of the most active representatives of the International in France. Here, signing himself secretary of the Circle of Economic Studies of the Arrondissement, he offered the liberal bourgeois readers of the paper an article titled "The Opinion of the Workers' Federation of the Arrondissement of Rouen about the Protests of the Industrialists of the District Against the Treaties of Commerce." Claiming to speak for 3,000 union members, Aubry repudiated the efforts of the industrialists to associate their workers in their complaints. "Experience has shown that workers' pay was no less menaced under the system of protective tariffs than under that called free trade," Aubry asserted. He concluded,

> The corporations of organized workers of the arrondissement of Rouen, declare that they shall leave it to the industrialists of the district to protest the risks and perils from the continuation of the treaties of commerce, knowing full well that these gentlemen would be the sole beneficiaries of their suppression; that on the contrary, the working classes, by lending their support to the re-erection of commercial barriers, would only help facilitate the establishment of new monopolies. Moreover, while actively pressing their own complaints, the industrialists have in no way demanded the eradication of the economic privileges which are leading our society towards a certain ruin.[9]

The ruin came, of course, neither from the pursuit of privileges on the part of industrialists nor from the waves of strikes that terminated only with the outbreak of the war with Prussia, but rather from the adventuristic foreign policy of Napoleon III. Yet, Aubry surely was right to fear the dangers of co-optation that the new protectionist movement posed for the nascent workers' movement.[10]

This confrontation in Rouen between the small band of industrialists that Pouyer-Quertier managed to assemble and the handful of industrial workers for whom Aubry spoke was to be a microcosm of the pattern of attraction and conflict, of class consciousness and class collaboration, of two new classes creating themselves in the

9. Emile Aubry, "Opinion de la Fédération ouvrière de l'arrondissement de Rouen sur la protestation des industriels de la circonscription contre le traité de commerce," *Journal des économistes*, 3rd ser., XVI (December, 1869), 476–78.

10. Fohlen, *L'Industrie textile*, 436; L'Huillier, *La Lutte ouvrière*.

process of confrontation, that lay at the heart of the social history of the new republic established in the train of defeat. In the conflict we may discern the awakening of an as yet ill-organized and ideologically naïve industrial working class; we may observe industrialists seeking at the same time to remain masters in their own house and to recruit their workers to their pressure-group politics. We shall later see industrialists grasping for tariff protection as a form of both commercial and social salvation.

It must be emphasized, however, that the troubles of the late Empire were only a microcosm of later events. For, in the late 1860s the cotton- and iron-producing industrialists were neither economically dominant nor politically influential. The visibility of financiers in the emperor's entourage and the conclusion of the free trade agreement with England in 1860 attest to that fact. As to the desires of the workers, modern industrial consciousness was only slowly pushing out artisanal, peasant, or simply passive or vengeful visions of the world.[11] In the confrontation in Rouen—and in the labor troubles between 1867 and 1869 in Alsace, Normandy, the Nord, and the Lyon region—we see a glimpse of that awareness of self and situation that guided workers of subsequent decades to support syndicalist and socialist movements.[12] But in the 1860s and 1870s

11. The industrial workers in the still relatively underdeveloped Loire Valley, even though they struck, were quite collaborative with their employers in protesting the government's commercial policy in 1869, which they believed injured themselves as well as the owners. The dedicated paternalism of the Protestant manufacturers of Mulhouse also earned them their workers' support when they organized protests against the commercial treaties. See Sanford Elwitt, "Politics and Social Class in the Loire: The Triumph of the Republican Order, 1869–1873," *French Historical Studies*, VI (1969), 96–98, 109.

12. Pierre Léon, "Les grèves de 1867–1870 dans le département de l'Isère," *Revue d'histoire moderne et contemporaine*, I (1954), 300. Robert P. Baker largely confirms Léon's judgment for that period in the Nord; he characterizes working class consciousness as relatively "backward" because of the large numbers of recently arrived rural migrants and, as yet, unintegrated Belgian workers in the labor force. See Robert P. Baker, "A Regional Study of Working-Class Organization in France: Socialism in the Nord, 1870–1924" (Ph.D. dissertation, Stanford University, 1967), 21. Although Aubry spoke for the feared International in Rouen and although its representatives were active in the strike movement of Alsace, the evidence is slim for its agitational successes in the late Empire's labor troubles (Fohlen, *L'Industrie textile*, 436), or indeed in the Paris Commune. But it is also a datum of historical consciousness that government officials and owners charged it with great influence at the time, banning it in France and harrying its members.

industrialists and workers were doubly in minority status. Within the society neither could yet claim significant social visibility, and within their respective classes, the industrialists were still not the most powerful stratum of the bourgeoisie, while the factory workers numbered very few in a still largely artisanal and overwhelmingly peasant laboring force.

The Beginnings of the Republic

If in some important respects the labor conflicts of the late Empire anticipated the important issues and struggles of the Third Republic, the eras differed in three ways: the Empire had never known the intensity and duration of depression, the degree and intensity of labor militancy, or the uncertainty of state power suffered by the France of the Third Republic. These were the peculiar discontents of republican modernity.

First, the depression of the years immediately preceding the Franco-Prussian War was neither as pervasive nor as persistent as the one that beset the economy in 1873, which held sway through alternating cycles of recession and recovery for two decades. In the late 1860s industrialists suffered sinking prices, but growers and bankers escaped relatively unscathed. The depression of 1873–1896 struck them all down.

Second, even though sales declined in the 1860s, the manufacturers' struggle with labor over who was to pay the costs of depression was less desperate than in subsequent decades of the century. Class-conscious workers like Aubry were few in number and rarely spoke for any large portion of the labor force. The emperor represented himself as a friend of the workers; indeed, he paid the way of the French delegation to the first meeting of the International in 1864.

Finally, as long as Napoleon III reigned—and France remained at peace with its neighbor Prussia—a powerful state stood guard over the peace of society. Not only did one hear workers' cries of "Vive l'Empereur!" during strike demonstrations, but despite deep economic and political differences with the imperial authorities, millowners knew that they could expect help from the army if a strike should become violent. Accordingly, although French industrialists were too weak to restore tariff barriers against the will of the emperor, they could always count on the police and judicial protection of the state.

The defeat in 1870 at the hands of the Prussians and the fall of Napoleon III suddenly left France without a government. The need to search for a principle of order was made all the more urgent by the descent of a Great Depression that struck both industry and agriculture soon after the defeat and by the slowly awakening militancy and growing organization among industrial workers. During the 1870s the French political scene was riven with conflict among Bonapartists, two varieties of monarchists, and, of course, republicans over what that order should be and who it was to benefit—or protect—the most.

The Third French Republic was born in a manner akin to those great shifts in the plates of the earth's surface that, after long periods of slowly increasing but hidden pressure, finally occur amid earthquakes and new upjuttings of land. The Franco-Prussian War and the Paris Commune shook the land; the Republic was extruded into existence. The creation of the Kingdom of Italy and the German Empire were contemporaneous. In each case war and power politics created new states. But none of these new political entities had a firm shape; they were still too new. In their first decades, each of the new societies—Italy, Germany, and republican France—had to weave those finely spun but powerful networks of influence, obligation, and cooperation between the great leaders of the economy and society and the new political order. Not to do so would have thwarted both orderly government and a necessary social peace. Each new state had to identify or establish the governing class, or coalition of classes, that would confer and maintain public order in the new polity.

The coalition building labors in the late 1870s and 1880s of Agostino Depretis, a republican-turned-monarchist, qualify him to be named as one of the founders of modern Italy. He created his new ruling coalition by means of *trasformismo*, the manipulation of social interests and of elections to guarantee the stability of the new state. Otto von Bismarck practiced *Sammlungspolitik*, the politics of conservative concentration in the new imperial Germany, but he did so on an *ad hoc* basis. His successors, Johannes Michels and Bernhard von Bülow, turned *Sammlungspolitik* into a conscious principle of government.[13]

---

13. Hans-Ulrich Wehler, *Das Deutsche Kaiserreich, 1871-1918* (Göttingen, 1973), is the leading spokesman for the group of historians who read late-nineteenth-century Ger-

France of the new republic had no great heroes on the order of a Bismarck or even unpopular men of vision like Depretis; it had only Adolphe Thiers. And although he mastered the immediate postwar crisis, he was seventy-four in 1871 and would die in 1877. At first the quarrels of the monarchists, and then the crankiness of the Comte de Chambord, the Bourbon pretender, darkened the hopes of a restoration. Bourgeois lawyers and industrialists, drawn largely from the provinces, found themselves leading a republican state in the late 1870s, the majority of male citizens of which a few years before had testified to their yearnings for peace by voting for monarchist parliamentary representatives. The Opportunist republicans, then, the party of Léon Gambetta, Jules Ferry, and Jules Méline, had to do the work of a Bismarck or a Depretis. They had to create the new conservative order so that social peace might reign, and to accomplish this they had to create a republican governing coalition.

The first founding of the Third Republic required nearly a decade of political struggle. In the successive political shifts of 1787, 1789, 1815, 1830, 1848, and 1850, nineteenth-century France had been layered over by the magma of past modes of existence. The military defeat and the abdication of the emperor during the war, followed by a major insurrection in the capital, put the political leadership of the state—indeed its very form—at issue. Confident that France would now understand the price of turning away from an order graced by God and the ages, and steadfast in loyalty to the Bourbon line, the party of Legitimist monarchists took heart. Orleanists, more attuned to the world of capitalism (or at least to the banking aspects of capitalism), wished to renew the political arrangements disrupted by the 1848 revolution. Their candidate for kingship, the

---

man history as a *Sonderweg*, that is, in terms of German exceptionalism resulting from late nationhood, the persistence of *Junker* authority in a highly organized capitalist society, and the continuity from Bismarck to Hitler. Geoff Eley and David Blackbourn have subjected the position of German uniqueness to strong criticism. Their longest and most systematic exposition is *The Peculiarities of German History: Bourgeois Society and Politics in Nineteenth Century Germany* (Oxford, 1984). Since Wehler is willing to concede that he overstated his case, and Eley and Blackbourn in the heat of the polemic have over-reached, it is likely that a vision of Imperial German history will emerge very much along the lines portrayed in the comparative sections of this study. On these often venomous polemics see James N. Retallack, "Social History with a Vengeance? Some Reactions to H.-U. Wehler's 'Das Deutsche Kaiserreich,'" *German Studies Review*, VII (1984), 423–50.

Comte de Paris, unlike Chambord, had male heirs. Their dream of a moderate, constitutional, and hereditary monarchy that had made its peace with the economic order of capitalism seemed possible to realize with the defeat of the upstart seed of the Corsican dynast. Yet even in defeat some Frenchmen—peasants for the greatest part—clung to the Napoleonic myth.[14]

The demise of the imperial system also heartened the republicans, of whom we may distinguish at least two generations. Both the red republicans, the survivors of 1848, and the new recruits to the vision of a social republic of 1871 suffered defeat, death, or deportation for their role in the Paris Commune. However, the 1848 heritage died with its second defeat in 1870. The more moderate republicans, who left insurrectionary Paris in 1871 and would soon accept the name "Opportunists," saw their hopes soar to the heavens in the course of the 1870s, much as the balloon of their leader Léon Gambetta had soared from the besieged city at the beginning of the decade.[15] If any political circle may be said to represent the new men of the provinces—professionals, men of commerce, and above all industrialists—it is that of the moderate republicans. The victory of a republicanism that made itself conservative enough to attract the support of economically powerful groups that were indifferent or even hostile to republican rule is our theme. Let us turn to the alignment of forces in 1870 and trace the first phase of republican success amidst the powerfully conflicting political currents set in motion in the years 1870 and 1871.

The defeat of the imperial armies of the last Napoleon discredited Bonapartist rule. But it revived the hopes of French monarchists. The elections for the National Assembly of February 8, 1871, seated 400 monarchists of a total of 645 elected representatives. Nearly half of the new representatives (250) possessed landed wealth. Division among the monarchists between the Legitimists, Orleanists, and even a group of loyal Bonapartists made conversion of the monar-

---

14. Daniel Halévy's two studies *La République des ducs* (Paris, 1937) and *La Fin des notables* (Paris, 1930) are still wonderful reading on the early days of the Republic. For the longer view see Guy Chapman, *The Third Republic of France: The First Phase, 1871–1894* (London, 1962), 188–203; and Pierre Barral, *Les Fondateurs de la Troisième République* (Paris, 1968). See also J. P. T. Bury, *Gambetta and the Making of the Third Republic* (London, 1973), 398–461; and Bury's *Gambetta's Final Years* (London, 1982), 285–315.

15. Bury, *Gambetta and the Making of the Third Republic*, 7–8.

chist sentiment of the nation into governing institutions frustrating for conservatives, as the monarchists were called. Then, too, their mandate was conditional: after the horrors of the war with Prussia and the shame of defeat and occupation, townspeople and peasants wanted peace. That is what the conservatives promised.

The names of Gambetta and his republican allies conjured up the fearful image in the minds of many war-weary Frenchmen of a military resistance to the Prussians fought to the bitter end.[16] While the provisional government ensconced in Versailles prepared for peace, Gambetta, having fled to the South, tried vainly to assemble battalions to march to the relief of Paris. Moreover, with that reductionist sensibility that takes hold in times of troubles, many *bien pensants* blamed the moderate republicans for the works of the red republicans in the Commune: had not Gambetta stayed in tainted Paris too long? Had not Jules Ferry, his collaborator, served briefly as mayor of the city and Jules Méline, their supporter, as a deputy mayor? Never mind that the future leaders of Opportunism—Gambetta, Ferry, Méline—had fled from the Paris of the Commune; many French voters wanting no more risks cast their ballots for peace and order by supporting monarchist candidates.

The by-elections of July, 1871, held after the dissolution of the Commune and the conclusion of peace, benefited the supporters of republicanism throughout France, with the exception of the ravaged city of Paris, where conservative candidates were returned in the majority. Of the 114 contested seats for representatives to the National Assembly, only 12 monarchists won places. More than 100 republicans were elected. If republicans could suppress red insurrection and conclude peace, the voters were not obliged to support monarchist candidates to bring these things to pass. However, even as late as 1875, when new constitutional laws making France a parliamentary republic passed the legislature, many Frenchmen continued to associate public order and social peace with the monarchist cause.

The laws of 1875 passed the Chamber of Deputies by only one vote, that of a monarchist newly converted to conservative republicanism. Contemporaries saw the laws as stopgaps. When the monarchist president, MacMahon, dismissed the premier Jules Si-

---

16. R. A. Winnacker, "The French Elections of 1871," *Papers of the Michigan Academy of Sciences, Arts, and Letters*, XXIII (1936), 473.

mon in May, 1877—despite Simon's support in the Chamber—he believed that he was simply preserving appropriate lines of authority for the eventual restoration of a king to an office for the moment called the "presidency of the Republic."

The ensuing crisis of the sixteenth of May, 1877, established the principle that the Prime Minister served at the pleasure of the Chamber of Deputies and not that of the (pro-monarchist) president. Despite this new republican victory, the political arrangements at the end of the 1870s cannot be unequivocally characterized as the Republic triumphant. Admittedly, a coalition of a portion of the grande bourgeoisie, the *nouvelles couches* (the provincial middle class), and a vast portion of the peasantry led by the republicans who followed the charismatic liberal Gambetta denied the disheartened and divided conservatives their hoped-for kingly rule for the moment. Yet, to thwart the monarchists was not to unite to lead France; the question of who ruled France was not thereby settled.[17]

The republicans aimed to make France republican, but not by means of social revolution. Almost immediately they purged the ranks of the prefects and subprefects of appointees from the old order, which—we must remember—were Bonapartist, not monarchist, in persuasion. That housecleaning in itself, therefore, did not weaken monarchist presence in government. In 1879 the Conseil d'Etat, the highest administrative court and an instrument of Napoleonic authoritarianism, was restaffed with republican personnel. In 1883 the tenure of magistrates was lifted briefly so that supporters of clerical privileges might be removed. The remaining judges and their new republican fellows regained the right of life tenure in office, dashing the hopes of some of the more radical republicans of introducing elected magistrates after the manner of the United States.

The army, the rest of the bureaucracy, the schools—the great sustaining public institutions of France—were left alone. The aristocrats of the officer corps, the members of the high state services including the diplomatic corps, and the priests and nuns who taught the children of France continued in their monarchist faith

17. Georges Dupeux, *Aspects de l'histoire sociale et politique du Loire-et-Cher, 1848–1914* (Paris, 1962), 460–89. Dupeux's characterization of the turn of the electoral tide between 1871 and 1877 away from the monarchy and to the republic in the Loire-et-Cher as signifying not a step forward but only a rejection of turning back applies to the rest of France as well.

unmolested. Although in the mid-1880s the reforming energies of Jules Ferry, Gambetta's rival and successor in the leadership of the republican forces, would bear fruit in the creation of the system of free, compulsory, lay education, the changes in outlook that this new system of education were to bring took generations to seep into public life.[18] The Church hierarchy not only remained loyal to the Bourbon dynasty, it worked actively to keep monarchism alive among the believers. And of course, a significant minority of both the Chamber of Deputies and the Senate nursed the hope of monarchical restoration. Thus as the century drew to a close, the stage was set for the conclusion of the understanding, which became an alliance, and finally for the rule of the Republic.

In the 1890s French agricultural notables and captains of both heavy and light industry, faced with the twin threats of deep decline in agricultural and industrial prices and profits, as well as growing dissatisfaction among the underclasses with a republic for the rich, concluded a historic alliance of iron, cotton, and wheat. Evidence of this union is embodied in the articles of the Méline tariff of 1892, in the Ralliement (the attempt by the Church to end its political isolation from republican life), in the movement to organize the peasants from above before they organized from below, in the consolidation of the colonial empire, and finally in the parliamentary support for the Méline government of 1896–1898. This study will examine this new ruling order, France's republican conservatism, from its emergence in the 1880s through its consolidation and institutionalization during the pivotal years in the history of the Republic, the 1890s.

Once industrialization has begun to shake the old institutions and the old verities of a nation, there arrives a moment in its economic and political development dangerous to social peace. Although old leaders of the state and society find it increasingly difficult to mobilize sufficient support to rule, they remain powerful enough to veto changes, because a new stratum has not yet sufficiently matured to lead with decision. In such moments the leverage of small groups of radicals to disturb the order of existing society is at its greatest. More importantly, when those contending for leadership of society are astute men, they are likely to perceive the challenges that radicalism poses at that moment. The late nineteenth

18. Eugen Weber, *Peasants into Frenchmen: The Modernization of Rural France, 1870–1914* (Stanford, 1976).

century marked that moment in the United States; for Prussia-Germany, the era coincided with the ascendancy of Bismarck. France reached such a juncture at approximately the same moment, during the latter years of the Great Depression of 1873–1896.[19]

The travail of transition to a more urban and more industrial society within a still-fragile political system requires a new sort of ruling class or coalition of classes. In newly made and depression-riven Germany, Prussian landowners and great industrialists concluded a historic governing alliance of iron and rye.[20] The coalition of the interests of iron, cotton textile, and wheat producers in republican France was less antidemocratic and certainly not as militaristic, but it was no less intent on gaining socioeconomic dominance and backing it with political power.[21] The Junkers dominated the alliance in imperial Germany by means of their overweening

19. Other than Barrington Moore, Jr., *Social Origins of Dictatorship and Democracy: Lord and Peasant in the Making of the Modern World* (Boston, 1966), especially 40–110, 413–32, the insightful analyses of Samuel P. Huntington, *Political Order in Changing Societies* (New Haven, 1968), esp. 93–98, 264–78, 344–62, have incited me to think about the question of social peace and state-founding as I have discussed it here. For my own preliminary thoughts on the *problématique* of social transformation, and the resistance thereto, see "The United States Suggests Land-Reform," *Cross Currents*, XXXIII (Spring, 1983), 52–60. James Livingston, "The Social Analysis of Economic History and Theory: Conjectures on Late Nineteenth-Century American Development," *American Historical Review*, XCII (1987), 74–75, 78–85, has placed the resistance of American workers to employer pressures for increased productivity at the center of the economic history of the United States in the years of the Great Depression. The problems were parallel; the American solution, marginalism in economic theory, was specific to the United States.

20. The great works on this alliance are Alexander Gerschenkron, *Bread and Democracy in Germany* (Rev. ed.; New York, 1966); Eckhart Kehr, *Der Primat der Innenpolitik: Gesammelte Aufsätze zur preussisch-deutschen Sozialgeschichte im 19. und 20. Jahrhundert*, ed. Hans-Ulrich Wehler (2nd ed.; Berlin, 1970); and Kehr, *Battleship Building and Party Politics in Germany, 1894–1901*, ed. and trans. P. R. and E. N. Anderson (Chicago, 1975).

21. On the puzzle of the French aristocracy—the social history of which we know little about for much of the nineteenth century—the comparative volume edited by David Spring, *European Landed Elites in the Nineteenth Century* (Baltimore, 1977) is a good place to begin. See in particular the essay on the French nobility by Theodore Zeldin, pp. 127–138. See also A. J. Tudesq, *Les Grands notables en France, 1840–49* (Paris, 1964); A. Girard, A. Prost, and R. Gossez, *Les Conseillers généraux en 1870* (Paris, 1967); Paul Bois, *Paysans de l'Ouest: Des structures économiques et sociales aux options politiques depuis l'époque révolutionnaire dans la Sarthe* (Le Mans, 1960); Suzanne Berger, *Peasants Against Politics: Rural Organization in Brittany, 1911–1967* (Cambridge, Mass., 1972).

power in Prussia, which had in turn overwhelming dominance in the *Kaiserreich*. The French upper class had few Junkers among them, although the gentry (called sometimes the *hobereaux*) of Brittany, for example, pretended to the role.[22] The French bourgeoisie set the tone of the alliance in France, but it was a bourgeoisie not completely at peace with the costs and conflicts of a modern industrial society.

We must beware of uncritically accepting the ideological pretensions of the upper classes of the two countries as they romanced their fellow citizens about their special mission or historic function: in both nations they operated as well as the market permitted as capitalist (even improving) farmers, investors, civil servants, parliamentary politicians, and, not infrequently, industrialists. These were people deeply enmeshed in the most modern activities of contemporary capitalism.

And yet we must not discount their own beliefs that in an important sense they were bearers of values from another, more noble era. In many ways, they acted on the self-serving belief that they were *in* the society and yet in significant ways not *of* it.[23] However they saw themselves, or were seen by their contemporaries, they took the extended hand of their bourgeois coalition partners when their own economic and social interests seemed to be threatened. Aristocrats and bourgeois together pressed for tariffs as a first line of defense of what both French and German protectionists were pleased to call "national production."

In the 1880s and 1892 the two chambers passed protective tariffs covering agricultural products (especially wheat, meats, and sugar beets) and industrial goods (especially cotton goods and iron). Manufacturers had pressed for tariff change since the days of the liberal

22. A. J. Tudesq, "Les survivances de l'ancien régime: la noblesse dans la société française de la première moitié du XIXe siècle," in D. Roche and C. E. Labrousse (eds.), *Ordres et classes: colloque d'histoire sociale* (St. Cloud, 1967), 199–214.

23. On this theme Hans Herzfeld, *Johannes von Miquel* (2 vols.; Detmold, 1938), is very much worth reading, as is the history of Bismarck's relations with his Jewish banker Bleichröder by Fritz Stern, *Gold and Iron* (New York, 1977). Gerschenkron, *Bread and Democracy*, and Ralf Dahrendorf, *Society and Democracy in Germany* (Garden City, N.Y., 1967), are two modern classics on the persistence of Junkers and of Junker attitudes respectively. Arno J. Mayer's *The Persistence of the Old Regime* (New York, 1981), marking a valuable reopening of the topics of national uniqueness in Europe and of the survival of the old order, should incite other researchers to pursue the topic.

empire of Napoleon III but had been unsuccessful in ending what for them was the unwelcomed competitive environment of free trade. The men who dominated the Republic after the defeat of the imperial regime offered them no relief. Only during the years after 1882, in the depths of depression and in response to the twin stimuli of the need to refound the Republic and to pacify a newly self-assertive working class in the provinces, did industrialists and their allies succeed in turning French commercial policy in a protectionist direction.

This study will argue that the new conservative alliance of industrialists and big agriculturalists, which imparted a legacy of social conservatism to the Third Republic, sprang from the tariff negotiations and the subsequent collaborations they made possible. This conservative alliance coalesced first in response to the economic dangers of long-term depression in the years 1880–1896. But their social goals were of equal importance. The conservatives closed ranks to resist the restiveness on the land and the growing militancy— expressed in strikes, riots, and new forms of organizations—of the protectionist industrialists' own workers. The Left pressured the state for reforms that, if implemented, would have interfered in the labor process. The republicans resisted this course of action. Social appeasement without structural reforms was the appeal of protectionism.

In France, the years 1890–1896 were a period of often deep economic depression that hurt industrialists and big growers, workers and peasants. Prices for domestically produced industrial and agricultural goods dropped to their lowest point in two decades of low prices. Industrialists tried to reduce costs, particularly their wage bills. The discontent of a new working class located largely in the provinces burst forth in strikes, militant May Day demonstrations, and new forms of organization. Rural strikes, previously unheard of, compounded landowners' anxieties about the ongoing exodus of the rural labor force. In the 1880s, parliament passed several tariff measures for protecting the prices of domestic grains, meats, and manufactured goods in an attempt to bring industrialists and farmers some relief. These did not suffice. To cope with the new economic and social troubles the two chambers passed the great general tariff of 1892, which became the keystone of French commercial and social policy and which bore the name of the dominant parliamentary figure of the decade, Jules Méline. At the same time, for the sake of the newly endangered social peace, Catholic conservatives muted their hostility to the secular Republic by embracing the movement called the Ralliement. Also, the colonial empire, in addition to being an effective crutch to the faltering industrial economy, appeared to many Catholic and secular conservatives as an arena for national reconciliation. Indeed, by the 1890s all the respectable parties of French political life accepted the idea of empire in varying degrees. Led by Jules Ferry and Jules Méline, the conservative republicans—the Opportunists as contemporaries called them—and moderate Catholic conservatives had actively promoted the tariffs, encouraged the Ralliement, secured help from the men of finance, and enlarged the colonial empire. In 1896, they capped their work with a two-year ministry of social pacification led by Méline and supported by parliamentary Ralliés. In so doing they completed the crafting of the fusion of a new republican ruling amalgam of classes, and of a new conservative ethos that would outlive the conjunctural Opportunist-conservative alliance by over a third of a century.

I

Toward a Second Founding

If the monarchists neither governed nor ruled after 1880 and yet were not broken, how was the political life of France regulated? How were those delicate and complex lines of communication and influence that link the social and economic leaders of a nation with the men who determine its laws and public policy established and maintained? A society that does not marry economic power to political authority risks chaos: its laws may be harmful for national prosperity or, contrarily, the priorities of the economic elite may confound the laws. In this sense the Republic of the late seventies had not yet found its rulers. It had its spokesmen to be sure: Léon Gambetta and Jules Ferry represented the Republic in political struggle both inside and outside the Chamber of Deputies. And Gambetta, understanding the needs of the hour, encouraged the new strata of provincial bourgeoisie to make their way to the forefront of the new polity.

But the lawyers, businessmen, and manufacturers of the provinces whom Gambetta summoned were not yet ready or able to govern France in the first years of the Republic. As a group, they had no experience in national politics. With their own affairs to run many could ill afford the time to manage those of the nation. Moreover, the postwar depression required them to tend first to their own narrow interests. Certainly they were ready to exploit the new possibilities for gaining wealth: the railroad boom, a few French possessions abroad, and the favors to commercial agriculture disguised as peasant relief.[1] But the vision of these new men did not yet

1. In this connection it is interesting to consider the changing nature of scandals from the first decades of republican life to the late nineties. The crash of the Union General Bank and the Panama scandal were *histoires* of the corrupt pursuit of narrow self-interest found out, a question of shady individual businessmen or cliques. By the time of the Dreyfus affair, self-consciously corporate interests were in conflict, for

extend to the political borders of France nor beyond to her colonial empire.[2]

As this study unfolds we will observe the rare phenomenon of many prominent French businessmen, especially industrialists, beginning to take an active role in political life in the last three decades of the nineteenth century. Augustin Pouyer-Quertier, the Norman textile millowner, and Léon Say, a Marseille shipper, commercial wine grower, financier, and the Rothschilds' man on the board of the Chemins de fer du Nord, took different sides on the issue of free trade versus protectionism in the legislature of the Republic. William Waddington, of a Norman textile family, became prime minister in 1879. Baron René Reille, head of the Comité des Forges from 1890 to 1898, opponent of Jean Jaurès in Carmaux and onetime Bonapartist, worked in his capacity as deputy to bring economic and social order to the Republic, as did the father and son of the formerly Bonapartist Schneider family. These men plunged into the politics of the Third Republic. Charles Ferry, of the Banque franco-égyptienne and brother to Opportunist republican leader Jules, as well as Joseph Magnin, former industrialist, minister of finance in 1879–1880, and governor of the Bank of France, mediated some of the connections to the banking community. Many militants of the largest organization of industrialists, the Association de l'Industrie Française, also served in the Chamber or the Senate. Most of the Ralliés were industrialists or commercial growers. As we encounter their names and involvements in the subsequent chapters on the 1880s and early 1890s we will discern a new ruling class in the midst of creating itself. In the early 1880s the process was just beginning.

The elections of 1885 represented a setback in the process of republican consolidation, as contemporaries referred to the struggle for a new hegemony. For suddenly, just as it appeared that the Republic was becoming stabilized, the conservatives dramatically doubled their numbers in the Chamber. Of 383 deputies elected, 201

---

example, the army, the republicans, the proletariat. With the affair even lawbreaking had become class-conscious and, with the exception of the *roué* Esterhazy, not the activity of petty financial cabals.

2. In *The Making of the Third Republic: Class and Politics in France, 1868–1884* (Baton Rouge, 1975), Sanford Elwitt argues that the republicans understood the need to create a national market, but he does not treat their ideas or efforts to create a national ruling coalition.

represented themselves as men of the old monarchist Right. Suddenly worsened economic conditions in the cities and on the land, for which the voters blamed the republican politicians in power, had brought the conservatives renewed support. But even worse for the political stability of the new republic was the consequent division of the Chamber into three political blocs—a conservative, a center, and a left faction—of roughly equal strength. How could President Jules Grévy name a government; how could France be governed? Only coalition governments were possible, and these would produce parliamentary stalemates once all the bargains had been struck. Moreover, French parliamentary coalitions in situations of such delicate balance tended to be unstable. In the autumn of 1885 Paul Cambon, republican stalwart and close friend of Jules Ferry, wrote to his wife from the capital, "The general impression here is that the Republic is at the end of its rope. By next year we shall have revolutionary excesses followed by a violent reaction. How will it end? Some sort of dictatorship, probably clerical and stupid." Writing to a friend the next day he despaired, *"France has no government!"*[3]

The rapid changes of ministries bore out Cambon's deep pessimism. In January, 1886, Charles de Freycinet took up the premiership for a third time, but in less than a year he fell before the combined votes of the Right and the Left. René Goblet, closer to the Radicals in the Chamber than his predecessor, replaced him for five months. He was succeeded by Maurice Rouvier, who served three months, and he by Pierre Tirard, who served ten months. In early 1889 the Chamber still sought its majority as the elites of France worked to form a viable ruling order both within and outside of the parliament. Some felt that forming a parliamentary majority seemed hopeless; others believed it to be worthless. Some of the discontented men of several camps—desperate monarchists, disillusioned republicans, and disappointed workers radicalized by both depression and republican political pusillanimity—turned to yet another man on horseback in French history, the *brav'* General Boulanger.[4]

Supported by Radicals who were disgruntled by lack of reforms

3. Paul Cambon to Mme. Cambon, November 7, 1885, in Paul Cambon, *Correspondance, 1870–1924* (3 vols.; Paris, 1940), I, 261. Italics in original.
4. See the work of Jacques Néré, who has attempted to connect the antirepublican politics of Boulangism with the economic depression, "La Crise industrielle de 1882 et le mouvement boulangiste" (Dissertation, University of Paris, 1959); and his *Le Boulangisme et la presse* (Paris, 1964).

in the new Republic, by antibourgeois workers to whom the Republic thus far meant only unemployment and employer wage pressures, and by opportunist monarchists, General Boulanger offered himself as the embodiment of a solution to the problem of authority in republican politics. However, his lack of resolve and flight to Belgium in 1889 revealed him to be not a man on horseback but rather a handsome soldier fond of appearing in public astride his fine white horse—a great figure of vanity, not of statecraft. Perhaps it would not have been possible even for a leader more gifted than Boulanger to unite behind him all the conflicting groups whose support he would have had to have to rule effectively.

In their turn, the Opportunist republicans, although they had repelled both the insurrectionary resolution of what was now a permanent crisis of state and the monarchical solution of the Right, had yet to find their own governing formula. The continuing industrial depression and the economic troubles of the commercial growers added an air of urgency to the Opportunists' efforts to complete their state building. More frequent and larger strikes, better organized unions and parties of revolt, and growing peasant disaffection and flight from the land that was filling the cities with a population potentially disruptive to the peace of society provided additional impetus for speeding up the work of republican consolidation. The Republic needed governors; it needed an undivided ruling stratum or its future was at risk.

By 1893 the solution to the problem of creating a viable new order had been found. The Republic, which had come into existence because it divided the deputies least, was refounded on a firmer basis.[5] The elections of that year "were not contested for or against the Republic," in the words of Jean-Marie Mayeur, "nor for or against

5. The idea of a second founding of the republic originates in the historiography of the foundation of the German Empire. The appropriateness of applying the concept to the Third Republic is striking, so compelling are the parallels. Bismarck's unification of 1870–71 was achieved by force and guile. Only beginning in 1878–79 were the sociopolitical foundations of the empire addressed. In those years the imperial German government gained a dependable parliamentary coalition in the Reichstag, promulgated the antisocialist laws, and introduced the first in a series of protective tariffs. The phrase "second founding" was first used by Ivo N. Lambi, *Free Trade and Protection in Germany, 1868–1879* (Wiesbaden, 1963). See also its application in Elisabeth Fehrenbach, "Die Reichsgründung in der deutschen Geschichtsschreibung," in Theodor Schieder and Ernst Deuerlein (eds.), *Reichsgründung 1870/1871* (Stuttgart, 1970), 289.

clericalism, but rather on the 'social question.' " Between 1889, the year of Boulanger's popular-monarchist adventure, and 1893, votes for candidates of the Right fell from 3,000,000 to less than 1,500,000. The ranks of monarchist deputies were halved, their supporters either not coming out to vote or voting for the Opportunists whose defense of order recommended them to many former conservative supporters.[6] Over two decades of waiting, crowned by the Boulanger fiasco, had taken its toll. With more than 300 seats in the Chamber, the support of former monarchist voters and of the Ralliés, and the disarray of the obdurate monarchists, the Opportunist republicans made the greatest gains. They had gained enough seats to form a governing majority. When in the course of the decade their poorly disciplined ranks broke, the conservative republicans could depend on the support of the thirty-two Rallié deputies. The nineties would be the Opportunist decade, for the republican parliament had gained a governing majority. It did so because a French ruling strata had finally coalesced. What had changed between 1889 and 1893 that permitted the completion of republican consolidation?

The Conjuncture

The beginnings of France's Third Republic coincided with the descent of the Great Depression of the late nineteenth century. Its second founding took place during the depression's deepest troughs while the consolidation of republican government, completed in the course of the Dreyfus affair, occurred as the depression's pall began to lift. In the two decades between the late seventies and the late nineties, the movements of the economy, or more specifically, of the cyclical fluctuations within the larger trend depression, conditioned the political moves of the participants in the public life of the Third Republic.

The identity that the hard-won Republic had forged for itself by the turn of the century—the identity it would retain until the next great depression in the 1930s—assumed recognizable form in these years of business and agriculture distress. That identity was fashioned, along with a new ruling and governing class, upon the armature of economic protectionism. While in Germany Bismarck was

6. Jean-Marie Mayeur, *Les Débuts de la Troisième République, 1871–1898* (Paris, 1973), 209; Alain Lancelot, *L'Abstentionnisme électoral en France* (Paris, 1967), 58.

presiding over the governing partnership of heavy industrialists and Junkers, the alliance of iron and rye, in France Opportunist politicians like Jules Ferry and Jules Méline mediated the republic's ruling *and* governing coalition of millowners and rural notables, the alliance of iron, cotton, and wheat. The French upper-class partnership, despite important differences from that of Germany, shared a key feature with it: it too grew out of a fear of the disequilibrating effects of modern forms of class struggle upon a still new and relatively fragile political order. In both countries, too, the partners wished to gain socioeconomic leadership and to ensure their hegemony politically.

In republican France, as in imperial Germany, the alliance of economic interests that was concluded in the articles of the various protective tariffs passed in the last two decades of the century lay the fundaments for the politics of the new conservatism of Jules Méline's and Jules Ferry's Opportunist republicans. One source of that industrial-agrarian unity originated in the threat that France's commercial rivals posed to her already deflated domestic economy. This danger of defeat before more powerful or better-placed international commercial rivals threatened the fragile social stability of both the new Republic and of the new Empire in a manner unimaginable for Great Britain, for example. Parallel domestic conflicts in the two new and still fragile political formations generated similar initiatives for conservative unity as well.

When in 1893 the socialists of all the various tendencies managed to increase their delegation in the Chamber of Deputies to an unprecedented forty-nine members, Friedrich Engels quickly sent Paul Lafargue, a leader of the Parti Ouvrier, his delighted congratulations. But he alerted his sometimes naïve young correspondent to a potential political danger for French socialism that the Germans had already experienced. He warned,

> Your victory could lead to the formation of "the grand reactionary mass," about which Lasalle warned us, a coalition of all the bourgeois parties against socialism. This mass always coalesces at the moment of danger, but usually dissolves once again into its component diverse and antagonistic interest groups of great landlords, industrialists, high finance, the small and middling bourgeoisie, peasants, and so forth. However, each time it forms again, it acquires greater solidarity, until at the moment of the crisis we will have to confront a well-unified enemy. This ongoing process of concentration and of dissolution has been the pattern

in Germany from the time our party counted more than twenty deputies in the *Reichstag*. But the concentration will develop more rapidly in your country, because [unlike Germany] your Chamber of Deputies possesses real power.[7]

Fears

If we employ the perspective of our own age, an age that experiences massive social upheavals on an almost yearly basis, the fears for domestic stability expressed by the founders of the Third Republic seem exaggerated. So do any suggestions that a few returned communards, radicalized workers, threatening anarchists, and discontented peasants could shake the foundations of French society. And yet, as the history of tariff agitation, the Ralliement, and the course of republican politics in the last two decades of the nineteenth century reveal, such fears played a part in the decisions of statesmen, business leaders, and growers. For the social peace, that is, the system of authority, of the embryonic republican government was fragile not so much because the Left was strong as because the forces of order of the unfinished state sensed themselves weak. The leaders of the Republic had inherited a defeated army, diplomatic isolation, accelerating foreign commercial competition, and eversinking prices and land values. They had to contend with a divided upper class, uncertainty about the loyalties of the peasants, a capital with rebellious inhabitants, and, in growing numbers, resentful workers in other parts of the country. Their sense of weakness was justified, for the situation was fluid. A small calamity could engender a great one.

Although it is necessary to confirm in a systematic fashion that policy makers suffered this sense of vulnerability it would be useful, as a preliminary, to capture a view, however fleeting, of the deep recesses of the minds of the educated, monied, and socially well-connected. Perhaps the techniques of the then contemporary impressionist painters might help us direct the light where it is needed. The impressionists applied small dabs of pigment to canvas. If one looks at their work closely one sees only bits of color; if one stands back to take in the entire canvas, these bits of color transform into

7. Engels to Paul Lafargue, January 22, 1895, in Frederich Engels, Paul and Laura Lafargue, *Correspondance*, ed. Emile Bottigelli (3 vols.; Paris, 1956–59), III, 394.

elements of a recognizable image. If we sample the insights of a number of the writers, add something from the private letters of a cultured and sensitive political figure like Paul Cambon, look at a bit of lurid anarchist propaganda, and recall the critical reception of Emile Zola's 1885 warning novel, *Germinal*—and step back—we can bring to light, however fleetingly, the often unspoken fears of those who possessed and those who feared to lose. Let us sample a decade and a half of accumulating anxiety.

First, there are the writers read by the *bien pensants* and the members of the Commune of Paris. Almost every important author active in the 1870s—and some later ones such as Zola and Anatole France—wrote against the Commune.[8] If we believe the writers, the insurrectionary violence of 1871 aroused a new *Grande Peur* in the hearts of the monied and titled that did not quickly abate. Soon after the Commune's suppression in May, 1871, the novelists Alphonse Daudet, Maxime du Camp, and Elémir Bourges published works of fiction in which participants and works of the Commune appeared variously as horrible, vicious, resentful, or simply unnatural. In *Les Désirs de Jean Servien*, written at a later period of labor insurgency and published in 1907, the year of the violent vintners' agitation, Anatole France wrote a vivid scene that began with one of the bloodthirsty women of the Commune urging the men to shoot their prisoner Jean Servien. But the cowardly *fédérés* fled at the sound of the soldiers approaching from Versailles. Impetuously, the monstrous revolutionary pressed the pistol to the prisoner's temple and shot him herself; "then the woman danced on the body shrieking with joy."[9]

But even after the revolutionaries of Paris were defeated, the literary sentinels of the well placed warned of persisting dangers. For the Comte de Gobineau, the theorist of racial superiority, Paris still housed "a profoundly perverted population, multitudinous and seething with rage." The Comtesse de Ségur claimed that "there

8. Paul Lidsky, *Les Ecrivains contre la Commune* (Paris, 1982), 10–11. The most commonly cited (hostile) literary appreciation of the Commune was in Vol. IV of the Journal of Edmond and Jules Goncourt, *Mémoires de la vie littéraire (1851–1896)* (9 vols.; Paris, 1872–96). See also Ernest Daudet, *L'Agonie de la commune: Paris à feu et à sang* (Paris, 1871); Théophile Gautier, *Tableaux de siège* (Paris, 1872); Maxime du Camp, *Les Convulsions de Paris* (Paris, 1889); Anatole France, *Les Désirs de Jean Servien* (Paris, 1882); and Emile Zola, *La Débâcle* (Paris, 1892).

9. France, *Les Désirs de Jean Servien*, 247.

were still 50 or 60 thousands of the radicals scattered in the faubourgs of Paris ready again to massacre and to pillage." Leconte de Lisle wrote, "Deport this Parisian rabble—men, women, and children." But even that measure, if carried out, would in the end prove futile, he despaired, because the future held the destruction of all that was precious: "The proletariat will inevitably triumph and that will be the end of France. After all, neither civilizations nor nations are immortal."[10] Many of the insurgents were indeed deported, but the Chamber voted to allow them to return in 1880. The republican politicians realized that the excommunards, even if any of them wished to return to political engagement, had been left behind by political developments. The dangers lay in other directions. Socialists ran for public office and their electoral victories alarmed even seasoned moderate politicians.

Cambon, now serving as prefect of the Nord, had at first discounted the chances of a socialist candidate for a seat on the general council of the canton of Lille in November, 1879. But as the campaign developed, it appeared that the worker would defeat the two republican candidates. "What worries me," he wrote his wife, "is that once the workers get involved in electoral politics no one can tell where it will stop. Today it is the General Council, tomorrow it will be the Municipal Council of Lille, the day after it will be the Chamber of Deputies." He dreaded the industrial conglomeration of Lille going the radical way of Paris and Marseille. He had racked his brains, but could think of nothing. "The current which draws the workers along is very violent; I do not know what we can do to stop it."[11]

If workers' engagement in electoral politics aroused feelings of alarm, proletarian violence was considered much more dreadful. The anarchists in their propaganda summoned the workers to violent deeds; they flung back into the faces of the *bien pensants* the charges of worker barbarity. What horrors could the powerful and comfortable not imagine if in the relatively peaceful year of 1883, before the wave of anarchist bombings and murders in Paris, they

10. A. de Gobineau, *Lettres à deux athéniennes (1868–1881)* (Paris, 1936), letter to Zoé, May 28, 1871; Comtesse de Ségur, *Lettres d'une grand-mère* (Paris, 1898), Letter of June 5, 1871; Leconte de Lisle, *Lettre à J.-M. de Herédia*, letter of June 2, 1871, and de Lisle, *Lettre à Jean Marras*, letter of November 3, 1871, both cited in Lidsky, *Les Ecrivains*, 81.

11. Paul Cambon to Mme. Cambon, November 4, 1879, in Cambon, *Correspondance*, I, 105–106.

heard tell of the violence of the anarchist press. *Le Drapeau noir* spoke for at least some French workers:

> All that is necessary to carry out a social revolution . . . is to develop the hatred and the desire for vengeance which lies in the heart of every one of the oppressed. Hatred is necessary for every revolution because it is the ferment which gives the needed courage to those whom poverty has reduced to faint-heartedness and stupification. The desire for vengeance is the first stage of revolt. . . . Let us promote hatred and vengeance, and we shall soon know the terrible awakening of the oppressed and hungry. To the task! Workers of all worlds [*sic*], the old society is dying: It needs only to be dispatched by an invasion of the barbarians.[12]

The good bourgeois and many a monarchist sensed that the old society was dying, perhaps dead. The future was indeed uncertain. What if that future contained millions of angry workers who grew from the industrialization of provincial France like the dragon teeth soon to sprout from the soil above the mine at the end of *Germinal*? Zola "foresees our old society smashed and overturned by this immense army of *misérables* which nothing can stop," wrote Edmond Deschaumes. In an essay that read more like an assessment of the social crisis than a book review, he continued, "When will the weak avenge themselves against the strong? [Zola] gives us no precise answer. But the hour of vengeance will surely come; that is the conclusion of *Germinal*." A "terrifying scene," wrote Philippe Gille, referring to Zola's evocation of life underground and to the workers "surging up, black and frightening, to demand a place in society." And to many, Zola's warning of the dragon's teeth sown over the mine yielding worker-warriors seemed correct: the workers' militancy and strike activity grew rapidly in subsequent years.[13]

The violence continued—sometimes initiated by one side, sometimes by the other—but in the language and, even more, in the fantasies of the bourgeoisie, a militant strike, labor violence, anarchist murders, the election of socialist deputies and social revolution blended together as one great threat to the public order. The support of General Boulanger by a majority of the followers of the old revolutionary Louis Blanqui and many workers of the industrial Nord alarmed cautious monarchists and threatened republicans alike.

12. *Le Drapeau noir*, August 26, 1883, p. 4.
13. Edmond Deschaumes, Review of *Germinal*, *L'Evénement*, March 2, 1885; Philippe Gille, Review of *Germinal*, *Le Figaro*, March 4, 1886.

Even though the general's cause crumbled in 1889, the May Day celebrations and riots of that year and the shootings of 1890 confirmed that the worker rabble continued to pose a danger to good order. The 1890s witnessed a new stage of workers' militancy, of workers' organization, and of reactive conservatism. The larger and more numerous strikes of the last decade of the century took on an increasingly political nature, especially when revolutionary syndicalists or socialists involved themselves. The rural exodus continued to alarm growers, who were losing their subservient labor force, as well as urban leaders, who did not relish the existence of rootless rural dwellers near their homes. The successes of socialist organizers and political leaders—most famous of whom was perhaps Jean Jaurès of Carmaux—who began to reach the peasants of the small communes of the South also evoked unhappy reactions from the propertied and the well-situated. Such worries extended beyond the circles of the Right and the Opportunist republicans. In the 1890s socialists began to push Radicals out of their positions of spokesmanship for the left-leaning workers and peasants of the provinces. (We shall look more closely at that leftward shift away from local Radical leadership in the case of the peasant woodcutters of the Nièvre and among the small farmers of the Var in Chapter IV.) Thus as the eighties gave way to the nineties the incidences of both urban and rural leftism were multiplying; in step with the coming of age of the class of French industrial capitalists, a modern French Left was making itself.

The upper economic strata of the society, however, continued to suffer from a deep division of interests. Men who made their money by selling abroad had not yet made their peace with producers for the domestic market (see Figure 1). Nor had the leaders of domestically oriented industries come to terms with the important agricultural notables. Indeed, in the course of the passage of the 1881 tariff, the pro-tariff industrialists had split from the growers and had reaped most of the rather limited benefits the new duties conferred. Only the tariff increases on grain and cattle in 1884, 1885, and 1887, which the spokesmen for industry in the Chamber permitted the growers, appeased the agriculturalists sufficiently to permit them to consider undertaking common action again. The big farmers had been burned in the arena of pressure-group politics; when in 1889 some of them tried to go it alone by embracing the cause of General Boulanger, they were burned again. But in 1889 the republicans, it will be remembered, also were shaken.

Figure 1

The Movement of Agricultural and Industrial Prices and the Passage of the Tariffs, 1848–1914

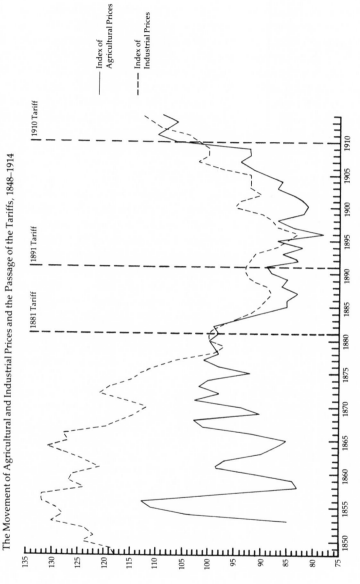

Source: Maurice Lévy-Leboyer, "L'Héritage de Simiand: Prix, profit et termes d'échange au XIXe siècle." *Revue historique,* CCXLIII (January, 1970), 108–11. 1880 = 100

It was in this state of economic and political disunity that the elites of agriculture, manufacturing, mining, and banking observed the mounting radicalism from below.[14] Although in future decades both urban and rural radicalism would grow more potent, not until the mid-1930s would the Left confront an upper strata so divided, so economically and politically vulnerable, and so aware of its weakness. At this already trying conjuncture from 1890 to 1895, agricultural and industrial prices and production plummeted to their lowest levels in twenty years.

The Great Depression

Perhaps because French economic historians have devoted so much work in the last decade to refuting the charge of French backwardness, there is no seminal study of the era of the Great Depression of 1873–1896.[15] We can make some statements about the clear trends, however. It is agreed that between 1873 and 1896 France—like other developed nations of Europe—suffered downturns of major indexes of prices, interest rates, and commerce.[16] Most commentators also agree that 1882 and 1890 were years of sudden falls in French production and prices ("crisis years" in nineteenth century language). But there is consensus neither on the periodicity of the combined index of industrial production nor on the individual in-

14. Many an industrialist or mine owner who fought for protection had experienced labor troubles in his own shop in the course of the depression. Where I could connect such troubles with a prominent protectionist's firm I have done so.

15. Hans Rosenberg, *Grosse Depression und Bismarckzeit: Wirtschaftsablauf, Gesellschaft und Politik in Mitteleuropa* (Berlin, 1967); François Caron and Jean Bouvier, "Les indices majeurs," in Fernand Braudel and Ernest Labrousse (eds.), *Histoire économique et sociale de la France* (8 vols.; Paris, 1977–82), vol. V, pt. 1, pp. 128–37 (hereinafter cited as *HES*); Jean Bouvier, "Mouvement ouvrier et conjonctures économiques," *Le Mouvement social*, XLVIII (July–September, 1964), 3–30. M. Lévy-Leboyer, "L'héritage de Simiand," *Revue historique*, CCXLIII (1971), 77–120; Lévy-Leboyer, "La croissance économique en France au XIXe siècle: résultats préliminaires," *Annales: économies, sociétés, civilisations*, XXIII (1968), 788–807 (hereinafter cited as *Annales*); Jean Lescure, *Des Crises générales et périodiques de surproduction* (3rd ed.; Paris, 1923) especially 60–118, 449–55; François Crouzet, "Essai de construction d'un indice annuel de la production industrielle française au XIXe siècle," *Annales*, XXV (1970), 56–99.

16. W. Arthur Lewis states that, although the Great Depression hit all of Europe in the late nineteenth century, its peaks and troughs—and to some degree, the reasons for the cycles—varied from country to country. See his *Growth and Fluctuations, 1870-1913* (London, 1978), 17–68.

dexes for various industries. Nor is there agreement on the causes of the downturn. In Keynesian fashion, Arthur Lewis blames the crash of 1882 on the government's cessation of funding of the vast railroad building scheme known as the Freycinet Plan. Others insist on the contemporary explanation of the decline that inculpated the fall in agricultural purchasing power.[17] As we shall presently see, the period was a transitional one making the weighing of factors in economic cycles especially elusive.

The price changes of both industrial and agricultural goods were readily noted and tabulated by nineteenth century observers. Prices hit peaks in 1880 and 1890, just before precipitous downward slides that bottomed out in 1887 and 1896 respectively. Contemporaries witnessed bank and bourse slumps in 1882 and 1889 and 1890. These various cycles will take on greater meaning when we relate them to the rolling waves of strikes that broke out throughout the new Republic with increasing force (see Table 1).[18]

Even without the detailed monographs and precise indices we have come to expect in contemporary economic history, we can discern the birth of a new kind of economic cycle during the Great Depression. Past cyclical crises both in France and other countries in Europe had tended to follow on crop shortfalls—usually grains—

17. *Ibid.*, 47–50. The demise of the Freycinet Plan had several causes. Many French politicians were persuaded that Prussia had ridden to victory on its rail network. Rational defense planning suggested that the French create a similar capacity. By 1882 that patriotic ardor had begun to cool and the bonds to fund the scheme were beginning to be difficult to place. The costs of construction were soaring. But probably most important were the attacks upon it by the militant free trader and opponent of state intervention in the economy, Léon Say, both in articles (for example, "Le rachat des chemins de fer," *Journal des économistes* [December, 1881]), and from his post as minister of finance. Lewis states that the beginnings of the decline in 1882 convinced the government to reduce expenditures and to abandon the railway construction, and that generated further decline, not fallen purchasing power in the agricultural sector. The other source of extraordinary government expenditure in 1882 was the military expedition to Indochina that ceased only two years later with the fall of Jules Ferry.

18. Caron and Bouvier, "Les indices majeurs," in Braudel and Labrousse (eds.), *HES*, vol. V, pt. 1, pp. 132–33; Jean Bouvier, "Mouvement ouvrier et conjonctures économiques"; E. Shorter and C. Tilly, *Strikes in France, 1830–1968* (Cambridge, England, 1974); Michelle Perrot, *Les Ouvriers en grève, France, 1871–1890* (2 vols.; Paris, 1974); J. Julliard, "Théorie syndicale et pratique gréviste," *Le Mouvement social*, LXV (October-December, 1968), 55–69. See also Jacques Néré, "La Crise industrielle de 1882 et le mouvement boulangiste"; and Néré, *Le Boulangisme et la presse.*

TABLE 1

Strikes, Strikers, and Days Struck, 1877–1882

Year	Strikes	Strikers	Days Struck (strikers × days)
1877	55	12,900	no data
1878	73	38,546	390,508
1879	88	54,439	760,959
1880	190	110,376	1,110,988
1881	109	68,037	596,216
1882	271	65,514	580,683

Source: Michelle Perrot, *Les Ouvriers en grève, France, 1871–1890* (2 vols.; Paris, 1974), I, 89–90, copyright © 1974 by the Ecole des Hautes Etudes and Mouton de Gruyter. Reprinted with permission of the publisher.

that so reduced peasant purchasing power that urban manufacturers were caught with too many goods and no customers. Thus in the first three quarters of the nineteenth century periodic crop failures in the countryside united with a relative overproduction of manufactured goods to produce the typically meteorologically driven fluctuations of the economy as a whole.[19]

Normally, too, the rhythms of agricultural prosperity and distress cycled out of phase with those of industrial production. For example, the distress of cultivators caused by an abundant harvest and low prices, benefited both urban workers and employers with low food prices and reduced tensions between them over wages. We may trace the troubled and often antagonistic relations between upper-class growers and modernizing industrialists throughout much of the nineteenth century to the inverse fates dealt them by the cyclical fluctuations of the economy for most of the century.

The Great Depression introduced a cycle of a new kind. The change was observable by the late seventies, and a decade later, the new rhythm thoroughly dominated the movement of the economy: agricultural and industrial prices now moved up and down together. France's economy was becoming unified. The spread of the

19. Ernest Labrousse, "A livre ouvert sur les élans et les vicissitudes des croissances," in Braudel and Labrousse (eds.), *HES*, vol. III, pt. 2, pp. 961–1024.

railroad network and the diffusion of literacy was bringing into being the national market that provincial businessmen and market agriculturalists needed to grow.[20] Heightened international economic competition reinforced the growing internal economic coherence to encourage distressed growers and industrialists to seek ways to unite the nation's producers for their mutual benefit. The possibilities for coalitions between the endangered producers of table wines, cattle, and wheat and the beleaguered manufacturers of iron goods and textiles could be seen in the parallel curves that told of their economic fortunes, or misfortunes, during the depression years (see Figure 2).

Initially these early agrarian-industrialist collaborations were simply alliances of pressure groups of a predictable sort pressing their representatives in the Chamber for tariff legislation of an accustomed variety. Throughout most of the nineteenth century the tendency of French commercial policy had been protectionist.[21] The high-handed opening up of France by Napoleon III to the commerce of the world in 1860—to the commerce of Great Britain, primarily—had political motives behind it: he wished to strengthen his alliance with Britain. Freer trade between the two countries was Richard Cobden's price. The defeat of Napoleon III discredited those free trade policies. The decade of the seventies was sufficiently prosperous for both agriculture and industry, and at the same time sufficiently politically uncertain, that no important pressure built up to return to protection. With the sharp economic decline after 1880, and the seating of a republican government that would listen to the industrialists' pleas for aid, Pouyer-Quertier, could finally mobilize industrialists and the big growers to demand relief from their distress of the legislature. What better protagonist of a new ruling-class unity of interest might serious economic leaders want: a self-made man under the empire, briefly a supporter of Boulanger, Pouyer-Quertier crafted the tariff agitation for republicans like Ferry and Méline to carry on but married off one daughter to a count, the other to a marquis. Elected as a republican senator in 1876, he was nevertheless widely identified as a Legitimist.[22]

20. Elwitt, *The Making of the Third Republic*, 19–52.

21. Andre Broder, "Le Commerce extérieur: l'échec de la conquête d'une position internationale," in Braudel and Labrousse (eds.), *HES*, vol. III, pt. 1, pp. 334–35.

22. On Pouyer-Quertier see Jean-Pierre Chaline, *Les Bourgeois de Rouen* (Paris, 1982), 114–17.

Figure 2

The Movement of Grain, Heavy Industrial Goods, and Textile Prices, 1848–1914

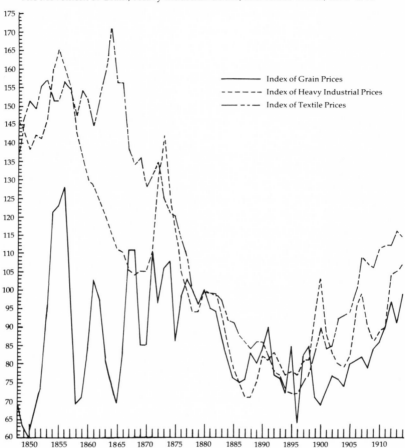

Source: Maurice Lévy-Leboyer, ''L'Héritage de Simiand: Prix, profit et termes d'échange au XIXe siècle.'' *Revue historique,* CCXLIII (January, 1970), 108–11.   1880 = 100

But more was at stake in the 1880s and 1890s than an upwardly mobile provincial bourgeois uniting representatives of vested economic interests around the revival of neomercantilist commercial legislation. Because this kind of business cycle was new, so were the affinities of interest it permitted. The new republic was untried and not yet shaped socially. And the provincial industrial workers, who in the course of the depression became increasingly conscious of how their needs and interests differed from those of their employers, were also a new breed. No longer social republicans like those of 1848, nor bearers of the traditions of the Paris Commune, they comprised the growing levies of modern socialism and revolutionary syndicalism. But even before they posed any serious threat to the political stability of the Third Republic, their demands in the years of declining prices, diminishing profits, and rising wages had a profound political impact on their employers.

Between 1883 and 1899 real wages rose faster than productivity. One estimate puts the increase at approximately 20 percent.[23] At least two factors account for the improvements in the material life of the French workers on whom we have statistics. First, the period of amelioration coincided with an accelerating rate of industrial strikes, echoing the growing social and political militancy of workers. Thus French workers fought successfully to improve their lives by means of the strike, or at least they fought against employers' attempts to depress wages or worsen work conditions in bad times. Second, the employers, especially those in cotton textiles, mining, and iron processing, simultaneously suffered serious declines in prices and profits. Agricultural prices declined as well. Falling prices, in turn, improved the purchasing power of the workers'

<hr/>

23. On the data see Lewis, *Growth and Fluctuations*, 94–111; he bases his calculations on E. H. Phelps-Brown with Margaret Browne, *A Century of Pay* (London, 1968). See also Michelle Perrot, "Les Classes populaires urbaines," in Braudel and Labrousse (eds.), *HES*, vol. IV, pt. 1, pp. 490–502. The improvement of the lives of European workers in the late nineteenth century was one source of intellectual crisis of European socialism in that epoch. Eduard Bernstein, Rosa Luxemburg, and V. I. Lenin each realized that current marxist orthodoxy was unsuited to explain this new reality. The theories of imperialism of Luxemburg and Lenin were in large part aimed at accounting for this violation of the immiseration tendency articulated by Marx. Bernstein called for a rethinking of Marxist theory because he extrapolated what he believed to be a trend of improved conditions for workers.

households, at least until the effect of the tariffs on their purchasing power made itself felt.[24]

Owners of textile mills, iron manufacturers, and mine operators struggled bleakly with the costs of raw materials, foreign competitors, and their own workers' demands in order to keep their firms afloat and to protect the family patrimony. We now realize the error of ascribing the poor performance of the major industrialists of depression-struck France to their lack of initiative. The sectors most hurt, on the contrary, were rather innovative. Even the Schneiders of Creusot, aggressive and pioneering entrepreneurs by any standards, complained about the unreasonableness of their workers and, with other major industrialists, turned to the state for relief. But throughout the Great Depression their dilemma persisted: foreign competition and workers' pressures compelled capital investment. This the threatened industrialists were prepared to do. However, the retained profits to pay for new investments were shrinking in the same depressed decades, as were the markets that any improved productivity presupposed.

Prominent spokesmen of French business interests, both inside and outside the Chamber of Deputies, reacted with perplexity. Did not Say's Law promise them that for every increase in production a proportionate increase in demand would clear the market? The trend depression had heartened Marxist theorists with the vision of the final crisis of capitalism; it filled the minds of many businessmen with growing misgivings. No one—neither at the Faculties nor in their world—could offer a systematic theory of business cycles. At meetings of the Association de l'Industrie Française, the main protectionist organization, and in testimony before parliamentary commissions of inquiry, there was much talk of a crisis caused by lack of markets exacerbated by high wage bills.

---

24. Strikes from 1899 to 1914 were more frequent and in many ways more militant. But by the turn of the century industrialists had ceased to be as disconcerted by what in the eighties and nineties was a relatively unexpected style of worker economic resistance. Moreover, in the new century industrialists' organizations were stronger and they themselves had grown more sophisticated about the social question qua wage problem. Most important, economic recovery made them less a hostage to their employees. In the decade and a half after 1899 real wages rose more slowly than productivity. See Lewis, *Growth and Fluctuations*, 107; François Caron, *An Economic History of Modern France* (New York, 1979), 144, 154. Pierre Léon, "Le Moteur de l'industrialisation: L'enterprise industrielle," in Braudel and Labrousse (eds.), *HES*, vol. III, pt. 2, pp. 614–16, discusses the divisions of opinion in the important literature.

Thus the Great Depression bathed French society of the eighties and nineties in its special hue. The demoralizing confusion it engendered among the business elite spread to the leaders of the new Republic. For the crisis coincided with the ascendancy of the Opportunist republicans; these moderate and calculating provincial bourgeois, grouped loosely first around the immoderate and passionate Gambetta and then Ferry and Méline, were compelled to create a new political order under its stresses. It was "a great stroke of historical bad luck," wrote Jacques Néré, "that it was precisely during their period of power that there occurred one of the worst and longest crises that the French economic system has ever had to endure."[25] Admittedly, the depression slowed the growth of the French economy. The material limits it raised, the impasses it set, and the commercial defeats it engendered left wounds in the French economy that did not fully heal until the years after World War II.[26]

Tariffs

From the often desperate commercial and political initiatives launched by the Opportunist leaders and their business and grower allies also emerged a resilient and triumphant new conservatism. The first move in the creation of the economically conservative Republic required its new leaders to respond to the long-term economic depression so that its potentially disruptive social consequences might be contained. Policy and self-interest went hand in hand in the legisla-

25. Jacques Néré, "The French Republic," in *Material Progress and World-Wide Problems, 1870–98* (Cambridge, England, 1962), 307. Vol XI of the *New Cambridge Modern History*, 14 vols.

26. Whether rapid or slow growth produces more serious problems of stability in a society is much disputed. See M. Olson, "Rapid Growth as a Destabilizing Force," *Journal of Economic History*, XXIII (1963), 529–52; R. G. Ridker, "Discontent and Economic Growth," *Economic Development and Cultural Change*, XI (1962), 1–15; Laurence Stone, "Theories of Revolution," *World Politics*, XVIII (1966), 160–76. In his *Bismarck und der Imperialismus* (2nd ed.; Cologne, 1970) and his essay "Bismarck's Imperialism, 1862–1890" in James Sheehan (ed.), *Imperial Germany* (New York, 1976), 180–222, Hans-Ulrich Wehler argues that rapid growth as a promoter of stability is "one of the dangerous legends of contemporary development-politics" ("Bismarck's Imperialism," 181). One of the benefits of the comparative approach of the present study is that it reveals social elites in France in a period of little economic growth as concerned about social stability as the *Sammlungspolitiker* in rapidly developing Germany. In short, the issue seems not to be growth but, as I argue here, the perceived fragility of the political frame holding together the society and economy.

tion that conditioned the other measures of socioeconomic protection passed through the Chamber to stabilize the Opportunist Republic.

Implementation was not simple. A part of the French bourgeoisie and most farmers were economic liberals; they abhorred state intervention in their affairs. And yet they also realized that it was on the level of national policy that any national ruling coalition had to be concluded. Liberals in general, and French liberals in particular, were prepared to permit government intervention in the economy in wartime. But France was at peace. Were there any other possible exceptions? In nineteenth-century Europe during times of commercial depression protective tariffs often seemed to political leaders of developing nations an attractive countermeasure. Tariffs, because they encouraged the illusion among liberals that their workings involved a minimum degree of tinkering with the supply price of commodities, functioned as an ideologically tolerable interference with markets.[27] Before the mid-1880s republican liberals envisioned any more active involvement of the state in the economy as both unnecessary and dangerous: unnecessary because neither economic distress nor the still nascent workers' movement was sufficiently acute to require great political measures; dangerous because it was not fully their state to use as their instrument.

Tariffs, then, were the answer to the long-term crisis. They were a known remedy, for other struggling nations of Europe were erecting commercial barriers as well. French tariffs could be represented as defensive in origin, and protectionists envisioned numerous benefits. First, protection would diminish the impact of the depression by shielding French industrial goods—and eventually agricultural products—from the competition of the exports from the New World and from the dumping of the exporting nations of Europe. High tariffs would tame the new industrial working class with the promise of real job protection—even a promise of improved wages—if only workers would cooperate with their employers in pressing for the repudiation of the imperial legacy of free trade.[28] To encourage

27. See Michael S. Smith's treatment of the ineffectuality of the agitation of the free-trade pressure group in *Tariff Reform in France, 1860–1900: The Politics of Economic Interest* (Ithaca, N.Y., 1980), 160–70.

28. Perrot, *Les Ouvriers en grève*, I, 160. She writes, "the repudiation of the treaties of commerce, the appeal to protectionism are the principal themes of a kind of fuge in which the voices of *patrons* and workers are intertwined. The economic crisis reinforced the sentiments of a community of national interests more than those of class

such cooperation, employers promoted the ideology of National Labor. They sought to unite employers and workers through the ideas that both labored to create the goods of society and both were all French. They stressed that shared tasks and a common *patrie* precluded ideas of class conflict, and that the enemies of French production were foreign invaders, as the Prussians had been, and foreign economic rivals, as the Prussian-Germans now were. For the good of France and of French prosperity, they proclaimed, both industrialists and workers had to recognize these truths.

But most decisively, the new tariffs laid the economic basis for the other agreements and understandings that completed the alliance of bourgeoisie and upper class in the last decades of the century.[29] Thus the Jules Mélines and the Jules Ferrys, the provincial lawyers who governed the new Republic, began in the tariff struggles the brokerage of a new conservative ruling power bloc of classes.

Even better than arranged marriages the tariffs served to bring differing economic interests closer together.[30] Whereas the Great Depression was easing the union of iron and rye in the neighboring German Empire, in France it was uniting the elite of the society around that which needed protection there—iron, wheat, and cotton. In both societies the depression created the willingness to deal; uncertain control of the peasants and increasingly militant working classes provided the push. Certainly Orleanist growers and financiers were not Junkers; the traditions of the Prussian and French aristocracies evolved under different circumstances. So indeed had

---

struggle" (178–79). General Boulanger employed the theme of National Labor during his rise.

29. Arno Mayer speaks of an "amalgam" of the top layers of upper and bourgeois classes at the turn of the century with wide influence among the governors of France. This argument is correct; we do not have to accept his larger Schumpeterian claim about the persistence of an Old Regime to acknowledge its validity. Mayer's argument fits Germany and Austria-Hungary (Schumpeter's homeland) better than it does France. There can be no doubt that even the most reactionary of the French aristocracy in the late nineteenth century would have felt uncomfortable being labeled a representative of the Old Regime. In Third Republic France the bourgeoisie set the tone and, as this study argues, took leadership of the nation. In building upon Mayer's signal contribution to political social history, as the present one attempted, future studies will have to focus especially on the nuances of the ruling alliances in the various lands of Europe (Arno J. Mayer, *The Persistence of the Old Regime* (New York, 1981), 105).

30. Everyone had an economic interest, but not every bourgeois or upper-class family on hard times had an eligible offspring.

TABLE 2

Division of the French Working Population, 1840–1906 (percent)

	Agriculture	Industry	Other
1840–45	51.9	26.0	22.2
1866	49.8	27.9	22.3
1896	44.8	28.6	26.6
1906	42.7	28.2	28.1

Source: François Caron, *An Economic History of Modern France* (New York, 1979), 33, copyright © 1979 by Columbia University Press. Reprinted with permission of the publisher.

those of Great Britain. But we should not be misled by the real varieties of national social development within Europe into missing the ongoing hybridization of the ruling strata and the ensuing shifts in political discourse and political practice in almost every European land during the course of the nineteenth century.

The Coalition Forms

Cotton textile manufacturers, shipbuilders, and iron founders— therefore both light and heavy industrialists—prompted the efforts to push tariff bills through the Chamber in the 1880s and 1892. The more sophisticated of them saw the tariffs as more than simply useful commercial legislation. France of the Third Republic did not carry out the kinds of social reforms that both British liberals and Bismarckian conservatives hoped would integrate workers into the order of things. Important proponents of tariff reform—certainly Jules Méline, their chief spokesman—saw the tariffs as acts of social policy and improvement, as means of granting machinists, miners, and textile, iron, and shipyard workers, steady employment and possible improvement of their lot. To accomplish all these goals the tariffs had to improve domestic sales.

But who would buy even the protected manufactured goods in the midst of an agricultural depression? Most of the nation still lived from the land; destruction caused by phylloxera (vine root lice), foreign grain and cattle, and the flight from the land depressed purchasing power or reduced the number of customers for urban

TABLE 3
Division of the Value of Physical Product, 1835–1913 (percent)

	Agriculture	Industry
1835–44	61	39
1855–64	56	44
1895–99	45	55
1905–13	40	60

Source: Caron, *An Economic History of Modern France*, 33, copyright © 1979 by Columbia University Press. Reprinted with permission of the publisher.

manufacturers. The agricultural interests had to be benefited, if they in turn were to confer their benefits on industrial sales (see Table 3).

Like the founders of the contemporary Bund der Landwirte in Germany, Méline and his friends in the Chamber represented themselves as spokesmen for all French agriculture.[31] Their efforts to speak on behalf of the peasant farmers were considerably more successful than those of the Junker-dominated Prussian organization. After 1881 the Opportunist protectionists managed to enlist not only the national spokesmen for the notables of market agriculture to their cause but also many small farmers and winegrowers. The influx of Italian wine in the 1880s moved many wine producers, especially in southern France, to embrace demands for higher tariffs in the 1890s, although by 1907 overproduction had turned the same peasants against the republican leadership and toward socialism.[32] In any case, as we will see, most peasants consumed or traded locally the little wine or few crops they grew, causing them to search their souls as to where their interests lay. The big growers, especially the monarchist dukes and counts of the Société des Agriculteurs de France, took the proffered hand of the republican conservatives. Sophisticated men whose ancestors had suffered one rural and sev-

31. The historian of the Bund der Landwirte is Hans-Jürgen Puhle. See his *Agrarische Interessenpolitik und preussischen Konservatismus in wilhelmischen Reich, 1893–1914* (Hanover, 1966); and his comparative study, *Politische Agrarbewegung in kapitalistischen Industriegesellschaften: Deutschland, U.S.A., und Frankreich im 20. Jahrhundert* (Göttingen, 1975).

32. See Chap. IV of this study on the complex role played by the peasantry in the shaping of the conservative alliance.

eral urban revolutions, they knew well the social dangers threatening French society. And they feared for their land rents.

They also feared for the continued docility of a peasantry entering the national market system in the worst decades for the French rural economy since the 1840s. At the same time socialists—both those sent from the cities and local converts—had begun systematically trying to win over peasants with their message of abolition of great holdings of land and of capital. Old conservatives had hoped to keep the countryside safe as a base for the eventual renewal of the Old Regime. However, the dangers of a social republic—perhaps like that of 1848, following on the bad economic conjuncture—encouraged them to make common cause with their new tariff partners, perhaps to employ the mass of the peasantry to brake the drive toward a social republic. During the years of tariff agitation landed conservatives worked through the Société des Agriculteurs de France to negotiate clauses of protective tariffs with their industrialist partners, while simultaneously proliferating syndicats agricoles under their tutelage. Agricultural duties eased the decline in land values and slowed the fall in agricultural rents; protecting French agriculture strengthened rural notables in an industrial age while at the same time rallying significant numbers of conservative-organized peasant farmers to the values of social conservatism.

The sociopolitical union for a new, republican conservatism followed upon the conclusion of the tariff coalition between industry and agriculture. The Ralliement, the development of the colonial empire, and the Méline ministry strengthened the ties that economic understandings had first knotted. In the decades of the Great Depression the ruling class of the Republic made itself in the process of re-creating a viable polity. Let us now look more closely at the stages of the creation of that ruling order from its first narrow economic beginnings to the test of its strength in the Dreyfus affair. First, before everything, came the tariffs.

II

Protection Against Labor Troubles
The Efforts of the 1880s

After the defeat of the Commune and a final flurry of the strike movement that had begun before the war with Prussia, Frenchmen of all classes turned away from the so-called social question. Many radical leaders had been killed, deported, or immobilized in the repressive social peace that accompanied the reoccupation of Paris. Many members of the bourgeoisie were eager to see in the recent horrors the work of foreigners, agitators, or "pathogenes" and considered the removal of these undesirables sufficient to restore public order. Probably because the mid-1870s were largely free of significant social and economic agitation from below, these illusions remained unchallenged. Indeed, the French upper strata could afford to take nearly a decade to negotiate the social and economic truces needed to permit the transition to republican government, a form that in midcentury their fathers had considered a most dangerous kind of rule.[1]

As the decade drew to a close the economic peculiarities and disruptions of the period of the Great Depression began to surface. Businessmen in iron, coal, and textiles—the nation's leading industries—began to grow ever more alarmed by the secular decline in prices that had started in 1873. They kept producing and even selling their wares, but their profit margins sank steadily. Profits declined in iron and coal production as well as in banking; the general index of industrial profits, reaching 193.8 for the period 1860–1864, declined to 112.9 by 1880–1884 and sank to 100 in 1890–1894.[2]

1. Michelle Perrot, *Les Ouvriers en grève, France, 1871–1890* (2 vols.; Paris, 1974), I, 73, 80, 82; David Thomson (ed.), *France: Empire and Republic, 1850–1940* (New York, 1968), 329.

2. François Caron, "La croissance industrielle: secteurs et branches," in Fernand Braudel and Ernest Labrousse (eds.), *Histoire économique et sociale de la France* (8 vols.; Paris, 1977–82), vol. IV, pt. 1, pp. 266–67 (hereinafter cited as *HES*); Donald

The farmers suffered also. Bad weather reduced the size of most of the harvests in the 1880s. Wheat and meats grown outside of Europe inundated the international markets, injuring the sales of French producers both at home and abroad. The winegrowers suffered the added misfortune of the infestation of phylloxera, which badly set back production of quality (that is, export) wines.[3] Because agriculture still generated over half the value of the aggregate national product, and French peasants were the chief customers for much of France's industrial production, the agricultural crisis reinforced the downward tendencies of industrial prices. Thus while French growers saw their economic fortunes eroding away, the industrialists had to witness the two new capitalist colossi, the German Empire and the United States, capture markets for manufactured goods all over the world. The domestic market was plagued by failing demand, and French colonial outlets were as yet undeveloped. But even the methods that many industrialists used to try to recoup their profits further threatened stability.

French entrepreneurs of the nineteenth century lacked neither initiative nor foresight.[4] As prices declined, many resourceful businessmen looked for ways to achieve economies and to rationalize their operations. In the late 1870s and early 1880s, for example, many manufacturers—especially the cotton thread and cloth producers of the Nord—invested heavily in modern equipment. They also pressed their workers for increased productivity, as they had done during the business recession of the last years of the Empire. And as in the late 1860s, the renewed assertiveness on the part of industrialists in the 1880s and 1890s brought them into frequent and repeated confrontation with their workers. It was this struggle over who was to bear the greatest costs of the depression that ignited the first national struggle between the working class and the increasingly class-conscious industrialists.[5]

Reid, *The Miners of Decazeville: A Genealogy of Deindustrialization*, (Cambridge, Mass., 1985), 75.

3. Charles Warner, *The Winegrowers of France* (New York, 1960).

4. See Richard Kuisel's summary of the backwardness debate in his *Capitalism and the State in Modern France: Renovation and Economic Management in the Twentieth Century* (Cambridge, England, 1981), especially Chap. I.

5. Jean Lambert, "Quelques familles du patronat textile de Lille-Armentières, 1789–1914" (Dissertation, University of Lille, 1954), 488; Michael J. Rust, "Business and Politics in the Third Republic: The Comité des Forges and the French Steel

The political and economic leaders of other lands also struggled with the social consequences of the worldwide price deflation. With no peasants and very few members of the upper classes living on incomes primarily derived from cereal production, the British held to the arrangement hammered out in 1846: the Corn Laws were not reenacted. However, the British government found the depression era a propitious moment to buy out British landlords in Ireland, thereby leaving it to the Irish peasantry to pay off their mortgages amid declining agricultural prices. Britain also increased exports of cotton goods to India and as a consequence destroyed for a second time the colony's renascent textile industry. Italy exported great numbers of economically redundant peasants, a well-established safety valve for social tensions. Danish farmers, who had given up cereal crops to specialize in dairy products, were beginning to enjoy brilliant marketing successes.

The more socially vulnerable societies of Europe reacted more defensively. Whereas a pattern of economic protectionism had been widespread in early-nineteenth-century Europe, the swing to free trade was marked after the 1850s. In the decades of the 1850s and 1860s the commercial policies of Switzerland, the Netherlands, Belgium, Piedmont, Spain, Portugal, Norway, Sweden, Britain, Russia, Prussia, and, of course, France shifted in the direction of lowered tariffs and trade treaties carrying most-favored-nation clauses. But with the deepening of the Great Depression many stricken nations reversed their commercial policy and closed their doors against their neighbors' goods.[6]

Lands in the midpassage of industrialization, nations moving from largely agrarian social relations toward industrial maturity—and therefore toward the social conflicts of newly industrializing societies—sought in protective tariffs a weapon of countercyclical social protectionism. In 1879 the German Empire began a series of tariff increases that culminated in 1902 with the passage of the Bülow

---

Industry, 1896–1914" (Ph.D. dissertation, Princeton University, 1973) 18–19; Michael S. Smith, *Tariff Reform in France, 1860–1900: The Politics of Economic Interest* (Ithaca, N.Y., 1980), 132–40; E. Shorter and C. Tilly, *Strikes in France 1830–1968* (Cambridge, England, 1974), 74–75, 307.

6. See Charles Kindleberger, *The Economic Response: Comparative Studies in Trade, Finance, and Growth* (Cambridge, Mass., 1978), 39–65; Hans Rosenberg, *Grosse Depression und Bismarckzeit: Wirtschaftsablauf, Gesellschaft und Politik in Mitteleuropa* (Berlin, 1967), 25–30.

Tariff. Italy and Austria-Hungary followed suit. Even the United States—at that moment experiencing both unprecedented industrial conflict and Populist disaffection—passed the strongly protectionist McKinley Tariff in 1890. The responses that societies made to the domestic social consequences of the depression—or prosperity, for that matter—were not supplied to them in abstract market analyses. How their elites reacted to the effects of depression depended much more upon both the values in their hearts and on the structural strengths and weaknesses of the given societies.[7]

This is not to affirm that calculations of profit and loss were not woven into French arguments for free trade and protection in the years of the depression. Advocates of free trade tended to be linked to international markets, but not necessarily to the French colonial economy. Thus firms in transport, shipping, and domestic railroad interests were fervent supporters of freer trade. So, too, were the chambers of commerce of Paris and of great port cities involved in world commerce such as Bordeaux and Marseille. Paris craftsmen, for example, procured raw materials from all over the world and sold their finely wrought luxury articles abroad. The capital was also the center of French merchant banking, classically a free market industry. Businessmen of Lyon, both because of the bankers the city housed and because of its dying silk export commerce, were initially in the forefront of the free trade advocates.[8]

Nevertheless, the economic courage of the free traders, even that of the bankers, was daunted by the persistence and cyclical depths of the world depression. With sales abroad sluggish, arguments for freedom of commerce must have struck many business leaders as a bit hollow. Moreover, in the case of none of these industries or cities can we find what already existed for example in Lille, Roubaix, Tourcoing, Le Creusot, even Epinal: a modern class-conscious labor force. By the last quarter of the century, Paris was no longer a center of modern industry.[9] And with the exception of Paris, France's in-

7. Sidney Ratner, *The Tariff in American History* (New York, 1972), 36; Kindleberger, *The Economic Response*, 38. See also William M. Reddy, *The Rise of Market Culture: The French Textile Trade and French Society, 1750–1900* (Cambridge, England, 1984), 330–36.

8. John Laffey, "Roots of French Imperialism in the Nineteenth Century: The Case of Lyon," *French Historical Studies*, VI (1969), 78–92; Smith, *Tariff Reform in France*, 65–89.

9. The array of free trade advocates from the Paris mercantile community involved in the Association pour la Défense de la Liberté Commerciale et Industrielle

dustrial workers were not concentrated in the regions or industries most closely associated with the cause of free markets. Pressures from workers played no important role in any discussions over commercial policy of these exporting cities or industries. Free traders confined their efforts to mobilizing support in Paris, but, with the Commune still a memory, not among Parisian workers.[10]

The strongest advocates of protection came from the ranks both of big agriculture and big business. Until the 1870s French growers hewed to a free market position: they retained control of the domestic trade while continuing to export their market products (primarily wines and wheat) and to import their manufactured needs at the lowest prices. But the diseases of the vineyards and of silk worm culture, the swelling rural outmigration, and the competition of new world wheat and cattle producers made many French growers rethink their economic philosophies in the late 1870s and early 1880s. The large landowners in northern and western France, the sugar beet producers in the north and on the Paris plain, the eastern grain growers, and economically threatened market farmers from many regions of France reached to protectionism as to a life ring. The wine-growers of the Gironde, the producers of champagnes and fine brandies, all of whom lived from exports, remained free traders. But they were neither numerous nor powerful in the newly arisen agricultural pressure groups. The most powerful of these organizations, the Société des Agriculteurs de France, was dominated by landowning nobility and entered the protectionist camp in the early eighties. Most French peasants, not yet fully integrated into the national communication or market networks, often suffered less than the growers who supplied distant markets. Consequently peasants played only a small role in the policy debates. Both free trade and protectionist notables spoke on their behalf; the protectionists won the propaganda war over who spoke for the small cultivators on the tariff question.

French heavy industry, more than any other discernible economic

---

et pour le Développement des Traités de Commerce is listed in Smith's appendix to *Tariff Reform in France*, 250–52. By the early twentieth century the bicycle, automobile, and aircraft industries would once again make Paris a great industrial center.

10. *L'Industrie française*, March 27, June 5, 1879. Free trade advocates put on a few banquets and discussions in the capital, depending on their influence with the Tirard government to protect their interests. Moreover, even if they had wanted to mobilize the masses, they had no masses of workers to mobilize.

interests group, actively promoted the abandonment of the imperial legacy of free trade. Manufacturers of producer goods, especially the spinners of cotton yarns and producers of pig iron, dominated the protectionist advocacy along with the owners of great coal and iron mines. Most large firms from every major metallurgical interest supported increases in industrial tariffs in the 1880s. The largest coal mining companies—Anzin, Grand-combe, Blanzy, Firminy-Roche-La Molière, and Aniche—adhered firmly to the cause of tariff protection even though distance and transport costs sheltered them from the competition of neighboring countries. Since the iron founders were their best customers, good sense suggested solidarity on the issue of tariffs. And both industries suffered from, and complained about, the manner in which labor costs cut into their narrowing profit margins; many believed that tariffs might correct that problem, too.

The textile industries, with the primary exception of the silk weavers of Lyon, advocated commercial exclusion. Wool, linen, and cotton processors, despite competition among themselves, united around tariffs. At the forefront of the interest group were not decaying little firms at the margins of the economy. Rather, the spinners and weavers of Rouen, the Nord, and the Vosges ran large plants (over five hundred employees, typically) and suffered modern (that is, antagonistic) labor relations. Their reaction to the depression was surely defensive, but they hoped to defend themselves by sharing a monopoly of national production. Neither the important leaders of the metallurgical industry nor the mineowners wished to thwart the developing cotton oligopoly; they too were intent on sheltering themselves from their workers' wage pressures and from foreign competitors during a period of depressed profits. When the Third Republic became a political reality in the late 1870s, the protectionist manufacturers argued their case both in a national propaganda campaign and in the Opportunist-dominated Chamber of Deputies, sometimes in their capacity as elected deputies.

They had reason to expect success from their efforts of special pleading on at least two grounds. First, in past moments of French economic history various governments had resorted to economic protectionism as a weapon of international conflict. Jean Colbert had put up trade barriers; the French revolutionary regimes had torn them down. Tariffs were reinstituted in 1822 as part of the economic conservatism of the Restoration government. France remained an essentially protectionist nation until Napoleon III came to power. Soon after he had consolidated his dictatorship in 1852, he unilaterally lowered the duties on selected imported industrial products such as coal, iron, cast iron, woolens, and slaughtered meats. Then in 1860, once again employing his power to make laws by imperial decree, and largely for political reasons, the emperor had his representative Michel Chevalier sign a treaty of commerce with Great Britain that greatly reduced the French barriers to the importation of British goods. Napoleon's policy of freer trade remained in force when state power fell into the hands of the republican politicians in 1877.[11]

The second reason protectionist manufacturers could hope to change the direction of French commercial policy, of course, was that they were well organized. The economic downturn of the mid-1840s, which culminated in the political explosion of 1848, also spurred a number of France's leading industrialists to seek and to receive the requisite legal exemption from the minister of the interior to form a commercial organization for the defense of their interests. In 1846 Eugène Schneider, the iron founder, Victor Grandin, the great cloth manufacturer of Elbeuf, and Léon Talabot, the Toulouse iron and railroad entrepreneur—to name just the most famous members—founded the Association pour la Défense du Travail National. The goal of the association, as they wrote the minister, was to oppose the free traders, whose ideas, they believed, "would lead to the overthrow of the economic system of the country."[12] The organization disappeared during the reign of Napoleon III, but reemerged immediately upon the resolution of the constitutional crisis of 1877. Pouyer-Quertier, Thiers's minister of finance in 1871, revived the defunct protectionist organization in 1878 amid mounting conflict between owners and laborers after a long period of tranquillity. The reconstituted association counted 128 members

11. Méline, to encourage passage of what would become the high tariffs of 1910, wrote a brief tariff history of France, "Traités de commerce et conventions commerciales," *Revue économique internationale*, I (1907), 7–37. I have used some of his formulations in these paragraphs to demonstrate that Méline had a good sense that he was involved in an advocacy that had a long tradition in France and that tariffs were one of the historic ways in which the French state solved a variety of problems. However, the reader should consult also Smith, *Tariff Reform in France*, 26–47.

12. Rust, "Business and Politics in the Third Republic," 7–9; Roger Priouret, *Origines du patronat français* (Paris, 1963), 81–84.

at its founding. It published its news in a weekly newspaper, *L'Industrie française*, from the start, adding a second organ, *Le Travail national*, in 1884 as it stepped up its activities. The association was founded on the principle of solidarity among French industrial interests. It united, in the words of the opening declaration, "in the same alliance the metallurgists and the colliers, the thread and the cloth makers, the shipbuilders and the machinery manufacturers, the producers of chemicals and the clothing manufacturers, indeed all phases of the textile industries."[13]

To call the Association de l'Industrie Française a pressure group would be to violate the principle of Ockham's Razor, which counsels us not to multiply entities beyond logical need. Many of the members and most of the leaders of the association were active Opportunists, the dominant party of the early Third Republic.[14] Rather than functioning as an external pressure group, the protectionists, beginning with Méline, Ferry, and their friends, constituted the most farsighted and socially sensitive members of the republican party. At a unique moment in French history, a subcommittee of the bourgeoisie united to regulate common concerns.[15]

The French bourgeoisie had tolerated imperial rule because they could not, they dared not, rule in their own name.[16] But with the defeat of Napoleon III and the failure of the monarchists to create a government, bourgeois republicans had to shoulder the task of creating a stable political order that encased and appeased the im-

13. *Le Travail national,* July 6, 1884 (the first issue); "Augustin Pouyer-Quertier," *Grand larousse encyclopédique* (10 vols.; Paris, 1960–64), VIII, 743; A. de Foville, *Pouyer-Quertier: souvenirs et documents* (Paris, 1911), 6.

14. Jürgen Hilsheimer's inaugural dissertation at Heidelberg treats the pro-tariff agitation in France as a case study in pressure group politics. In view of the tight connections between the conservatives and the Société des Agriculteurs, and the Opportunists and the Association de l'Industrie Française, however, it seems difficult to conceive the state as a neutral arbitrator of competing interests. See also Hilsheimer's *Interessengruppen und Zollpolitik in Frankreich: die Auseinandersetzungen um die Aufstellung des Zolltarifs von 1892* (Heidelberg, 1973).

15. See the appendix in which the leadership and supporters of the Association de l'Industrie Française are listed for different times up to the war. After 1892 the membership gained not only agriculturalist spokesmen but also free traders who had reconciled themselves to a protectionist France, making the organization a truly national representative of big business and big agriculture.

16. Karl Marx's *Eighteenth Brumaire of Louis Bonaparte* is still the best explanation of why and how this was so.

portant sectors of the society. However, the preliminary task of unifying the party of the bourgeoisie was difficult. The republican voting system initiated in 1875, modified in 1885, and changed once again in 1889 (to thwart any future multiple candidacies in the manner of General Boulanger) made maintenance of strict party discipline difficult to enforce.[17] Clearly support from the candidate's constituency—or from the men of high standing in the arrondissement or department—plus the necessary deals that two rounds of elections required had to find a place in the electoral tactics of most candidates. Against these pressures party discipline and party whips could not readily prevail. Thus we must characterize the group of politicians known at various times as Progressistes, Modérés, and Opportunists—the dominant group that, starting with tariffs, fashioned the hegemonic bloc to sustain the Third Republic against present and future labor troubles—by saying something about the political philosophy that linked them and about the parliamentary leaders who spoke for them.

The Opportunists dominated the Chamber of Deputies in the 1880s and controlled both houses of the legislature for nearly all of the 1890s. Not since the Restoration was the class bias of the leadership of the French state made so manifest. In the realm of social organization, the Opportunists championed the proliferation of political self-help organizations: they were drawn to Proudhonian mutualist ideas of class reconciliation. Politically, of course, they were liberals whose prime unit of analysis was the individual. We may describe them as laissez-faire in theory but agreeable to state intervention in the economy if their interests so required.[18] Growing accustomed to the exercise of real power, they eschewed doctrinaire posturing.

We would misunderstand the role of these politicians of the early Republic if we were to dismiss them simply as inconsistent liberals or self-serving rascals. They fashioned a sociopolitical governing bloc in the difficult years of the depression. They did so because, as Pierre Sorlin has written,

17. Peter Campbell, *French Electoral Systems and Elections, 1789–1957* (London, 1958), 71–81.

18. Marie-Geneviève Raymond, *La politique pavillonnaire* (Paris, 1966), 187–88; Richard Kuisel, *Capitalism and the State in Modern France,* 15–20.

They believed themselves menaced by the awakening of the workers. The fear of socialism became their common denominator. Incapable of defining a precise program, they at first contented themselves with fashioning electoral alliances with all the partisans of the established order; they soon wound up aligning themselves with the natural defenders of capitalism. . . . The Progressiste republic, the republic of the Méline Ministry, was characterized at the same time by its conservatism and by the close ties which bound the world of business and that of politics.[19]

Or, as Jules Ferry put his sentiments about how to deal with workers' claims for the solicitude of the state to his fellow deputies in a speech to the Chamber on January 31, 1884—at a moment of plunging agricultural and industrial prices *and* of extensive unemployment—too many republicans and the great majority of the workers erred in believing "that they had the right to demand from the government the solution to the social question. It was on this misunderstanding," he warned, "that the Republic of 1848 had foundered." Workers should not expect from the Republic measures of social welfare or insurance such as Bismarck was then instituting across the Rhine, he was saying. And if they pressed for such measures, he was also warning, they could expect another experience of the June Days of 1848.[20]

After Léon Gambetta, Jules Ferry was the great hero of the Opportunist republicans. Upon Gambetta's death at the end of 1882, Ferry became their most prominent parliamentary spokesman. His friend, fellow Vosgien, and minister of agriculture in his cabinet, Jules Méline, was the leader of the center-right in the 1890s.

Like his compatriot, Méline was one of the provincial lawyers who dominated the early Third Republic.[21] Born in 1838 in Remiremont in the Vosges mountains, then largely a center of lumbering and agriculture but soon to become a center of textile production, he went to Paris like so many ambitious small-town bourgeois before him to make his fortune as a lawyer. There he fell in with the opponents to the rule of Napoleon III. The unexpected fall of Napoleon opened the path for Méline's first political step: on September 6, 1870, two days after the fall of the Empire and the proclamation of

19. Pierre Sorlin, *Waldeck-Rousseau* (Paris, 1966), 364.
20. Paul Robiquet (ed.), *Discours et opinions de Jules Ferry* (7 vols.; Paris, 1893–98), VI, 226.
21. Sanford Elwitt, *The Making of the Third Republic: Class and Politics in France, 1868–1884* (Baton Rouge, 1975), 10–18.

the Republic, he took up the post of deputy mayor in the first arron-dissement. His friend Ferry, then mayor of Paris, had nominated him for the position. Although elected to the municipal council on March 26, 1871, Méline attended only the first meeting on the twenty-eighth. He had been in the city ten days before, when the Paris mob had executed Generals Lecomte and Thomas, whom Thiers had sent to secure the cannons on the heights of Montmartre. The radical senti-ments of the Parisians who proclaimed the Commune on March 28 convinced Méline that that piece of insurrectionary violence would not be the last one Parisians would perpetrate or witness. Like Ferry, who had already left the city, he was appalled by the radicalism he saw there. Resigning his seat, he hurriedly left the next day to spend the months of the Commune in his tranquil home in the Vosges. The direct experience of the violence of insurrection, of worker revo-lutionary radicalism, impressed him deeply, as it did Ferry. He de-voted a good part of his parliamentary career to building dams against it. Méline returned to Paris in May as soon as the victorious Versailles forces of Adolphe Thiers had pacified the city.

Méline's long career in national politics began the next year with his election as deputy from the Vosges. His parliamentary career was relatively undistinguished until 1876, when he was named to the parliamentary commission charged with formulating recom-mendations for a law of amnesty for the Communards. He opposed amnesty. If the parliament inclined to permit the deportees to re-turn, he urged that they be pardoned rather than amnestied, wish-ing thereby to hold over the heads of the insurrectionists the cul-pability of their acts. The Chamber of Deputies supported a pardon bill of the sort Méline could accept, but the reactionary Senate re-jected it, causing the fall of the Dufaure government. On December 14, Jules Simon, declaring himself "deeply conservative," managed to form a ministry.

Simon appointed Méline to his first post in national government by naming him undersecretary of state for justice and cults. At this new position he pursued moderately anticlerical policies but with-out excessive Masonic fervor. It is unlikely that he shared Gambet-ta's judgment, "Clericalism, there's the enemy!" declaimed on May 4, 1877, in the Chamber. In any case he was not tested, for two weeks later President MacMahon forced Jules Simon from office and for the third and last time called upon the Duc de Broglie to form a government.

Méline experienced the crisis year of 1877 by having to run against an "official" monarchist candidate for his seat from Remiremont. In his electoral campaign he denounced bellicosity, suggesting that not the republicans but the supporters of Bonapartism and monarchy were eager to embroil France in new wars. Nevertheless, Méline urged Frenchmen to support MacMahon, despite what he vaguely termed MacMahon's "errors." But he balanced those conservative affinities with, for him, uncharacteristic sentiments of anticlericalism. His able political trimming brought him electoral victory. On his return to Paris in March, 1878, he allied himself once again with his countryman Ferry and was appointed to the parliamentary committee directed to examine French customs duties. So began his famous and long-term association with protection and protectionism.[22]

While Méline began to find his way around the corridors of power in the Chamber, his chief backers, the cotton manufacturers of the Vosges, met at the city hall of Remiremont late in March, 1879, to discuss what common action was possible to reverse the serious depression in the prices of cotton goods. After some deliberation, they decided that one course of action to avoid was the reduction of wages. They realized, according to the prefect's report of the meeting, that such a course would only exaggerate the overproduction and underconsumption that was fueling the decline in sales. After all, they agreed, their workers were important consumers of their products.[23]

The industrialists of the Nord, who also shared the notion that economic crises originated in the combined effects of overproduction and underconsumption, faced the added worry of an especially explosive work force. That same March the textile manufacturers of Armentières sent a delegation of their foremen and managers to the prefect, Paul Cambon, to gain his influence in Paris for higher duties. The industrialists' representatives argued that in Armentières, at least, a wage reduction was enough to put the workers in this mill town "into motion," and although they were hard to arouse, "once

22. For a discussion of Méline's life and career before 1878, see Jean-Paul Gérard, "Jules Méline, député des Vosges à l'Assemblée Nationale et à la Chambre des Députés (1872–1877)," *Annales de l'Est*, 5th ser., XVI (1964), 329–48.
23. Archives Nationales (hereinafter cited as AN) F12 4655, Vosges, cited in Perrot, *Les Ouvriers en grève*, I, 152–53.

in motion, they were difficult to stop." For their part, the owners would of course warehouse their surplus production, but they urged Cambon to press their case for immediate tariff protection.[24]

The explosion of labor militancy around the turn of the decade was not restricted to Armentières or even to the Nord. In the mid-1870s the annual number of strikes on the average was approximately the same as in the early 1840s. After 1877, the frequency of industrial conflicts and numbers of workers involved in them shot up. Contemporaries were amazed by the increases of the year 1878, a third more strikes affecting twice as many workers as the year before. Those of the year 1880 marked a new height of industrial conflict in France; the great strike wave of 1869–1870 was surpassed in scope. After a reduction of tensions in 1881 the number of strikes shot up again dramatically, although the numbers of strikers involved or days lost did not reach the peak attained in 1880 (see Table 1).[25]

With strike activity also rose the involvement of workers belonging to unions in the strikes. The percentage of the strikers who belonged to a union rose from a low of 1.9 percent in 1875 to 19 percent in 1878 and 39 percent in both 1881 and 1883. Labor was therefore organizing more, and striking more, as the 1870s gave way to the 1880s. Workers did so because of disputes centered largely on issues of pay, hours, and work rules.[26]

To many members of the Association de l'Industrie Française these strikes were nasty personal experiences, perhaps even threats to the survival of the family business. Consider these examples of strikes in firms in the North owned by important members of the association. In 1880 the Roubaix weaving firm of Delathe père et fils was struck twice. In early January two hundred strikers sat at their looms refusing to work until they received an increase in pay. After closing down the factory for over three weeks, the weavers returned

24. *Ibid.* The cotton spinners of the Nord held something on the order of a half year's unsold production of finished yarn worth two million francs (François Caron, "Dynamismes et freinages de la croissance industrielle," in Braudel and Labrousse (eds.), *HES*, vol. IV, pt. 1, pp. 266–67).

25. Shorter and Tilly, *Strikes in France*, 47.

26. *Ibid.*; Perrot, *Les Ouvriers en grève*, I, 406. Shorter and Tilly, *Strikes in France*, 342, specifically deny the importance usually ascribed to wage disputes in the occurrence of nineteenth-century industrial disputes. They see wage demands as "merely a mobilizing device, not a real issue."

with a small pay raise. Between February 9 and 12 a smaller number struck again but could get nothing more for their efforts. They returned to work "without conditions," as the official record of the ministry of commerce phrased it.[27]

In 1882, Julien LeBlan, president of the Lille chamber of commerce, member of the executive committee of the Association de l'Industrie Française, and manufacturer of linen thread in Lille, twice personally confronted workers on strike over pay cuts he had initiated. Both strikes were defeated and the thread workers went back to work "under the old conditions."[28]

Even the reputedly docile workers of the Vosges resisted employers' attempts to make them pay for the commercial crisis. Just before Christmas, 1882, in Saint Dié 160 workers employed in the weaving firm of Dietsch frères, whose owners were also members of the Association de l'Industrie Française, walked off to protest alterations in the shop rules. These strikers won. The rule modifications were withdrawn, and production resumed.[29]

The pattern obtained in other regions and industries. In 1882 important strikes shook Le Creusot, where Henri Schneider, another executive committee member of the association, ruled. The coal mines of Carmaux and shops in the iron-working regions of Saint-Etienne, Grenoble, and Vienne were struck as well. That fall labor troubles broke into violence at the Blanzy coal mines in Montceau-les-Mines. In brief, the industries, and in many cases the firms, most crippled by the price plunge of the turn of the decade were also attacked in the new surge of labor militance. These industries and firms comprised the core of the Association de l'Industrie Française. In many instances owners personally suffered the animosity of their workers in the course of labor actions and often perceived the demands of their workers as threats to the livelihoods of their families.[30]

But it was also in centers of association-related industries that owners tried to persuade their restive workpeople to make common cause against the policy of commercial free trade. The association

27. AN F¹² 5749, Grèves en France.
28. *Ibid.*
29. *Ibid.*
30. See the list of members, their firms, and officers of the association in the appendix of this work.

orchestrated a national campaign of rallies and petitions. Early in 1879 in Lille, member Gustave Dubar, the linen manufacturer, had his foremen and managers gather workers' signatures on a protectionist petition. Claiming to have assembled thirty thousand names, they presented the document to President Jules Grévy in May. In Amiens association militants also gathered the signatures of their workers and held public meetings as well to promote protectionism. Nicolas Claude, senator, textile manufacturer, and Méline's mentor in the Vosges, organized similar efforts in the textile mill towns of the Vosges valleys. Petition campaigns, rallies, and meetings between workers and officials blossomed all over Normandy. At Rouen yet another large protectionist demonstration collected thousands of workers' names on petitions against free trade that in due course were presented by association stalwarts Lucien Dautresme and Richard Waddington, at the head of a delegation of foremen, to Premier William Waddington, Richard's brother.

Many contemporaries saw such tactics as playing with fire. An alarmed contributor to the resolutely free trade *L'Economiste français* voiced the fears of many of the well-off when he wrote of the protectionist rallies that the agitation was going well beyond the usual speechmaking and passing around of petitions: "they were trying to unite with the workers [by telling them] that they [were] going to starve, and that it [was] the fault of the treaties of commerce."[31]

As soon as the constitutional crisis had been settled and right-thinking Frenchmen hoped to settle back to profit from the republic that had fallen from the spastic grip of the monarchists, another wave of depression once more drove industrial and agricultural prices down, while a surprising new labor militancy drove their anxieties up.[32] Emile Zola used the violent strike at Anzin in 1884 as a

31. Pierre-Armand Dufrénoy, "La dernière manifestation protectionniste," *L'Economiste français*, May 10, 1879. The references and data of the last two paragraphs I owe to Michael S. Smith's *Tariff Reform in France*, 163. In the sense of strengthening or weakening pressure group politics, his judgment that "for all the drama and notoriety of such rallies, they played a relatively minor role in the protectionist campaign," is surely accurate. But this tells us little about their role in the larger struggle for social appeasement and class collaboration rather than conflict.

32. See the excellent article on the lack of class consciousness among the workers of the Nord textile mills before 1870 and its sudden emergence in the next decade by Jean-Paul Courtheoux, "Naissance d'une conscience de classe dans le prolétariat textile du Nord? 1820–1879," *Revue économique*, VIII (1957), 114–39.

model for the explosion of workers' militancy he portrayed in *Germinal*, published a year later. The horrors of class conflict that the novel conjured up warned its bourgeois readers that they were experiencing just the springtime of workers' discontent; the hot summer was yet to come. Contrary to the assertion of some literary scholars that the specter of the Commune haunted *Germinal*, Zola and his readers were more deeply troubled by the surges of contemporary labor conflict, which, unlike the Commune, could not be put down with a great, bloody, but short struggle.[33]

And in this moment of economic crisis the industrialists could do little to improve the wages of their workers. On the contrary, many tried to reduce them in various ways. That made the ideology of National Labor very tempting. The first number of *Le Travail national* voiced the industrialists' intentions clearly: they sought no conflict with their workers. "Our guiding principle is the solidarity of employer and worker. We reject the categories of 'capital' and of 'labor,' for the patron, like the worker, also labors. Rather, we propose solidarity of all French workers before the threat of foreign competition."[34]

At the first full-dress national congress of the new-born socialist movement held at Marseille in October, 1879, the participants had debated the issue of free trade versus protectionism. Ferrand of the Parisian hatters defended protectionism as policy good for the French workers suffering from the industrial crisis, especially in the north, and good for the nation, "for our dear Republic." The several other speakers admitted of no difference between free trade and protectionism, or between free traders and protectionists, from the point of view of the interests of the workers. Taking essentially the position advanced by Emile Aubry in 1869, the congress adopted a resolution claiming to see no advantage for the proletariat of either policy. The delegates therefore refused to consider taking a position in support of either course.[35]

33. In this I endorse the view of Perrot, *Les Ouvriers en grève*, I, 73, 89.

34. *Le Travail national*, July 6, 1884, p. 2.

35. *Congrès ouvrier socialiste de France tenu à Marseille du 20 au 31 octobre 1879* (Marseille, 1879), 671–703, 815–16. By 1884 at least one socialist leader, Paul Brousse, offered a keener analysis of the social strategies in play, as would Paul Lafargue and Jean Jaurès some years later. On Brousse's advocacy at the Marseille congress of the strike as the chief weapon for improving working conditions, see David Stafford, *From Anarchism to Reformism: A Study of the Political Activities of Paul Brousse Within the*

In the early eighties a relatively disorganized, inconscient working class might be expected to cooperate with their employers.
Moreover the provincial industrial bourgeoisie—still unsure of its
strengths and place in French society as well as those of its employees—had good reason to envision themselves arm and arm
with their workers, on the order of the artisan shop writ large and
run in paternalistic fashion.[36]

Even the economic discourse of their spokesmen promoted the
ideology of industrial harmony. In early February, 1881, Méline, as
reporter for the tariff commission of the Chamber, presented the
draft tariff law that the protectionists had so strenuously promoted.
He claimed in his speech introducing the bill that in the often narrow
and detailed discussions of duties on this or that item, he had held
tightly to two ideas: "The first of these principles is that labor is the
source of everything, that it is labor which creates capital, and that
the greater the labor the more accumulation of capital and the more
national wealth. . . . The second . . . is that the greater capital
accumulation, the more there is for wages, the more pay increases,
and as a consequence, the more the working class—for which we
have so much solicitude—gains in well-being and in morality."[37]

Therefore he offered the tariff as that spur to the accumulation of
capital, to the increase in profits in essence, that would benefit
workers and capitalists alike.[38] Méline was proposing, in effect, that
perhaps industrial tariffs might be raised high enough to permit
sufficiently ample recovery of sales and profits to grant some of the
workers' economic demands. He wooed the representatives of the
growers in the Chamber, while keeping peace with his industrialist
friends, by endorsing the extension of protection to agricultural
products to stimulate revival of flagging rural purchasing power. It
is likely that the deputies were more smitten by his less abstract
proposals about supporting cotton thread, pig iron, and beef prices

---

First International and the French Socialist Movement, 1870–90 (Toronto, 1971), 156–58,
188.

36. See Peter Stearn's valuable study of the extent of harmony and paternalism
in French industry in the earlier part of the century, *Paths to Authority: The Middle
Class and the Industrial Labor Force in France, 1820–48* (Champaign, Ill., 1978).

37. *Journal Officiel*, Chambre des députés, Débats, February 3, 1880, pp. 1202–
1203.

38. *Ibid*.

that followed the disquisition on economic philosophy. The tariff, as we know, passed.

The tariff act of 1881 was the first approximation at fulfilling the protectionists' commercial and *social* hopes—albeit, to many of them, a disappointing first effort.[39] Among the agriculturalists only the livestock breeders gained heightened protection. They also gained an effective veto power over any tariff decreases the government might negotiate in the future. But the 1881 measure offered nothing for the hurting winegrowers, nor the wheat farmers. And although the industrialists received a 24 percent boost in duties on manufactured goods and conversion from duties expressed on an *ad valorem* basis to listed duties on each item (permitting them better surveillance and quicker reaction), they were not content. The pages of *Le Travail national* continued to carry their lamentations and expressions of need.

Moreover, less than a half year after the tariff's passage, between October, 1881, and February, 1882, the protectionist industrialists and deputies, still smarting from their poor showing in the tariff fight with the parliamentary supporters of free trade, could not prevent the conclusion of a series of trade treaties between France and Belgium, Italy, the Netherlands, Portugal, Sweden-Norway, Spain, and Switzerland. The treaties were negotiated at the behest and to the benefit of the free traders. Existing understandings with Russia, Austria-Hungary, and Turkey continued in force, and the German Empire retained the right, accorded in the Treaty of Frankfurt that had ended the Franco-Prussian War, to receive any of the beneficial trade arrangements negotiated with any other trading partners. The British, too, retained this right of most-favored-nation treatment despite the expiration of the 1860 treaty.[40]

The commercial crisis, although for the moment not as acute as in the years before 1880, went on. The curve of prices (and with them, profits) continued to sink, heading downward at an alarming slope. The numbers of strikes, if not the numbers of those participating, continued to increase.[41] After waiting to see whether the tariff, and

39. Smith, *Tariff Reform in France*, 180–82.

40. *Ibid.*, 151.

41. Although there was a clear upsurge of strike activity in the years 1880–82, Shorter and Tilly (*Strikes in France*, 110–12) do not include that peak in their survey of strike waves. They discuss the wave of 1869–70, which they characterize as "still

time, would not heal cuts both in profits and in the social fabric, the Opportunist majority in the Chamber decided on the need for additional action, however tentative.

First, the move was an attempt to contain the workers in organizations which would tame their growing radicalism. It is in the context of the growing labor conflicts of the depression that we should understand the passage of the 1884 law, a measure permitting workers to form legal trade unions. Despite the opposition of many socialist leaders, who saw Waldeck-Rousseau's bill as a legal trap (an early version of the law required registration of the names of all the members of the union) and as an attempt to co-opt workers into the politics of mutual aid advocated by the ideologues of *Solidarité*, the measure passed in the parliament. Waldeck-Rousseau hoped the 1884 law would structure peaceable and orderly relations between labor and capital.[42]

And second, the Opportunists sent to the provinces for guidance and help. Unsure of what further might be done to reduce distress, or at least to explain its occurrence, the Opportunists undertook a parliamentary inquiry. Questionnaires were sent off to chambers of commerce all over France to solicit the views of the business community in systematic fashion. Hearings were scheduled as well. From the pattern of responses we may clearly discern the lining up of free traders against protectionists, not simply according to industry and region, as one could expect, but also according to the intensity or lack thereof of industrial conflict.

Consider the attitude of the chamber of commerce of the wine-exporting (and therefore free trade) city of Bordeaux. Although other parts of France had suffered intense strike activity, Bordeaux had been quiet; the response of the Bordeaux merchants denied that

---

part of the artisanal pattern" and then go on to discuss the industrial conflicts of 1893 ("near the front end of the long transition from artisanal to mechanized production"). They tend to discount the connection of business cycle fluctuations with strike activity. They discount, as well, workers' assertions that wages were the overwhelming issue in the majority of strikes—as well as work rules, which often translate into wage issues (pp. 335–43). *Employers* do not figure in their account of industrial conflict. On the economic climate at the turn of the decade see Caron, "Dynamismes et freinages de la croissance industrielle," in Braudel and Labrousse (eds.), *HES*, vol. IV, pt. 1, pp. 266–67.

42. Edouard Dolléans, *Histoire du mouvement ouvrier* (3 vols.; Paris, 1936–53), II, 25–26.

workers were suffering any important new difficulties. They were about as well off, asserted the returned questionnaire, as they had been twenty or twenty-five years before. Bad harvests, which could have sent bread prices up, had been compensated for by the temporary admission of foreign-grown wheat. Moreover, the optimistic statement concluded with a dig at the cotton manufacturers; its authors claimed that increases in the scale of production in recent years had reduced clothing prices, which had held down increases in the cost of living.[43]

Certainly, this was the extreme free trade position, coming from citizens of a nonindustrial port who made their livings from processing and exporting luxury wines. The chambers of commerce of Saint-Quentin and Nancy, both industrial cities (Saint-Quentin largely a textile manufacturing city), took exception to questions in the inquiry that sought to discover whether prices for workers' essentials and their rents had gone up. Nor did they consider questions about the existence of workers' mutual aid societies appropriate. Such questions implied a certain distrust of employers, the chamber of commerce admonished; the parliamentary inquirers should realize the current crisis was *industrial* (that is, hurt the industrialists) in nature, not just related to the narrow problems of workers.[44]

The chambers of commerce of Chalon-sur-Saône, Autun, and Louhans, towns situated in a region of fine wine production that was also the home of the great Schneider-owned Le Creusot works, was well-situated to restate the article of faith of French protectionists: that the best means of improving the lot of industry and commerce would be to take measures to benefit French agriculture, "the principal source of profits in our region."[45]

The most revealing written response to the inquiry came from the business spokesmen of the great metallurgical and textile producing center in the north, Lille. The authors of the return from Lille complained, above all, that other nations' industrialists had both tariffs to hide behind and the services of a relatively cheap labor force. Because French workers' wages, "the principal component of cost,"

43. *Enquête parlementaire sur la crise économique et sur la situation industrielle, commerciale et agricole en France, 1884.* AN C³³²⁹ *Réponse*, Bordeaux.
44. *Ibid.*, *Réponse*, Saint Quentin, Nancy.
45. *Ibid.*, *Réponse*, Chalon-sur-Saône, Autun, Louhans.

had risen in the past few years and because of the wretched effects of "strike upon strike," foreign customers could depend neither on the stability of French prices nor on promised delivery dates. Only "foreign competitors . . . profited" from the pay gains French workers exacted in strikes.

There followed in the response from Lille a long diatribe against workers' organizations, both for turning the workers against their employers and against capital in general, and their efforts to reduce the length of the work day, which only hurt production without benefiting labor. And finally, the respondents complained about the high taxes that weighed so heavily upon the industrialists of the Nord. The workers would have to work harder and more intelligently, concluded the analysis, and they should not allow themselves to be misled by "outside agitators."[46]

The views expressed by the Lille manufacturers manifested a bedrock belief widespread among the protectionist industrialists: that profits, wages, and foreign competition were linked in a triangle of forces. Foreign competition reduced profits, which in turn drove down wages. Conversely, reduced foreign imports permitted higher profits that allowed wage improvements. But wages (that is, labor) stood at the pinnacle of the production triangle. Practical men, the Lille manufacturers operated according to a rough-and-ready Ricardianism. Wages, they claimed, were their principal cost of production. The vise squeezing their profit margins and thus squeezing their family's patrimony had as one jaw their wage bill, the other, foreign competition. The debate-at-distance between the socialist Paul Brousse and Senator Nicolas Claude, one of the founders of the Association de l'Industrie Française, in their testimony at the hearings of the inquiry demonstrates this point rather graphically.

On March 8, 1884, Paul Brousse, speaking on behalf of the Fédération des Travailleurs Socialistes de France, the so-called Possibilistes, appeared before the commission to present his views on the depression. His theme was that the wages of French workmen were not the cause of the economic crisis, as so often had been alleged. Rather, he reminded the members of the commission the reason that French textiles could not compete in world markets lay in the high domestic costs of coal, machinery, and labor. Apparently unable or unwilling to do anything about the first two costs, he charged, French capital-

46. *Ibid., Réponse,* Lille.

ists had decided to make the wages of their workers "the great battlefield." Indeed, he continued, "they claim that French workers are better paid than workers in other lands, and that as a result it is not possible to hold out against the foreign competition." The rest of his testimony expounded the theme that, if French workers were paid well, it was because they were more productive than workers elsewhere.[47]

A few weeks later, Senator Claude, a thread and cloth manufacturer from Saulxures, a few kilometers down the road from Méline's home in Remiremont, appeared before the commission to challenge Brousse's testimony and, in so doing, to articulate in succinct fashion the position of most protectionist industrialists for the coming decades. Claude, like the spokesmen of the chambers of commerce of Chalon-sur-Saône, Autun, and Louhans, saw that the French agricultural crisis lay at the center of the general economic crisis and that "from the difficulties of agriculture flowed, in part, those of industry." What of the problems originating in the industrial sector? To be sure, something had to be done about the high price of domestic coal, as well as high internal transportation costs, he argued. And especially, the senator emphasized, "the fact of the inflation of wages" had to be confronted. To that purpose, he concluded, "We must bring about a good understanding between labor and capital, that is, we must arrive at the elimination of the strikes, which cripple our production to the profit of that of other nations."[48]

The rate and intensity of labor conflict slowed between 1885 and 1890. An observer inclined to optimistic judgments might hypothesize that the tariff and the 1884 law legalizing trade unions were beginning to effect Claude's hoped-for "good understanding between labor and capital." Although the steep decline of both industrial and agricultural prices had halted, they remained in a deep depressionary trough, with agricultural prices resting five index points below the levels for industry. The agricultural interest needed attention; its recovery would aid that of industry. However, no responsible political leader could depend on the continuation of industrial peace in planning for the future. The suffering growers had to be mobilized against the free traders in the Chamber. United, the

47. *Enquête*, 1884, Procès-verbaux, séance du avril 1, 1884, p. 343.
48. *Ibid.*, séance du mai 8, 1884, pp. 141–50.

leaders of national industry and national agriculture could raise the tariff wall still higher. That measure, they believed, might also serve to protect them from the discontent and anger of a class of workers still in its germinating state.

III

The Alliance of Iron, Cotton, and Wheat

The passage of a new, more protective tariff in 1882 ended neither the crisis of French industry nor that of agriculture. Although collaboration was by no means inevitable, powerful producers in the two potentially antagonistic sectors of industry and agriculture continued to work together to encourage state policies for their mutual benefit.

First, all interested parties started from the same, almost canonically repeated premise: peasants, or individuals drawing their incomes from agriculture, made up the bulk of the consumers of French industrial production.[1] Therefore, decline in agricultural revenues created industrial gluts. The great renewal of railway construction in the late 1870s and early 1880s and the proliferation of branch lines bearing the name of its promoter, the railway-engineer-turned-politician Charles de Freycinet, was aimed at tying the rural sources of raw materials and rural consumers more closely to the centers of urban production and at the same time creating urban outlets for rural products.[2]

Second, the relative inelasticity of French domestic demand required not only that the home market be as fully and as efficiently exploited as possible but also that the peasant market be shielded from foreign competition. In the eighties the phylloxera continued to destroy the vines, hitting especially severely the extensive plantings in grapes destined for the *vins ordinaires* of the Midi. Only the rich commercial growers could afford the drastic remedy of grafting the French shoots onto American roots; nor could poor peasants afford the several years' wait for the new vines to start producing

1. See, for example, *Le Travail national,* August 17, 1884, p. 73–74.
2. Sanford Elwitt, *The Making of the Third Republic: Class and Politics in France, 1868–1884* (Baton Rouge, 1975), 103–35.

acceptable wine grapes. American, Argentinian, and Canadian wheat came in growing volume and with declining prices onto the world and French domestic markets. Meat from American, Argentinian, and Australian livestock, even before the widespread use of refrigerator ships in the 1890s, was imported into France at competitive prices.[3]

For a short time the manufacturers fared better. The duties of 1882 benefited the textile interests somewhat. The iron and coal producers kept busy by supplying the needs of the railroad construction that the Freycinet Plan had called forth. In addition, the modernization and, for the moment, the relative prosperity of the textile industry of the Nord required more coal production.[4] Still, isolated moments of relative prosperity were not good enough for the cotton industry, which had to buy its raw materials abroad and could not undersell English producers in most branches of production. Moreover, what invasions would they have to repel, the French iron and steel producers wondered, when the French railway boom ended and the efficient American and German mills disgorged their products at prices below the barrier set by French tariffs?

Third, insofar as industrialists and growers alike needed the state to perform fiscal, judicial, police, and defense functions, whatever else might divide them, they had to see to it that the state received the wherewithal to function. Sales taxes on agricultural products, especially wines and spirits, paid an appreciable portion of the state's expenses. Contemporary public officials, industrialists, and growers knew this. In a year of good wine harvests in pre–World War I France excises on wine and spirits might finance 15 percent of the state budget; they were the greatest single source of governmental revenue. Moreover, wine exports represented the second most valuable source of foreign exchange.[5] In first place, still, were textile

---

3. Paul Lafargue, leader of the Marxian Parti Ouvrier, displayed a keen understanding of the fecundity of capitalist agriculture in the United States and the grave dangers it posed for the French growers in "Le blé en Amérique," *Journal des économistes*, VII (1884), 42–61, 195–214.

4. The power needs of the textile industry fostered the development of the coal industry, and in turn the coal industry created demand for textiles. See Roger Priouret, *Origines du patronat français* (Paris, 1963), 212.

5. Charles Warner, *The Winegrowers of France* (New York, 1960), 1. Warner writes of the *value* of the taxes paid on wine and brandy consumption; I am discussing *who* paid the excise.

exports. Opportunist ministers, even if tempted by calculations of class advantage, could scarcely afford to allow the already fiscally undernourished state to lose more revenues.[6]

Thus the state protected the possessions of both growers and manufacturers. Workers and peasants—in their capacity as consumers—paid the bill for a protective system aimed as much at themselves as at foreign competitors. Just as excise taxes shifted the costs of government onto the shoulders of the poor, so did tariffs.[7] The elevated prices they engendered would expand the profit margins—or reduce the losses—of growers and manufacturers. To the degree they were not prohibitive (and the Opportunists' duties were not), they would supplement state revenue. And the state, then, could better function to keep the public order.

Because they considered themselves *the* party of the Republic, the Opportunists took the initiative in assembling a broad social coalition that would support the new state that had begun taking form in the late 1870s. In the concrete reality of the newly created Third Republic this meant, of course, winning the peasants away from any lingering loyalty to Bonapartism and the large growers away from loyalty to monarchism.

The leaders of the party promoted the right man for the key post in the struggle. In 1883 the urban lawyer and industrialists' spokesman, Jules Méline, assumed the unlikely post of minister of agriculture in the government of Jules Ferry. Much has been made of Méline's lack of knowledge or experience with the concerns of his ministry, but technical competence has never been an important asset for a politician's career. It was sufficient that Méline understood the need for building coalitions based firmly on the economic interests of the participants, and that he had the confidence of Jules Ferry.[8]

As the eighties gave way to the nineties, the task of propitiating or cowing the relatively new but growing modern industrial working

6. Should the penury of the French state have proved dysfunctional, the mounting pressure for a graduated income tax would have been even harder to resist—not on grounds of fiscal justice but simply to collect the wherewithal to keep the state's business going.

7. Jean Bouvier, "Sur l'immobilisme du système fiscal français au XIXe siècle," *Revue d'histoire économique et sociale*, L (1972), 482–93.

8. Michel Cointat, "Jules Méline: Mérite agricole et protectionnisme," *Revue politique et parlementaire*, LXXIV (1972), 1–12.

class also forced its way on the Opportunist political agenda. Since that working class was weak, small, and concentrated largely in the towns of the provinces, the newly emergent industrial bourgeoisie in modern mining, iron, and textile manufacture was inclined to deal with the workers' economic grievances directly. When the strikes of the late 1870s and early 1880s began to convince the more astute of their number that the workers' discontent was *structural* and therefore not soluble by a kind word or even by means of paternalism, many industrialists turned to the government to provide the means whereby the ideology of the unity of owner and employee at the workplace could be maintained. Owners and workers alike confronted rapacious foreign competitors, the owners reasoned. Their common interests would be served by tariffs. But as we have seen, many workers seemed hesitant to take up the owners' offers. Moreover, there was no possibility of governing with the workers, and there was some danger of having to govern against them.[9]

Thus, very much like the emerging ruling coalition of the neighboring German Empire, the troubled industrialists held out their arms to another distressed stratum, the large, often aristocratic, agriculturalists.[10] Although they produced for the market, these

9. For the refusal of some textile manufacturers of the Nord to recognize workers' unions and treat with them see Maurice Petitcollot, "Les Syndicats ouvriers de l'industrie textile dans l'arrondissement de Lille" (Thesis, University of Lille, 1907). Gambetta called the provincial bourgeoisie the "new strata"; Elwitt calls them "moderate men of order."

10. The economic and political collaboration of republicans and conservatives, growers and industrialists, often originated on the local level over local concerns. In the Pas-de-Calais during the tariff struggles, for example, leaders of the local agricultural societies collaborated with industrial leaders on the Conseil Général of the department. The sugar manufacturers and brewers of the region played leading roles in the agricultural organizations. And by 1905 the regional republican-oriented agricultural organization was holding its general assemblies in common with the parallel conservative body. For this region see Ronald H. Hubscher, *L'Agriculture et la société rurale dans le Pas-de-Calais: du milieux du XIXe siècle à 1914* (2 vols.; Arras, 1979–80), I, 602, 608–09, 618. To learn something of the local convergence in the Loire-et-Cher, see Georges Dupeux's discussion of the newly emerged political tendencies in the department toward the end of the century, the Ralliés and the socialists: *Aspects de l'histoire sociale et politique du Loire-et-Cher, 1848–1914* (Paris, 1962), 460–489, 490–541. For some information on local affinities and criticisms of André Siegfried's *Tableau politique de la France de l'Ouest sous la IIIe République* (Paris, 1913), which traces the pervasiveness of conservatism in western France to the special rapport of the local

growers nevertheless lived uneasily within the newly created republican version of a capitalist society.

The French Revolution was not as great a calamity to the fortunes of the nobility as is sometime supposed. The noble families that left the country lost their lands, it is true; however, those who stayed behind managed to retain their estates.[11] In 1825 the restored monarchy indemnified the returned émigrés. Although many placed the money in more modern sorts of investments, a large number managed to reconstitute their landed holdings. As the century progressed, aristocrats increasingly invested in state bonds, railroads, and insurance companies. As in England they were involved early in mining and metallurgy.

But the removal of the legitimate line of French kings in 1830 caused great disappointment to the loyal aristocracy. Thereafter, as they pulled back from public life, increasing numbers took on the practice of living on their country estates for at least part of the year. There they took up a philanthropic concern for *their* peasants and occupied themselves with the improvement of local agriculture. In the province of Brittany and the departments of the Sarthe and the Mayenne, for example, the resident aristocracy elevated the level of agricultural practice on their estates—and through the agricultural societies—in the larger region. The defeat on the national level as a result of the revolution of 1830 resulted in the Legitimist aristocracy enhancing their local power, while at the same time managing to keep up in wealth with the newer Orleanist and Napoleonic nobility.

More modern in spirit and principal investments, the aristocratic

---

priests and nobles with the peasants, see Paul Bois, *Paysans de l'Ouest: Des structures économiques et sociales aux options politiques depuis l'époque révolutionnaire dans la Sarthe* (Le Mans, 1960), 117–35. See also Gilbert Garrier, *Paysans du Beaujolais et du Lyonnais, 1800–1970* (2 vols.; Grenoble, 1973), particularly Vol. I. Less helpful is Pierre Brunet, *Structure agraire et économie rurale des plateaux tertiaires entre la Seine et l'Oise* (Caen, 1960). This topic deserves additional regional studies.

11. The suffering that Patrice Higonnet discusses in *Class, Ideology, and the Rights of Nobles During the French Revolution* (Oxford, 1981), 37–56, 257–72, was real enough, but he focuses primarily on the personal price the aristocracy paid during the Revolution, not their financial fortunes, nor that which was recovered after the Restoration. On the situation of the nobility in the eighteenth century, Guy Chaussinand-Nogaret, *La Noblesse au XVIIIᵉ siècle: de la féodalité aux lumières* (Paris, 1976); Chaussinand-Nogaret, "Aux origines de la Révolution: noblesse et bourgeoisie," *Annales: économies, sociétés, civilisations*, XXX (1975), 265–78 (hereinafter cited as *Annales*).

supporters of the Orleanist and Napoleonic dynasties also maintained a certain social distance from the grands bourgeois. They, too, like many a successful bourgeois, saw land as something more than a good investment: the land was a way of life. And one did not reach the upper strata of French society without some connection to appreciable hectares of it.

Like the Prussian Junkers and the southern planter class of pre–Civil War America, members of the various French aristocracies had enmeshed themselves in contemporary capitalist society. The landowners among them closely followed the fluctuations of the world markets for agricultural goods. But they also served the state—although not necessarily its government—in the ranks of the officer corps, the higher civil service, and the diplomatic corps. The various levées of the French aristocracy of the nineteenth century, like their Prussian and English peers, had accommodated well to the capitalist society in which they lived without entirely jettisoning their aristocratic heritage. Even when, by the epoch of the Third Republic, the French aristocracy had ensured its social and economic survival by diversifying its sources of wealth, the land continued to cast a magic spell.[12]

The spokesmen and ideologists of the Legitimist aristocracy repeatedly urged those who had taken up primarily urban existences once again to return to the land. Emmanuel de Curzon, for example, traced the depopulation and demoralization of the countryside to the loss of its elite. Urbain Guérin, the Le Playist spokesman and future librarian of the Musée Social, held up the rural family rooted on the land as the main guarantee of that stability that gave a society strength. He too urged the upper class to return to the land. There they could bind themselves with other rural families by means of the form of sharecropping known as *métayage* and together better hold out against the ravages of the agricultural crises while maintaining the stability of property.[13] I have found no general study in the vast

12. François Crouzet, in the preface to Hubscher's study *L'Agriculture et la société rurale,* underscores Hubscher's conclusion that, although smallholders increased and middling farmers declined in numbers in the years 1850–1914, "the large holdings, in particular those of the nobility, held their own" (p. 8).

13. The *fermier* was usually a cash-paying tenant much like the English type. The *métayers* leased the landlord's land in exchange for a certain part of the yield. This latter form of arrangement was the favorite of French ideologists of "agrarianism," since it shared the risks of cultivation between owner and tenant while locking both

literature on agriculture in the Third Republic that investigates to what degree this frequent exhortation to the landowning upper classes to live among "their" peasants bore results, but there is the famous case of Emile Duport and the conservative and active agricultural society of the Lyonnais-Beaujolais region he inspired. The Union du Sud-Est, as it was known, brought all classes of growers in this rich region into active collaboration under the leadership of local aristocrats. Contemporary conservatives often held it up as a model worthy of emulation.[14]

The census of 1882 elicited, for the first time, the information necessary to determine what portion of the agricultural population and land were involved in sharecropping. Briefly, direct ownership and cultivation were practiced by 80 percent of the people cultivating agricultural land, and 60 percent of the land was so used. Rent tenancy (*fermage*) and sharecropping accounted, therefore, for only 20 percent of the agriculturalists and 40 percent of the soil. But the extent of sharecropping was half that of rental tenancy. The modest presence of sharecropping should have discouraged those looking for organic unity in the countryside. However, the 60 percent of the holdings worked directly by their owners were on the whole very small, many too tiny to support a family trying to live from the fruits of the family farm alone. Many peasants may have owned their own land, but 40 percent of the rural population had to work as rural laborers (*domestiques* and *journaliers*) to survive. Rural notables, especially those involved in local or national politics, wanted to believe that they could count on the political reliability of their servants and day laborers.[15]

This wonderful mix of values—agrarian romanticism (or as much fear of the urban masses of workers) linked to concern for property values—lay at the heart of the late-nineteenth-century alliances of

---

parties firmly into their respective social and economic statuses. See Emm. de Curzon, "Le devoir et le rôle des propriétaires ruraux," *Réforme sociale*, III (1882), 502–10; and Urbain Guérin, "La crise agricole et ses remèdes," *Réforme sociale*, 2nd ser., III (1887), 421–92.

14. See Louis de Vogüé, *Emile Duport, la leçon de ses oeuvres* (Lyon, 1909). Gilbert Garrier, "L'Union du Sud-Est des syndicats agricoles avant 1914," *Mouvement social*, LXVII (1969), 17–38; Garrier, *Paysans du Beaujolais et du Lyonnais*, I, 417–42, 506–22.

15. For more details, see Robert Laurent, "Les cadres de la production agricole: propriété et modes d'exploitation," in Fernand Braudel and Ernest Labrousse (eds.), *Histoire économique et sociale de la France* (8 vols.; Paris, 1977–82), vol. III pt. 2, pp. 653–58 (hereinafter cited as *HES*).

TABLE 4

The Decline in Land Values, 1851–1908

Land	Rental value/hectare (francs)			Sale value/hectare (francs)		
	1851	1879	1908	1851	1879	1908
Land of superior quality	81	104	108	2,815	3,382	3,013
Arable land	42	57	49	1,479	2,197	1,496
Fields and pastures	73	97	65	2,256	2,961	1,878
Vineyards	69	130	76	2,067	2,968	2,033
Woods	20	23	17	642	745	573
Heath and waste	5	6	4	155	207	159

Source: J.-P. Houssel, *et al., Histoire des paysans français du XVIIIᵉ siècle à nos jours* (Roanne, 1976), 319, copyright © 1976 by Editions Horvath.

iron and rye in Germany and iron, textiles, and wheat in France (see Table 4).

Although we must not make of the Prussian experience a misleading norm, to refuse to recognize any analogies, as does Theodore Zeldin, impoverishes our understanding of a very significant aspect of economic development.[16] It cannot be doubted that the landed interests of both France and Prussia would have agreed that agriculture was an industry like the others, as we read repeatedly in the proceedings of meetings of the Société des Agriculteurs de France. The Prussian growers, like their French counterparts, hit by a long-term and severe agricultural depression, believed they too had a right to special help. Only the industrialists could furnish the aid, and they did so because they in turn needed the political support of the growers to gain aid and benefits for themselves. For their part, the industrialists of Germany and France were prepared to allow an increase in the costs of their workers' sustenance, only because the growing intensity of the political and economic pressures of the industrial workers narrowed their policy options.

16. Theodore Zeldin, "France," in David Spring (ed.), *European Landed Elites in the Nineteenth Century* (Baltimore, 1977), 127–33.

The promotion of agricultural tariffs, especially on wheat and livestock, benefited big growers ideologically by showing the peasants that the big farmers looked out for their interests and at the same time counteracted the ongoing decline in land rents that injured the largely absentee landlords. Although by no means the majority of large landowners, the aristocrats, through the agency of the Société des Agriculteurs de France and the associated syndicats agricoles, proclaimed themselves spokesmen for all of French agriculture.[17]

At the general assembly of the Société des Agriculteurs de France held in late February, 1884, Méline's mentor in protectionism, the indefatigable Pouyer-Quertier, appeared to offer the aid of the Association de l'Industrie Française to help mitigate the effects of the latest phase of the agricultural crisis. After some reflection, Baron d'Avril, who had recently returned home after having spent most of the years since the collapse of monarchism (1876–1883) representing France in South America and was now devoting himself to literature and farming, rose to praise the industrialists' remarks as "illuminating."[18] When the assembled leaders of French industry met in December, they voted their support "for the proposal adopted at the meeting of the Agriculteurs de France regarding the increase of the duties on agricultural products."[19]

17. Harvey Goldberg argues that holdings between 25 and 100 acres, which made up about 20 percent of pre–World War I French farms, belonged to (absent) doctors, lawyers, military officers, and the like, thus representing an important bourgeois participation in rural investment. See Goldberg's "The Myth of the French Peasant," *American Journal of Economics and Sociology,* VIII (July, 1954), 353–79, in which he tries to make a case for an overwhelmingly capitalist-dominated French countryside in the late nineteenth century. We would find aristocratic owners in possession of the largest units, those both most oriented towards the market and at the same time viewing their estates as part of a great family's heritage. As the work of Thorstein Veblen reminds us, a family not in long-term contact with money must decline in its social pretensions. There is no contradiction between seeking both efficiency and good market position on the one side and maintaining what could be saved of aristocratic heritage and privilege. The British aristocracy had done so for centuries; the Junkers were doing so in the period of the new Empire.

18. *Bulletin de la Société des agriculteurs de France,* Travaux de l'Assemblée Générale, February 25, 1884 (hereinafter cited as *SAF*). Adolphe Baron d'Avril, other than serving the expansion of French influence as a diplomat in Chile, also participated in the founding of the Alliance Française, the organization intended by its proponents to further French influence abroad by spreading French language and culture.

19. *Travail national,* December 21, 1884; the meeting was held December 9.

But there remained one important flaw that might complicate the conclusion of the great social alliance. Would not raising the duties on sugar, wheat, and meats raise the workers' cost of living? Would they not in turn press their employers for relief? In mid-August, as the French wheat grew golden in the fields, *Le Travail national* gave an answer to this concern of Méline and his industrialist friends. An editorial entitled "Les petits agriculteurs français" decried the sad circumstances of the peasant farmers and reminded the readers that millions of French agricultural workers were also consumers of agricultural products. French bread prices had remained steady in the days of freer trade, according to the article, despite the declines in foreign wheat prices. And conversely, it concluded, the price of bread would not be affected by "a rise of a few centimes in the duties."[20]

The aristocrats of the Société des Agriculteurs de France also worried about the price of the workers' bread. Indeed, they confronted the social-policy implications of the tariff movement directly and with a great deal of lucidity. At the next annual meeting of the society, early in February, 1885, the president, the Marquis de Dampierre, addressed the issue of food prices in his opening speech.

From a distinguished Legitimist family, Jean-Baptiste-Elie-Adrien-Roger de Dampierre had retired from public life upon the Orleanists coming to power in 1830. He returned to politics in 1848 as a representative of the Landes in the Constituent Assembly. Thereafter he supported the government of Louis Napoleon but rejected the coup of December 2, 1851. In the National Assembly of 1871 he again expressed monarchist sentiments on behalf of the Landes. A supporter of the Duc de Broglie, he failed to gain a seat in the legislative elections of 1876. Throughout his political career he had continued to interest himself in agriculture and agricultural improvement. For example, he employed the enforced leisure that the proclamation of the Empire conferred on him to write a book on cattle breeding in France, England, and Switzerland. With the eclipse of the monarchist cause in 1877 he turned again to agriculture. His election to lead the Société des Agriculteurs de France in 1878 serves as a good example of how the Legitimist nobility withdrew from public life in the Third Republic—but not too far from it—to work for change in other ways.

20. *Travail national*, December 21, 1884, pp. 73–74.

In his presidential message, Dampierre reviewed the sad and by then well-known tale of pervasive agriculture distress in France. He reported on the uncertain prospects for relief via parliamentary measures. He then turned to the issue that most threatened the fruition of the blossoming agrarian-industrial coalition, the Left's and free traders' charge that raised import tariffs would make the workers' bread more expensive. In response he recalled the position taken by the society's delegation when it called upon the minister of agriculture (still Méline) to present their problems: "Would it not be better for the urban workers to have work and pay five centimes more for their kilogram of bread, than for them not to have work and get their loaf for five centimes less?"[21]

The next day M. Le Trésor de la Rocque, the aristocrat who headed the national organization of syndicats agricoles, the link between the large growers and the peasantry, took up the theme. He stated: "There are two alternatives for the workers: they could accept perhaps a slight increase in the price of bread and keep the job which furnishes the wherewithal for paying for their bread or indeed accept a reduction of wheat prices by going along with free trade in agricultural products, but by so doing, expose themselves both to the risk of being entirely dispossessed of their work and of losing the means of gaining their bread."[22] One can discern the search for a social policy that would not violate the free market, however tentative and unsure, in these growers' discussions of the costs of workers' bread and the risks to their jobs if French commercial policies were not made more protectionist.

A surge of industrial conflict had encouraged the passage of the 1881–1882 tariff on industrial goods. Now in mid-decade the strikes and lockouts had abated for the moment; but the prices of grains, textiles, and extractive and heavy industry products were on the decline.[23] The unity that a sense of common distress confers eased the conclusion of the alliance of so-called national production.

21. *SAF*, Travaux de L'Assemblée Générale, February 9, 1885, p. 18; H. Temerson, "Dampierre, Jean Baptiste-Elie-Adrien-Roger de," in R. d'Amat and R. Limouzin-Lamothe (eds.), *Dictionnaire de biographie française* (16 vols; Paris, 1933–82), X, 67.

22. M. Le Trésor de la Rocque took up the presidency of the SAF in 1896 on the death of the Marquis de Dampierre.

23. Ernest Labrousse, "A livre ouvert sur les élans et les vicissitudes de croissance," in Braudel and Labrousse (eds.), *HES*, vol. III, pt. 2, pp. 1002–1009. Indexes of prices were calculated by Lévy-Leboyer, P. Léon, and F. Crouzet.

Méline and Ferry worked in the Chamber and the Senate to transform the fragile understanding into laws. However, each partner in the blossoming friendship of national production supported the other in promoting legislation protective in the largest sense, for their legal obstacles differed.

For the growers, protection meant a need for immediate tariff increases. They still resented their meager gains from the duties that the industrialists had pushed through the legislature in 1882. In 1884 Méline, playing the role of a domestic "honest broker," procured the passage of raised duties on the importation of foreign sugar and sugar beets, for decades a commercial crop produced by large growers in the Paris Basin and the Nord for sale to industrial distillers.[24] Méline also promoted a raise in the duties on imported wheat; he managed to get those on imported cattle doubled in 1885. In 1887, the growers, supported actively by the industrialists, exacted yet another elevation of wheat duties.[25] Representatives of the growers addressed the annual meeting of the Association de l'Industrie Française in February of that year. With domestic grain prices now going up, but the index of industrial prices still declining, potential divisions between the partners had to be managed.[26] And since neither interest felt sufficiently protected, everyone in the audience whole-heartedly applauded Pouyer-Quertier's bombastic unity speech.[27]

However, in the 1880s succor for the industrialists was not possible via legislative relief. Unlike agricultural products, industrial

24. Many years later, when head of an Opportunist ministry, Méline addressed the annual banquet of the association of sugar refiners with the words, "I have for you and your industry real fatherly feelings. You were so tiny before 1884" (*République française*, April 10, 1897).

25. I have refrained from giving the statistics on tariff rates in this paragraph and generally throughout this study, for they tell us little about whether they were prohibitive enough or not. We are dealing here with hopes and expectations rather than fine economic calculations, which, in any case, contemporary growers and industrialists were incapable of making with any kind of precision. Michael S. Smith, *Tariff Reform in France, 1860–1900: The Politics of Economic Interest* (Ithaca, N.Y., 1980), has samples of tariff rates according to different legislative acts for livestock and foodstuffs; coal, iron, and steel; machinery and metallurgical manufactures; and textiles in his Appendix 2.

26. Labrousse, "A livre ouvert," in Braudel and Labrousse (eds.), *HES*, vol. III, pt. 2, pp. 1002–1009.

27. He concluded by expressing the common resolve to struggle together and, united, to win. See *Travail national*, February 6, 1887, pp. 61–63, 83–86.

goods were covered in the trade treaties concluded in the late seventies. These treaties would not expire until 1892; the industrial protectionists acted as soon as it was possible to do so. Meanwhile the protectionists worked to integrate Ferry's new colonial empire into the existing tariff system of 1882.

Delegates to the general meeting of the Association de l'Industrie Française held in December, 1884, voted a resolution to demand of the government "a privileged position" for French business in the colonies and for protection against the commerce of foreigners. Algeria was covered by the tariff of metropolitan France later that month, and in 1885 Réunion, Guadeloupe, and Martinique were similarly walled off.[28] Only the populous French possessions in Indochina still remained outside France's protective barrier. The protectionists at this point had the support of the settlers' business community and of their chief political spokesman, Eugène Etienne.[29] In 1887 the proposal of active association members in the Chamber, Thompson, Richard Waddington, and Dautresme, to levy duties on foreign goods imported into Cochinchina, Cambodia, Annam, and Tonkin at the levels in effect for the national territory passed by a vote of 416 to 96. Not only had the onetime enemies of Ferry's colonial policy, the Radicals, voted for the measure, but so had the representatives of the conservative agrarian interests.[30]

The tightened commercial connection with the colonial possessions immediately improved the market for French manufactures. In 1885 and 1886, cotton goods of French origin supplied only 0.75 percent of the needs of Indochina. By 1887 France's share was 2.5

28. *Travail national*, December 21, 1884, pp. 298–99; February 1, 1885, pp. 54–55.

29. Michel Augé-Laribé's claim in *La Politique agricole de la France de 1880 à 1940* (Paris, 1950), 279–80, that neither Méline nor the growers showed any interest in the colonial empire is inaccurate, as Chap. VIII herein will further demonstrate. Here, it is sufficient to point out that throughout the eighties, as the Chamber vote shows, the agrarians joined the industrialists in trying to find ways that the new possessions might benefit France.

30. *Travail national*, February 2, 13, 1887, pp. 73, 82–83, June 26, 1887, p. 305. The Conservative interest in the colonies flowered relatively early and remained strong. See, for example, Urbain Guérin's support for colonial acquisition in Indochina in "La France dans l'Extrême Orient: Le Tonkin et L'Annam," *Réforme sociale*, V (1883), 155–63; and that of A. Delaire, "La France et la colonisation," *Réforme sociale*, IV (1883), 108–115; A. Noguès, "La question coloniale," *Réforme sociale*, V (1883), 71–75; and Charles-Marie Le Myre de Vilers, "Address before the Union de la Paix Sociale," *Réforme sociale*, 2nd ser., VI (1888), 58–61.

percent, and by 1888, 18 percent. French refined sugar exports to Cochinchina rose in value between 1887 and 1888 from 75,000 francs to 800,000 francs. In the same short period French crude and worked metals achieved a new high of 48 percent of Indochinese metal imports.[31]

Yet these improved colonial sales were not sufficient for some French businessmen, and too much for others. French producers were a long way from pushing foreign competitors out of their colonial market, even with the help of the 1882 tariff.[32] Moreover, many of the colonial businessmen began to grow unhappy with the restrictions the tariffs placed on their enterprises, for freer trade would cheapen their own imports. The passage of the Méline tariff worried them greatly. Jules Ferry had to quiet their complaints soon after the new measure went into effect.[33]

Although in the mid-eighties the agrarians worked to increase their tariff protection, and the industrialists to develop the colonial market, both interests looked to the expiration of the trade treaties in 1892 as the real moment to effect their salvation. As the eighties came to a close, although the prices for grains and manufactured goods (especially textiles) were once again recovering, anxiety heightened in business and grower circles about the threatening disintegration of society. The political discontent, associated with Boulangism and the escalation of anarchist violence, contributed to socially conservative fears.[34] Nor could the centenary celebration of

31. *Travail national*, October 6, 1889, pp. 465–67, October 13, p. 485, October 27, 1889, pp. 501–502. The Indochinese bought relatively little French cloth; rather, they purchased thread and made their own cloth, to the regret of the French cloth manufacturers.

32. *Travail national*, December 9, 1888, pp. 601–608, April 21, 1889, pp. 134, 218, June 21, 1889, pp. 285–86; May 11, 1890, pp. 231–32.

33. When some of the settler businessmen in Indochina thought to get around the new tariff inhibitions, Méline called on Etienne (June 22, 1887), newly installed as undersecretary for colonies, to urge him to gain the cooperation of M. Filippini, governor of Cochinchina, in the enforcement of tariff regulations. The growing split between colonial and metropolitan businessmen eventually turned the colonial party against protectionism. Metropolitan business interests, that is, the continued inclusion of the colonies within the national tariff walls, prevailed. *Travail national*, June 26, 1887, p. 305.

34. François Caron and Jean Bouvier, "Les indices majeurs," in Braudel and Labrousse (eds.), *HES*, vol. III, pt. 1, pp. 132–34; Guy Chapman, *The Third Republic of France: The First Phase, 1871–1894* (London, 1962), Chaps. 16, 17, 20; Frederic H. Seager, *The Boulanger Affair: Political Crossroad of France, 1886–1889* (Ithaca, 1969).

the French Revolution, crowned by the display of French industrial prowess, the Paris Exposition of 1889, banish ruling-class worries for long.

In 1889 the number of industrial strikes increased only slightly over the count for 1888 (188 to 199), although the number of strikers involved rose from 51,500 to 89,100. But dramatically, in 1890 industrial France had to endure 289 strikes involving 119,400 workers. We are right to judge this new militancy as "the total rehabilitation of the strike, and its elevation into the irresistibly growing theme of the general strike." Increasingly, working class militants saw the strike as a preparation for the coming social revolution. The May Day strikes and demonstrations of 1890 radiated a mood of almost messianic hope.[35]

It is important to recognize that these were not strikes of the radicalized and volatile construction workers and skilled artisans who had in the past played a large role in Parisian labor unrest. These were overwhelmingly modern *industrial* strikes, centered in the areas of the Nord and the Pas-de-Calais involving the textile workers and miners of northern France. Metalworkers were not far behind. "The proletariat of the large factory now occup[ied] center stage; they act[ed] no longer simply to protect themselves, but to attack; they [were] organizing," writes Michelle Perrot.[36]

The problem of labor came up repeatedly in the answers of affected industrial centers to the 1890–1891 questionnaire of the Conseil Supérieur du Commerce et de l'Industrie about renewing or terminating the expiring treaties of commerce. The chamber of commerce of Roubaix, the textile center, criticized the damaging consequences of the treaties and inculpated for their commercial difficulties "the low price of labor in Germany." The chamber of commerce of neighboring Tourcoing urged that, because competition of neighboring nations threatened, "it was high time to safeguard our national industries and the pay of our workers by means of compensatory duties." The cotton manufacturers of the Vosges, especially of

---

35. E. Shorter and C. Tilly, *Strikes in France, 1830–1968* (Cambridge, England, 1974), Appendix B, 360–76; Michelle Perrot, *Les Ouvriers en grève, France, 1871–1890* (2 vols.; Amsterdam, 1974), I, 96–97.

36. Perrot, *Les Ouvriers en grève*, I, 96, 118. For 1889–90 Paris was the site of only 7 percent of the strikers and 3 percent of the strikes. In 1889, 59 percent of the strikers were textile workers largely from the North; in 1890, 35 percent of the strikes and 53 percent of the strikers were involved in textile production.

the town of Epinal, offered as general causes for the difficulties of their industry "foreign competition, the rise in labor costs, finally, and especially, overproduction." Exports of many French industries were down, the statement continued, while thanks to insufficient protection, foreign imports had risen. The chamber of commerce of Albi, a region of coal mines, metalworking, wine-bottle manufacture, and fierce class struggles, responded that neither their commerce nor industry was prospering.[37] It blamed primarily "the strikes of the coal basins, which have increased the price of coal and, as a result, of other products employing coal in their manufacture." The response went on to urge more protection for French agriculture as a way to bring back "the fine weather of industrial prosperity."

The chamber of Valenciennes, the coal-mining region of the North, although it claimed that the tariff policy affected them little, closed ranks with the rest of "national industry" by advocating non-renewal of the treaties and raised duties on coal and coke. The iron manufacturers of the Jura complained of the German competition, the American, Italian, Spanish, and Russian iron tariffs, and especially of the decline in French military orders and the slowing of railroad construction. Although the majority of the responses, some 150, did not focus on the question of labor, like those of the chambers of the Jura and of Valenciennes, those that did were sent from regions of strike-ridden industries; their members were militant supporters of Méline's Association de l'Industrie Française and of new tariffs.[38]

The election of 1889, although not contested as a battle of free traders versus protectionists, returned a large protectionist majority to the Chamber. It was, however, the national election held immediately after the flight into exile of General Boulanger and the collapse of his popular but Royalist-backed, antiparliamentary movement. His defeat tamed the antirepublican Right. "For their part," concludes one student of the period, "the Opportunists . . . could relax their guard against the Right, especially as the rise of socialism was providing a common enemy for the defenders of the bourgeois social order." *Le Travail national* well understood the benefits of the

37. Joan Scott, *The Glassblowers of Carmaux* (Cambridge, Mass., 1974); Harvey Goldberg, *The Life of Jean Jaurès* (Madison, Wisc., 1962).

38. The responses may be found in the folders of the Archives Nationales F[12] 6418 and F[12] 6916: "Réponse au questionnaire du Conseil supérieur du commerce et de l'industrie sur le renouvellement des traités de commerce, 1890–91."

incipient rapprochement between the conservative liberals and the monarchist Right: "A certain spirit of reconciliation animates all the members of the Chamber. We hear today in the meetings in which members of the Right hold the majority, the same language as we heard yesterday at those attended almost exclusively by Republicans." At one such meeting Paul de Cassagnac, the leading parliamentary Bonapartist, nominated Méline to head a unified liberal-Right agrarian interest group in the Chamber. He was easily elected. Méline had himself named reporter of the Chamber's tariff commission as well.[39]

Outside the Chamber the Association de l'Industrie Française mobilized its members and allies for the forthcoming struggles for a new tariff. Representatives of the Comité des Forges, the Comité Central des Houillères, the Chambre Syndicale des Fabricants de Sucre, and the Société des Agriculteurs de France (to name the most important participants), appeared at a great unity meeting organized by the Association de l'Industrie Française on December 17, 1890. They listened to speeches denouncing Bordeaux merchants, export-import expediters, shippers, the businessmen-bankers of Lyon, and the members of the Paris association of commercial agents (the last of which President Aclocque denounced as "cosmopolitan," the contemporary code word for Jews). In his address, Méline defended the maximum-minimum provisions of the proposed tariff as both allowing for bargaining with other protectionist nations and still setting a limit below which protection would not fall. The meeting closed with the participants' endorsement of a resolution that dismissed the calumnies of "persons, who, for the most part, have neither factories, nor lands, nor workers depending on them" and affirmed that the protectionists sought nothing more than to protect "national labor." At their meeting the next month, the members of the Société des Agriculteurs de France listened to their leader, the Marquis de Dampierre, connect the salvation of agriculture with "safeguarding social peace."[40]

The debates on the tariffs began in the Chamber at the end of April, 1891. As the first of May approached, government and indus-

39. R. D. Anderson, *France, 1870–1914: Politics and Society* (London, 1977), 14–15; *Travail national*, December 1, 1889, p. 564, 570.

40. *Travail national*, December 21, 28, 1890, pp. 622–56; *SAF*, XXII (1891), Meeting of the Assemblée Générale, January 28, 1891, p. 18.

trialist circles grew apprehensive. They remembered the previous May 1, the first French May Day, when great demonstrations and parades took place in Paris, Marseille, Bordeaux, and Lyon, the free trade strongholds. They also had witnessed the explosion of working-class militancy in Lille, Roubaix, Tourcoing, Saint-Quentin, Calais, Sète, Roanne, "in the mines, the textiles of the Nord, and the Massif Central."[41] Choosing to see the upcoming May Day as potentially insurrectionary, the Opportunist government moved troops to or near important industrial centers.

In the Nord, workers of the little wool textile town of Fourmies, population sixteen thousand, took the day off to celebrate the workers' holiday. A confrontation developed with the troops arrayed before the town hall; they fired into a crowd of men, women, and children, killing nine (eight of them children) and wounding thirty. The minister of the interior in the Freycinet government, Ernest Constans, tried to place the blame on socialist agitators. He had Paul Lafargue, a leader of the growing Parti Ouvrier, indicted for inciting murder and pillage. (Lafargue had toured the North the month before the massacre.) Hippolyte Culine, the party's secretary in Fourmies, was also indicted. The government readily obtained a conviction of the two socialist agitators. As the socialist leaders were being sent off to prison for a government-caused bloodletting, the Chamber majority worked out the details of the new tariff. Méline worked for passage actively behind the scenes and from the rostrum of the Chamber.

Less than two weeks after the Fourmies shooting, with news of the trial of Lafargue and Culine filling the newspapers, Méline seized a moment in the deliberations on the tariff to address himself to the causes of, and remedies for, socialism. Although it was true that socialism "raged" in neighboring Germany, he asserted, it was even more menacing in France because "in this land of free trade wages are of necessity lower than they are in Germany." He realized, he said, "that the movement of socialism results from causes much more profound than the commercial policy of a country." It is fed, "in my opinion, from the very legitimate desire of the disinherited classes to improve their situation. . . . [We] must concern ourselves ceaselessly with the questions that these aspirations engender. He continued, "I believe . . . that the best form of social-

41. Daniel Ligou, *Histoire du socialisme en France, 1871–1961* (Paris, 1962), 114.

91

ism—I do not shrink back from the word—would be that of providing work for our workers, of improving their conditions, and, to the degree possible, of raising their wages and improving their welfare." Writing in the August issue of *La Revue socialiste*, Adrien Veber angrily charged Méline and the rest of the tariff commission of the Chamber with using the tariffs as "a weapon of civil war and perhaps of external war as well." Their work would only reimpose the "reactionary yoke" on France and solidify "the privileges of the soil and of industrial monopoly."[42]

When a Radical deputy from Lille died in September, the Parti Ouvrier, led in the North by the astute Gustave Delory, decided on the stratagem of nominating Lafargue for the seat in this heavily working-class district. As the protectionists in the Chamber ironed out their final disagreements about the provisions of the pending tariff, Lafargue sent speeches from prison to the electors of the district and the entire country hammering home his attack on the Opportunist government as murderers and starvers of the workers.[43]

He won the seat, and the authorities, forced to honor his parliamentary immunity, released him from prison. He triumphantly traveled around the industrial North that fall and winter speaking everywhere against the tariff. But neither his speeches nor their echoes heard at the National Congress of the Parti Ouvrier at Lyon in November could halt its passage. By the end of December the measure had passed both the Chamber of Deputies and the Senate by large majorities.

The protectionists expressed complete satisfaction. The new tariff law, wrote Auguste Michel in *Le Travail national*, "is, on the whole, what we wanted from the beginning, what we have never ceased to hope for and to back."[44] But still to be answered was the question of in what ways did the protectionists believe that tariffs were suitable

42. *Journal Officiel*, Chambre des députés, May 12, 1891, p. 867; Adrien Veber, *Revue socialiste*, XIV (August, 1891), 129–45.

43. Michael S. Smith, *Tariff Reform in France, 1860–1900: The Politics of Economic Interest* (Ithaca, N.Y., 1980), 203–35, gives the details of the delicate bargaining over the tariff.

44. *Travail national*, January 17, 1892, p. 29. *Travail national* reprinted a text of the new tariff on p. 34. Although there had to be bargaining among the various interests seeking advantages, my reading of the sources does not confirm Smith's emphasis on the exclusive role of the tariffs in the creation of ruling-class collaboration. Class alliances are not worked out over the duties on low-numbered cotton threads. Classes fear not things, but other classes. Smith's treatment leaves out the larger sociopolitical issues—and the working class.

instruments to achieve the twin goals of industrial pacification and ruling-class unity in the late nineteenth century.

The protectionist industrialists—if we are to believe their organic intellectuals—operated with the widespread classical notions that labor was the source of value in a commodity, and that wages and profits were inversely and rigidly related. Thus they embraced the ideology of National Labor as much to justify their taking a profit for their own labors as to encourage class collaboration in the face of the threat of foreign enemies. Moreover, they estimated the new sort of economic crises of the last part of the century—such as the one that they then suffered—to be the consequence of some combination of overproduction and underconsumption.[45] In the 1880s and 1890s they were hemmed in by powerful competitors and crippled by the collapse of domestic purchasing power. They lacked a well-developed colonial market. Thus they despaired of ending the business depression through expansion of sales. Domestically, efforts to increase worker productivity by means of capital investments, speed-ups, increased labor discipline, paternalism, and sending for the army had too often broken on the rocks of workers' resistance. The hard-pressed industrialists of Roubaix even reintroduced child labor late in the century.[46]

Tariffs promised to stabilize existing industries, increase prices and profits, *and* permit concessions to pacify the growing militancy of the new class of industrial workers of the provinces. Accordingly they offered an ideal economic solution to the ever more insistently raised social question. Having no reforms to offer, the industrialists offered their workers safe jobs and steady pay to ensure the fragile social order of their new republic. They offered as well the illusion of agrarian protection to the stricken peasants. Moreover, that same policy invited large growers to join a socially conservative alliance at a particularly precarious moment of economic development. And as an added, if perhaps unplanned, benefit, the tariffs that held forth promise of protecting both their grains and industrial goods might set peasant producers against industrial workers over the rising costs of workers' bread and peasants' manufactured needs. Fi-

45. See Michael Bleaney, *Underconsumption Theories: A Historical and Critical Analysis* (New York, 1976), 9–21, and the section on Sismondi, 62–79.

46. David Landes, "Religion and Enterprise: The Case of the French Textile Industry," in Edward C. Carter II, Robert Forster, and Joseph N. Moody (eds.), *Enterprise and Entrepreneurs in Nineteenth and Twentieth Century France* (Baltimore, 1976), 41–86.

nally—taking into account the business ledgers of industrialists and of the large growers—urban workers, the multitude of peasant consumers, and the native inhabitants of the colonies would pay for any increases in what they received with higher prices for what they had to purchase. Tariff policy in France, therefore, was social policy. Yet, it was not simply a negative social conservatism; rather, it was a far-sighted look backward.[47]

The jubilation of the protectionists over their new tariff was tempered immediately, for while still under indictment for high crimes, a gifted and energetic spokesman for social revolution had been elected to a seat in the chamber. *Progrès du Nord*, the newspaper of the Lille textile interests, interpreted the election of the first Marxist deputy this way: "M. Lafargue elected from Lille. That means ceaseless agitation in the factories and the workshops."[48] On assuming his seat Lafargue justified the protectionists' apprehensions by calling for the immediate abrogation of all duties on food products. In a pamphlet of the same year he denounced the government as that of the possessing class, which had passed a tariff that would "burden foodstuff to the value of a billion francs a year . . . for the sole purpose of elevating ground rents."[49]

But Lafargue at that moment spoke only for a small, if growing, party. The Opportunists might justly have put his electoral success down as a fluke, if socialists, running in the May elections of 1892, had not won majorities in the municipal governments of Roubaix, Marseille, Narbonne, Montluçon, Commentry, and Toulon, to name just the major victories. Socialist minorities won seats in Calais, Montpellier, Saint Nazaire, Darnétal, and Wattrelos. Throughout

47. See the new study on the obstacles to social reform in the early decades of the Third Republic by Judith Stone, *The Search for Social Peace: Reform Legislation in France, 1890–1914* (Albany, 1985), 161–68.

48. For the story of Fourmies and the socialist breakthrough in its wake, see Claude Willard, *La Fusillade de Fourmies* (Paris, 1957), especially 77–78; Robert P. Baker, "A Regional Study of Working-Class Organization in France: Socialism in the Nord, 1870–1924" (Ph.D. dissertation, Stanford University, 1967), 64–67; Ligou, *Histoire du socialisme en France*, 111–20; Jürgen Hilsheimer, *Interessengruppen und Zollpolitik in Frankreich: die Auseinandersetzungen um die Aufstellung des Zolltarifs von 1892*, (Heidelberg, 1973), 426–27. For the feel of the moment, rather than for information on the election, see Laura Lafargue to Engels, November 22, 1891, in Friedrich Engels, Paul and Laura Lafargue, *Correspondance*, ed. Emile Bottigelli (3 vols; Paris, 1956–59), III, 132–33.

49. *Travail national*, February 21, 1892; Paul Lafargue, *Le Communisme et l'évolution économique* (Lille, 1892), pp. 22–23.

France, but especially in the iron-working and textile-manufacturing North, they won places on the department and arrondissement councils. Clearly a social pacifier, like the appeal to National Labor of the new tariff, was much needed. It was clear, too, that any such pacification would neither develop quickly nor automatically.

The year 1893 brought vindication for the those who wished to take measures that would bring social peace to the Republic. In that year both the need for the tariff and the agonizingly slow workings of a tariff policy conceived as a social policy were demonstrated. A new surge of strikes in 1893 dampened the post-passage optimism of the tariff coalition partners. In 1892, 45,900 workers participated in 268 strikes. By the end of 1893, France had experienced 634 labor conflicts involving 172,500 employees. Once again the militancy of the industrial textile workers put them in the forefront: in March, the Saint Quentin lacemakers walked out; in April and May, the dyers, cotton spinners, and garment workers of Amiens; in May, the dyers of Roubaix; and in August, the wool spinners of Vienne. All over France there were strikes of skilled construction workers: carpenters, joiners, and cabinetmakers. But the growing proletariat of modern industry was increasingly resorting to the weapon of the strike: the mechanics and fabricators of Nantes, the metalworkers of the Rive-de-Gier, and the thousands of miners of Béthune.[50]

Perhaps the most disquieting labor problem of 1893—beyond the clear signs that an industrial working class in the modern sense was coming of age—was the intensification and spread of the strikes of the woodcutters of the Cher and the Nièvre. Was urban radicalism finding an echo in the countryside? When the results of the parliamentary elections of August and September, 1893, revealed that forty-nine socialist deputies had "penetrated into the Chamber," to use Méline's alarmed words, industrial and agrarian social conservatives discovered yet another font of danger.

Jean Jaurès, a Radical deputy when he held a seat in the years 1885–1889, was also returned to public office. In the new legislature he brought his genius and oratorical brilliance to bear now on behalf of parliamentary socialism. Although not a Marxist, and thus held in some suspicion by both Jules Guesde and Lafargue (who nevertheless collaborated with him), Jaurès' election posed a serious threat to the class allies who had united industrial wealth and agricultural wealth around means of protecting the social order. To win election

50. Ligou, *Histoire du socialisme en France*, 117.

from the second electoral district of Albi, Jaurès had had to defeat both the Marquis de Solages, the incumbent, a director of the Mines de Carmaux and a Rallié, and his father-in-law, the local political boss, Baron René Reille, also a Rallié, chairman of the mine company and, until his death in 1898, head of the Comité des Forges. Both men were active members of Méline's Association de l'Industrie Française; Reille served on the governing council until his death. Reille had precipitated a bitter eighty-day strike in August, 1892, when he fired Jean-Baptiste Calvignac, an official of the miners' union, on the occasion of Calvignac's election as mayor of Carmaux. It was in the wake of the successful struggle to have him reinstated to his job in the mines, followed by the resignation of the humiliated Solages from his seat, that Jaurès, running as a socialist, won election to the Chamber.[51]

To bring off his return to the Chamber of Deputies, Jaurès had had to combine the support of the miners and factory workers with that of the small peasants who also voted in the district. He had had to create on the bottom of society the kind of alliance that had been created in the pro-tariff coalition at the top—in part, by the men he had defeated. Could the tariffs of 1882 and 1892 hold back the proliferation of Jaurès' sort of agricultural-industrial alliance? Or failing that, could the protectionist allies fashion bulwarks against the domestic enemies of National Labor to complete the system of defenses begun with the tariffs? The decade of the nineties would bring answers to these worrisome questions.[52]

51. See Michael J. Rust, "Business and Politics in the Third Republic: The Comité des Forges and the French Steel Industry, 1896–1914" (Ph.D. dissertation, Princeton University, 1973), 67–68, and Rolande Trempé's article, "Contribution à l'étude de la psychologie patronale: le comportement des administrateurs de la Société des mines de Carmaux vis-à-vis des mineurs (1856–1914)," *Le Mouvement social*, XLIII (1963), 53–91. Leo Loubère offers additional insight into the connection of the local struggles in the lower Languedoc with the national issues. He concludes his case study of coal miners' strikes by writing that English competition distressed the mine owners and that they determined to cut labor costs as a means of lowering prices to meet the competition. After many defensive strikes the miners decided that only socialist politics could improve their situation ("Coal Miners, Strikes, and Politics in the Lower Languedoc, 1880–1914," *Journal of Social History*, II (1968), 42–43).

52. The strike data come from Tilly and Shorter, *Strikes in France*, 112–13, 361. As they admit, we do not yet know what role, if any, socialists and/or anarchist organizers played in "mobilizing" the striking workers. The writers of the *République française* seemed firmly to believe that agitators of the Left played an important role.

IV

Mobilizing the Rural Democracy Against the Workers' Democracy

The parliamentary articulation of the conservative concentration began immediately with the opening of the new legislative session in the autumn of 1893. The agricultural group of the Chamber, a relatively loose caucus comprising some three hundred deputies from the Right and the center, honored the hero of the tariff struggle of the last legislature by electing Méline as its spokesman. In thanking his fellow deputies for their expression of confidence, Méline sketched his own view of the causes and remedies of the commercial depression that had for so long crippled both industry and agriculture.

The key step to resolving the economic crisis, he believed, was to improve the lot of the countryside. The so-called army of the unemployed, which socialists blamed on the "unjust" organization of French industry, was recruited, according to Méline, in "the depths of the countryside," from the mass of peasants whom poverty had driven off the land and into the cities. If only the peasants could manage to live on their homesteads as agreeably as the urban population lived, they would not leave the land, "which most certainly they loved better than the factory." Social peace in the factories, reduction of urban unemployment, and the revival of the domestic market would be the benefits of stemming the rural exodus. He urged the members of the agricultural group to align themselves with what had been his personal project for at least a decade. "It is to achieve this goal [of ending the flight from the land] that we have to strain all our efforts."[1] His fellow conservatives were prepared to entrust this mission to him.

On taking his place in the Chamber in that same parliamentary session, Jean Jaurès also devoted one of his first speeches to the lot of the peasantry. He challenged what he perceived to be the grand strategy of the forces of social order. "You shall not use the rural

1. *Travail national,* November 26, 1893 p. 582.

97

democracy against the workers' democracy," he warned the tariff partners. He accused the ruling Opportunists of pursuing a "retrograde course": of bringing former enemies of the Republic into government, of embracing the politics of Leo XIII, and even of trying, however covertly, to destroy the workers' unions. Presciently, he reproached the right republicans, saying, "Because you wish to combat socialism, you are condemned to a labor of reaction in all spheres of public life—reaction in politics, reaction in fiscal policy, and reaction in your policies towards organized workers."[2]

His own recent experiences in Carmaux with attempts of the governing Opportunists and their conservative allies to use the peasantry as a dam against the political ascent of the working class was not the only evidence Jaurès could draw upon. He knew that in 1891 in the aftermath of Paul Lafargue's victory for the parliamentary seat from the second electoral district of Lille, the Opportunist government redistricted the city to include the voters of sixteen rural districts in the previously largely urban constituency. When he ran again in 1893, Lafargue could not persuade the peasant voters of his new constituency of the merits of socialism, as he had been able to do the industrial workers of Lille.[3] Clearly, the Parti Ouvrier and the other working-class parties involved in parliamentary politics had to reach the peasants. Otherwise, as a consequence of perpetual redistricting and the organizational efforts of rural notables, antisocialist peasant voters would continue to overwhelm the urban adherents of socialism.[4]

Movement on the Land

But not all peasants shared the values of the young Breton recruits who had breached the defenses of Paris to bring down the Com-

2. *Journal Officiel*, Chambre des députés, November 21, 1893, p. 83.

3. Paul Lafargue, *Neue Zeit*, XII (89–94), 145; Hans Georg Lehmann, *Die Agrarfrage in der Theorie und Praxis der deutschen und internationalen Sozialdemokratie: Vom Marxismus zum Revisionismus und Bolschewismus* (Tübingen, 1970), 77–86; Claude Willard, *Le Mouvement socialiste en France, 1893–1905: Les Guesdistes* (Paris, 1965), 366–74.

4. The gerrymandering of electoral districts to serve socially conservative ends has been a given of French republican history right up to the present Fifth Republic. See François Goguel, *Géographie des élections françaises de 1870 à 1951* (Paris, 1951) and François Goguel and Georges Deupeux, *Sociologie électorale: esquisse d'un bilan* (Paris, 1951), respectively volumes XXVII and XXVI of the Cahiers de la Fondation nationale des sciences politiques.

mune, or of those who had voted Lafargue out of office. In certain regions of France many peasants kept alive a Left tradition going back at least to midcentury. Their inherited values resonated with the new tidings brought to them by the urban socialists during the Great Depression. Other country people contributed to rural radicalization by simply leaving the countryside in that movement contemporaries called the rural exodus, thereby thinning the ranks of the forces of subservience and fatalism in longtime conservative areas. Let us first look briefly at the social impact of the flight from the land before we turn to France's leftist peasants.

After steadily increasing from the time of the Restoration, the numbers of rural dwellers, people living from agriculture, and males working in agriculture all leveled off around 1850 (see Table 2).[5] Louis Chevalier gives us a sense of the disquiet and apprehension with which the authorities and members of the upper strata observed the cities (especially Paris) filling with *déraciné* countryfolk in the first half of the century.[6] Contemporary observers in the course of the decade 1850–1860 began to note with various degrees of misgiving the movement of population from the land into urban centers.

Until the 1880s this demographic movement comprised mainly superfluous nonfarming population, particularly displaced rural artisans. Industrialization and the creation of a national market had rendered such rural skills as weaving, cloth dyeing, woodworking, metalworking, pottery making, and utensil making redundant. The peculiar result, however, was that despite a loss in absolute numbers, the countryside lost very few of the males who farmed the land (cf. Table 5).[7] The rural artisans departed, as did women who could

5. See Gabriel Desert, "La grand dépression de l'agriculture," in Georges Duby and Armand Wallon (eds.), *Histoire de la France rurale* (4 vols.; Paris, 1975–76), III, 399–404; Paul M Hohenberg, "The Transformation of Agricultural Labor Supply in Nineteenth-Century France," *Economic History Review*, XXXII (1974), 260–66; George W. Grantham, Jr., "Technical and Organizational Change in French Agriculture Between 1840 and 1880: An Economic Interpretation," (Ph.D. dissertation, Yale University, 1972), 124–200; J. Guillou, "L'Emigration des campagnes vers les villes" (Thesis, University of Caen, 1905); Philippe Ariès, *Histoire des populations françaises* (Paris, 1971), 284ff. For the Lyonnais region see the splendid study by Yves Lequin, *Les Ouvriers de la région lyonnaise, 1848–1914* (2 vols.; Lyon, 1977), I, 142–43, 156–57.

6. Louis Chevalier, *Classes laborieuses, classes dangereuses* (Paris, 1958), 167–308.

7. Relatively few males left the land between 1872 and 1892 compared to the years before and after. See the graph in Desert, "La grande dépression," in Duby and

TABLE 5

The Rural Exodus, 1872–1911

	According to Lévy-Leboyer	According to Statistique Générale
1872–1881	1,053,000	1,238,691
1881–1891	852,000	1,040,757
1891–1901	1,040,000	1,246,893
1901–1911	1,092,000	1,328,608

Source: François Caron, *An Economic History of Modern France* (New York, 1979), 122, copyright © 1979 by Columbia University Press. Reprinted with permission of the publisher.

readily find work in nearby cities as servants or unskilled help in a small business. Those rural inhabitants who remained behind made up a less heterogeneous and more peasantlike population than before.[8] As the countryside drained of people, the number of smallholders increased, for if people were to remain on the land, farming—not cottage industries—had to be their work. Henceforth, more than ever before, the family work team, led by male cultivators, would be the norm on the small and medium-sized farms. As no other force had since the French Revolution, urban industrialization strengthened peasant family farming.

By the third quarter of the century, the growing economic development of the countryside by the larger growers and the expanding connections to urban markets had introduced on the land a genuine market for agricultural labor.[9] Rural laborers and poorer peasants began to bargain over wages with their employers or, by leaving the land, improved the bargaining position of their fellows who re-

Wallon (eds.), *Histoire de la France rurale*, III, 400. The relevant figure is "Active Males Working in Agriculture." The curve depicting the loss of males between 1872 and 1892 is relatively flat, compared to those showing the outmigration of other parts of the population for the same period.

8. On Gers, Oren, Isère, and the Marne, see Michael Burns, *Rural Society and French Politics: Boulangism and the Dreyfus Affair, 1886–1900* (Princeton, 1984), 38–54.

9. Hohenberg, "The Transformation of Agricultural Labor Supply," 265–66.

mained behind. In the nearby small town they—or more likely their children—could hope to find a position on the lowest levels of state employment as postal workers or policemen, or eventually, under the Republic, as village schoolteachers. In the years of depression when small farmers had to compete for hired hands with local growers and with the lures of the cities, they tended to be unsuccessful; consequently, in the last decades of the century they had to depend primarily on family members as their labor force. When this source of labor was not available, they worked primarily for their own subsistence.

Tenant farmers, too, could exploit the labor shortage and the depression to strengthen their bargaining position vis-à-vis the landowners. For however much they themselves might suffer from the effects of the shortage of laborers, or phylloxera, or the depressed prices for their products, they could always attempt to pass the loss on to the owner of the land by demanding lowered rents. They often succeeded in doing so. In the years of the depression annual rents sank by more than half in the Loir-et-Cher, from a third to a half in the Pas-de-Calais, and by a bit less than a third in lower Normandy (see Table 4).[10] Thus, even the conservative agricultural regions of France, where all would shut their doors to itinerant socialist agitators, felt the pains of class struggle over land rents. One thoughtful estimate suggests that the owners of rented land lost perhaps a quarter to a third of the real income from their lands.[11]

Of course, the sales price of land sank as well, making farm land a not very attractive investment, however rooted landownership made one. For with the title to a piece of land during the years of depression and out-migration, owners also had to reckon on labor shortages or even indocility, low rents, and low yields from the sale of crops. In the first decades of the Republic we may note also the passing of that tradition of deference—if it had existed locally—that had made rural landownership a bit more worthwhile. The rich, and especially the aristocratic, turned increasingly from high farming to high finance.[12] In the decades before World War I, the movement of

10. Desert, "La grande dépression," in Duby and Wallon (eds.), *Histoire de la France rurale*, III, 402.

11. *Ibid.*, 403.

12. J. P. Houssel, *et al.*, *Histoire des paysans français du XVIIIᵉ siècle à nos jours* (Roanne, 1976), 319; Desert, "La grande dépression," in Duby and Wallon (eds.), *Histoire de la France rurale*, III, 403. See also Hohenberg, "The Transformation of Agricultural Labor Supply," 266.

wealth out of agriculture into financial ventures permitted the peasant republic of France to become one of the great financial powers of the world, as we shall see in Chapter VII. For the purposes of this chapter, however, it is more important to underscore the trend that grew more marked as the century went on: the transformations of the countryside allowed the peasants of various regions to see themselves more and more as members of communities embedded in a class. The sifting of the countryside in the early years of the rural exodus had contributed greatly to that new self-understanding.

Only in the 1880s, when the full impact of the agricultural depression began to be felt in the farming communities, did true peasants begin to leave the land, in addition to rural artisans and surplus women. Hard times were etching their scars on the land. But the contemporary urban distress did not entice very many of these small farmers off the land; on the contrary, the general movement from the country to the cities slowed down during the years of depression (see Table 5). Closing ranks and seeking ways to defend their communities was an alternative to leaving on the part of the peasant cultivators. It would not be the first time the peasants of some parts of France had united for struggle.

France had a tradition of rural radicalism that was just as rooted and authentic as the tradition the Right could mobilize to defeat socialists. In 1849, for example, many peasant voters supported the *Montagne* in the May elections. The only militant resistants to Napoleon's coup d'etat of 1851 were the peasants of the central West, the Northwest, the Southeast, the Basses Alpes, the Drôme, and the Var. They fought then to keep their hopes of a peasant republic alive. Even after defeat and the return to a politically numbing prosperity under the Empire, the peasant-cultivators of these regions reaffirmed their loyalty to republican principles in 1877 as the *Démocrates socialistes* of 1849 had done.[13]

The spread of the depression in the eighties and early nineties forced many peasants to rethink what kind of republic they desired,

13. The great illuminator of that tradition has been Maurice Agulhon, *La République au village: Les populations du Var de la révolution à la Seconde République* (Paris, 1970); he has been seconded by Ted Margadant, *French Peasants in Revolt* (Princeton, 1980). See also Tony Judt, *Socialism in Provence, 1871–1914: A Study in the Origins of the Modern French Left* (Cambridge, England, 1979) and Philippe Gratton's attack on Pierre Barral's effort to treat the countryside as a politically uniform entity under the rubric of agrarianism, *Les Luttes de classes dans les campagnes* (Paris, 1971).

now that the "clericals," as the pro-monarchists were known in some villages of the South, had been checkmated. In the southern village of Cruzy, for example, smallholders had coexisted comfortably with rich winegrowers throughout much of the century. The small farmers had produced their *vin ordinaire* for marketing on their own account while supplementing their income by tending the vines of the bigger growers for wages. But hard times drove a wedge between the two strata. In the last two decades of the century the marginal small growers of domestically produced wines, who had to accept employment to finance their bit of independence, were transformed into a rural proletariat as competitive market agriculture came to dominate the region. Socialist organizers from nearby Béziers and Narbonne found the poorer farmers suddenly receptive to their message. In Carmaux, too, where the miners supported socialism and Jean Jaurès, one of the great issues heightening the militancy of these workers was their struggle to control hours and job rules at the mine so that they could continue to lead their double life as miners *and* peasant cultivators.[14]

Certainly, the story of how socialism came to the countryside in the years of the Great Depression might be deepened by examining the records of many more of the approximately thirty-six thousand communes of France than we have done. Surely local loyalties, feuds, and family networks were not trivial factors in why one village went Left and another Right.[15] And yet we must not assume peasant behavior to be so idiosyncratic from place to place that we despair of discovering larger patterns of peasant political response. Nor are we warranted in concluding that issues of national politics

14. J. Harvey Smith, "Work Routine and Social Structure in a French Village: Cruzy in the Nineteenth Century," *Journal of Interdisciplinary History*, V (1975), 357–82; Maurice Agulhon, "Les transformations du monde paysan," in Duby and Wallon (eds.), *Histoire de la France rurale*, III, 480; Rolande Trempé, *Les Mineurs de Carmaux, 1848–1914* (Paris, 1971); Pierre Barral, *Les Agrariens français de Méline à Pisani* (Paris, 1968).

15. Eugen Weber, "Comment la Politique Vint aux Paysans: A Second Look at Peasant Politicization," *American Historical Review*, LXXXVII (1982), 359. The issue of peasant politicization will need to be resolved on the basis both of more local *and* national studies than we currently have. Rather than taking a position on the complex issues raised by Weber and the other participants in the debate, I seek only to assess the national–political implications of the peasants' entrance into the public life of the nation, whatever may have been the purely local circumstances prompting their entrance into national politics.

only intruded into village life when they touched some local problem. It may be that the effects of the rural exodus, the fall in market prices for many agricultural products, and the activities of socialist organizers, for example, made themselves felt in profoundly different ways in different parts of France, or even in neighboring villages. But an important *national* change was the main result. For example, each bourg or village undoubtedly had its own special political mix, as each village of Normandy had its own Calvados and each bourg in the Midi its own mix of *herbes de Provence*; yet in the first several decades in the life of the Republic the peasant growers of Brittany and Normandy regularly returned conservative deputies to Paris where they legislated for the whole country.

Certain regions were strongholds of the Right. Brittany and the inland regions of the West held to a staunch conservatism. The cultivators of the East, in particular of Lorraine and Champagne, remained untainted by socialist politics. This was true as well for the Basque country of the Southwest and the strongly Catholic departments of the southeastern Massif Central, l'Ardèche, la Lozère, and l'Aveyron. However, by the last years of the century important regions of the country—the Cher, Nièvre, Hérault, the Pyrénées-Orientales, the Aude, Lot-et-Garonne, Isère, Seine-et-Marne, and the Aube—began with growing fervor to send socialists to represent them in the Chamber of Deputies, where they legislated for all of France.

The new socialist voters were perhaps moved by economic hardships, or the Left traditions of the locale; however, during the depression years there emerged a new concern with equality and dignity on the part of small farmers in several regions of France. In the republican South especially they resented the power of the former lords; socialist leaders could touch a responsive cord by denouncing overbearing local notables and their archaic pretensions. Addressing the Chamber, for example, Pierre Brizon, socialist schoolteacher and deputy from the Allier, heaped scorn on the great landowners and their parliamentary allies, not just because of their greed but also for what he believed to be the values motivating them. He told them, "You believe that you have fulfilled your obligations to the peasant class when you vote for higher agricultural duties. But such measures profit only the great landowners, those feudal *seigneurs* who, despite the revolution of 1789–1793, still remain in our countryside with their tithes, their corvées, and their great châteaux which cast a socially mortal shade over the peasants who work themselves to death under their dominion." The urban socialist organizations were sometimes slow to understand the material and spiritual needs of the peasants. Those that did focus on work in the countryside worried inordinately about peasant conservatism, judging the peasant's attachment to his small parcel as the main source of that conservatism.[16]

As modern French socialist tendencies had begun to take form in the aftermath of the Commune, only the faction around Jules Guesde, the Marxists of the Parti Ouvrier, took any systematic interest in creating a program to win the support of the peasantry. And to the degree that Guesde hewed closely to Marxian orthodoxy, even the Guesdists offered the landowning peasants only the bleak prospect of extinction.

The party congress of 1880 in Le Havre proclaimed the necessity for the nationalization of the land, mineral resources, and instruments of production; it made no distinctions between rural or urban property, or size of holdings, or whether labor was exploited on the site. It took a stand against any improvement of the lot of the peasant-proprietor. That would only reinforce the capitalist order, it believed; such betterment would "furnish [the capitalist system] with the sword and the shield of a satisfied peasantry [to brandish] against the workers' revolution."[17] Not surprisingly, socialist organizers were often greeted in the countryside with rebuffs and denounced for their alleged desire to expropriate the land and redivide it.[18]

But the crisis of the 1870s and 1880s began to change the minds even of landowning peasants. From the 1860s onward, as the modern market system spread to the French countryside, the tendency

16. Houssel, *et al.*, *Histoire des paysans français,* 362. In the *Eighteenth Brumaire of Louis Bonaparte* Marx wrote of his hopes that the French peasants might some day lose their dedication to their small holdings so that they might join the French proletariat in making the social revolution. Nearly a half-century later, in the "The Peasant Question in France and Germany" (1894), Engels chided both the French and German Marxist parties for seeking to confirm the peasantry in their private property.

17. Léon Blum, *Les Congrès ouvriers et socialistes français* (Paris, 1901), I, 62; Barral, *Les Agrariens français,* 154–55.

18. *Partageux,* meaning "dividers up," "expropriators," in the largest sense, was the reproach hurled at them in the villages.

toward monoculture—already advanced in the grain lands of the East and the Paris Basin, as well as in the dairy farms of Normandy—began to spread to the South. Many small Provençal farmers began to specialize in crops that the improved road system and the proliferating railway network could hurry to urban markets. They continued to produce their customary crops of olives and olive oil, of course, but in declining amounts. Their cut flowers, too, remained in demand in the cities. But their inexpensive wines could now be shipped to urban buyers, and the profits from them could buy their families the urban amenities slowly softening country life.

The small landowning peasants, therefore, were sufficiently integrated into the market economy to suffer economic distress when the Great Depression swept over them. However, their special griefs divided them economically from the large growers. In particular, three features of the contemporary economic malaise brought out their latent radicalism. First, because many peasants cultivated small holdings in France in an age when economies of scale were still possible, they constantly sought to increase their lands. In depressed periods they encountered great difficulties getting credit for land purchases, as distinct from credit for improvements or the occasional emergency loan. Their credit position both for current operations and new purchases worsened in the late seventies and eighties.

Secondly, there was the special suffering engendered by the spread of the phylloxera from the late 1870s onward. Larger growers and growers of expensive export wines, such as those in the Gironde, could afford the drastic step of uprooting their old root stocks and planting relatively resistant American varieties onto which they grafted the French vines.[19] But the smaller growers of less noble wines could not secure enough credit to make the switchover easily, and when they finally did make the switch (missing the profitable seasons of 1891–1897), they overplanted and, in the first decade of the new century, suffered from a crisis engendered by too much *vin ordinaire* on the market.[20]

---

19. On this disaster, see Charles Warner's *The Winegrowers of France* (New York, 1960), 23–51; Gilbert Garrier, *Paysans du Beaujolais et du Lyonnais, 1800–1970* (2 vols.; Grenoble, 1973), I, 418–27.

20. Tony Judt, *Socialism in Provence*, 148–49. The winegrowers' rebellion culminating in 1907 originated—at least economically—from this boom-bust cycle.

The third economic factor in the incipient radicalism of many of the landowning peasants—especially of the South—was connected directly to the tariff question. Because of the smallness of the holdings of many peasants or because of the trend toward one-crop culture (or often both) many peasants had to purchase their daily needs. Thus, while they were producers of agricultural products for the market, and therefore in principle interested in tariff protection, they were (like the urban workers) purchasers of wine, meat, and especially bread. We have no evidence indicating anti-tariff sentiment among the dairy farmers of Normandy or the poor potato farmers of Brittany. But in the Var, we know of meetings to protest increases in the tariffs for imported wheat. By the spring of 1891 the small-holding, wine-producing peasants of the central and southern Var were angrily damning the passage of the new Méline tariff. As a consequence, the urban socialists' professed animosity to protection struck a responsive chord in the hearts of the Provençal peasants.[21]

The tariff initiatives of Méline and his friends not only conferred the benefits of uniting the forces of what they liked to call "National Production," but at the same time they sowed division in the ranks of active, and potential, enemies of the new conservatism. The disputes over the passage of tariffs divided peasants who viewed themselves as consumers of necessities, as in the bourgs of the South, from peasants who produced for distant markets and who identified with the wealthier capitalist growers, like those of Normandy, Anjou, and Lorraine. The dispute between free trade and protectionism was also a source of potential division between peasants and urban workers over the issue of wages, retention of jobs, and the price of bread versus concerns about mounting debts, retention of family farms, and the weak sales of farm products. The tariffs of the 1880s and that of 1891 served as Méline's golden apple cast into the landowning peasants' paths to send them this way and that, and, compounding differences of wealth, region, and local traditions, to divide their resistance to the capitalist social order spreading through the countryside.[22]

21. *Ibid.*, 149–50, 325 n17. Judt points out the ambivalence of the Radicals on the tariff issue: they had collected a large following in the wheat-growing areas of France, especially among the local notables. Out of political power, the Radicals had no great social coalitions to build; they could trim.
22. See Robert Estier, "Les temps des dépressions," in Houssel *et al.* (eds.), *Histoire*

The new defensive tariffs played a role in an important, unprecedented instance of peasant radicalism in 1891. In the forests of central France, located in the departments of the Cher and the Nièvre, many poor peasants supplemented their household incomes by working as loggers in the winter months. Suddenly in the early winter of 1891 many of these loggers struck their woodcutting jobs. An initial look at the economics of that industry would suggest that the distress of both the industry and the loggers stemmed from technological changes. L. H. Roblin, the first to study the *bûcherons*, as they were called, believed that as French households switched from wood to coal for heating, and industry from wood to coke, the demand for the timber of the Cher and the Nièvre declined. Moreover, with the completion of the national railroad network and with the increasing substitution after 1860 of iron and steel for wood in construction, by the late eighties the industry—and the woodcutters—had begun to suffer serious distress.[23] Ironically, the magnificent steel and glass Gallery of Machines and the Eiffel Tower, both erected for the Paris Exhibition of 1889 as symbols of the hopes for the industrial future, served also as monuments to a dying trade. Improved technology certainly cut into the demand for lumber.[24]

But if iron and steel were driving out wood, why had so many powerful *maîtres des forges* like E. Lehayne of the Comptoir métallurgique de Longwy, Baron Robert de Nervo, president of the Société anonyme des forges et aciéries of Denain and Anzin, Henri Schneider of Le Creusot, and of course, Baron René Reille, president of the Comité des Forges, united in the Association de l'Industrie Française to fight for protection? For all the markets the steel producers were taking from the lumber industry, the new trade was insufficient to ensure the prosperity of heavy metal processors. T. J. Markovitch reports an appreciable decline in the rate of growth in the iron and steel industry between 1860 and 1892, and François Crouzet finds 1889 second only to the crash year of 1873 in the severity of the drop in the annual index of production of primary

---

des paysans français, 363–83; Gabriel Desert and Robert Specklin, "Les réactions face à la crise," in Duby and Wallon (eds.), *Histoire de la France rurale*, III, 409–51.

23. L. H. Roblin, *Les Bûcherons du Cher et de la Nièvre, leurs syndicats* (Paris, 1903), 51–55.

24. Philippe Gratton, *Les Luttes de classes dans les campagnes*, 62; Pierre Barral, *Les Agrariens français*, 144–45.

metallurgy and metal-working.[25] It was the weakening of the prices for their products that drove the *maîtres des forges* to seek shelter in the 1880s and, of course, the wage pressures of their workers. And it was in turn the fall in coal and iron prices of the late 1880s, not increased demand for them, that put downward pressure on the price of their substitute product, wood.

To return now to the strikes of the *bûcherons*, the response to the sinking prices for their products on the part of the lumber dealers of the Cher and Nièvre was to cut the price per cord paid the woodcutters. In November, 1891, with winter coming on, a baker in Uzay-le-Venon in the Cher refused any more credit to his already deeply indebted customers. (Consider the irony of peasants who could not afford to buy bread.) The majority of them, peasant-lumberjacks, turned to the lumber merchants and demanded a higher rate for cut wood. In a few days a strike committee was formed and, receiving no reply from the amazed lumber dealers, it called the woodcutters off their jobs. The movement spread to the surrounding villages. By early December seven hundred to eight hundred lumberjacks were on strike. At first the local Radical politicians spoke for the grievances of the strikers. But quickly their popularity was eclipsed by the socialist deputy from nearby Bourges, Eugène Baudin. By the end of February the resistance of the merchants had crumbled; the loggers won their demands for higher rates soon after they formed a Syndicat Central des Bûcherons that united the local groups of the whole southern half of the Cher. The loggers of neighboring Nièvre themselves began to form syndicats in the wake of their comrades' victory. In May, 1892, many of them walked off their jobs just as labor trouble was starting up again in the Cher and spreading to the Allier. Once again socialist deputies—Baudin from the Cher and Christophe Thivrier from the Allier—encouraged the strikers to resist. These strikes were won, but the conflicts rekindled again in February, 1893, and sporadically through the year, culminating in the region of Vierzon where three hundred strikers walked off their job sites for a

25. T. J. Markovitch, "L'industrie française de 1789 à 1964. Conclusions générales," *Cahiers de l'Institut des Sciences Economiques Appliquées*, series AF, VII (1966), 139. He gives the average annual (negative) growth rate, expressed as a percentage, for iron and steel as −4.26 for 1830, −2.58 for 1860–62, and −4.01 for 1892–1913. See also François Crouzet, "Un indice de la production industrielle française au dix-neuvième siècle," *Annales, économies, sociétés, civilisations*, XXV (1970) (hereinafter cited as *Annales*). Employing 1913 as the base year (100), Crouzet shows two deep troughs in both the metallurgy and metal working industries, one in 1873 (28.6 and 30.1, respectively) and the second in 1889 (33.2 and 37.5).

month and a half. On April 29, 1894, in addition to resolutions calling for better pay and improved working conditions, delegates to the seventh congress of the Fédération des Bûcherons du Cher at Bigny-Valleray passed the following resolution: "The delegates protest with energy against the reactionary actions of a government which takes its direction from the Vatican, [and] aver that collectivist socialism alone is capable of bringing the emancipation of the workers. [We] endorse the socialist group in the Chamber [and] thank all its members for the revolutionary socialist propaganda which they diffuse throughout the country."[26] Unfortunately, we do not have a complete picture of how the various sects of socialists worked out their positions on the peasantry. That of the Parti Ouvrier was the most elaborate and systematic.

However, neither Lafargue's correspondence with Engels nor the Guesde papers supply much information on the deliberations of the Parti Ouvrier about how the party might win the peasants to socialism. However, in the Guesde archives there are sixty-nine returned questionnaires that had been disseminated to rural supporters to gain systematic information about agricultural conditions in various regions. The questionnaires (it is not known how many in all) were sent out in July, 1892, during the protests against the tariff in Provence and in the midst of the strikes of the woodcutters. Divided into twenty-six items, the questionnaire inquired about the dominant forms of local property holding, the extent of mechanization of farming, the economic circumstances of the smallholders, food prices, rents, mortgage rates, and out-migration. There were questions about the pay rates, hours, and working conditions of the local rural laborers, as well as ones about the impact of industry on the region. The focus of interest of the Parti Ouvrier's National Council, which had authorized the canvass, was clearly on the lot of the small farmers and rural laborers. Although an examination of the responses reveals them to be often monosyllabic or incomplete, they were probably the best systematic information on rural France available to the drafters of the agrarian program of the upcoming party congress in September, 1892.[27] The agrarian program worked out at the tenth congress of the Parti Ouvrier Français at Marseille was to be the most complete and elaborate political program for the coun-

26. Roblin, *Les Bûcherons du Cher et de la Nièvre*, 134.

27. The questionnaires are filed with the Guesde Papers at the Internationaal Instituut voor Sociale Geschiedenis in Amsterdam. The announcement of their dis-

tryside proclaimed by any French left-wing or reformist party in the period. The 1892 program can be read as a concerted effort to win peasants, already on the verge of political engagement, to support parliamentary candidates of the Parti Ouvrier. Because France had a parliamentary form of government, peasant votes were the key to changes in factional strength.

The program contained proposals for economic reforms tailored to the differing needs of the rural cultivators. For the agricultural workers it called for the establishment of a minimum wage, councils of arbitration, reversion of communally owned or state-owned land to landless families, and invalid and old-age insurance to be paid for by a special tax on the large landowners. For tenant farmers and sharecroppers, it called for lower rents and reimbursement for improvements. All small farmers were to benefit from the communal purchase of machinery and their rental at cost to villagers, communal purchases of grain and fertilizer, and communal sale of products. The right of the landlord to claim the tenant's harvest in the event the tenant fell in arrears on his rent was to be abolished. And, of course, the socialists championed tax reform. This program did not offer the orthodox Marxist prediction of the erosion and eventual demise of peasant farmers with the advance of capitalism.[28]

The party reproduced its new agrarian program in leaflet form and distributed it in the countryside during the election campaign of its historic breakthrough with peasant voters in the fall of 1893. Although local notables continued to encourage *their* peasants to view these urban radicals as hostile invaders on the land, Lafargue and the party celebrated the new electoral support from peasants around Narbonne, Carcassonne, and in the Loire-Inférieure. Jaurès, although not a member of the party, was one of the authors of the draft program; he ran in Carmaux on its provisions and won peasant voters in a contest against the Association de l'Industrie Française leader, Baron Reille.[29] Jaurès and nearly fifty other socialists won

---

semination may be found in *Le Socialiste*, XVII (July, 1892); see Gratton, *Les Luttes de classes dans les campagnes*, 37, for his judgment of the usefulness to the 1892 Congress of the information contained in the returned questionnaires.

28. The text of the program can be found in *Dixième congrès national du parti ouvrier. Tenu à Marseille du 24 au 28 septembre 1892* (Lille, 1892), 34–36. See also Lehmann, *Die Agrarfrage*, 77–80; Gratton, *Les Luttes de classes dans les campagnes*, 37–45. Unfortunately, we have no stenographic proceedings of this Congress.

29. Paul Lafargue, "Les dernières élections législatives," *Almanach du parti ouvrier pour 1894* (Lille, 1893), 15–16.

111

seats in the Chamber, as other socialists had breached industrialists' strongpoints such as the Lille agglomeration and the mayors' offices and municipal councils of the countryside. The defenders of peace and order had now to look to the dangers in the countryside, as well as those in the cities.

In 1893, when the strike wave of the peasant woodcutters was at its height, the lumber dealers tried to enlist the support of the local landowners. Those same lumberjacks who struck and looked to the revolutionary socialists for ideological leadership in the winter months, they pointed out, were the agricultural workers whom the large farm proprietors hired to perform agricultural labor in the growing season. The peasants would surely not limit their socialist activities to the winter months. The publications of the lumber dealers repeatedly called upon the members of the Société des Agriculteurs du Cher et de la Nièvre to close ranks with them to protect "their common interests."[30] There is no direct evidence as to what form of aid the regional Société des Agriculteurs de France supplied the local businessmen—if it offered any at all. They probably turned to the Paris office of the society for advice, for in that same strife-filled year, the national society asked the conservative sociologist, Urbain Guérin, to investigate the situation of the agricultural laborers, and to report his findings to the next general assembly of the society.

When, on January 31, 1894, the annual meeting of the Société des Agriculteurs convened, Guérin was ready to give his preliminary report. Like the inquiry initiated by the Parti Ouvrier in July, 1892, Guérin had solicited information from as many local and regional agricultural societies as had ties with the Société des Agriculteurs de France.[31] Guérin's report—and a fleshed out, follow-up version prepared for the society's meeting the next year—is as valuable a historical document as the more famous Agrarian Program of Marseille. Guérin was a leading Le Playist social scientist and librarian of the Musée Social, the newly created conservative research center. He served as one of the most important full-time organic intellectuals of

---

30. Roblin, *Les Bûcherons du Cher et de la Nièvre*, 205; Gratton, *Les Luttes de classes dans les campagnes*, 59–80.

31. Not that the questionnaire sent around by Guérin was novel—that was an old and trusty Le Playist method of discovering the "facts." In this the socialists were the emulators. The issue here is the *timing* of the two inquiries—and rural strikes that were their common impetus.

the Catholic landowners grouped in the Société des Agriculteurs de France and of the industrialists with social consciences.[32] That he was not notably an original thinker makes us more comfortable about asserting that his insights and ideologies rendered more coherent the fears and hopes of his listeners and readers.

Guérin began his presentation to the elite of French agriculturists by frankly admitting the concern behind his inquiry: the recent strikes of the woodcutter-agricultural workers were very troubling. The Société des Agriculteurs de France had to confront the new realities that these events revealed, he believed. He then proceeded to offer an analysis in what by now had become the classical Le Playist style: one at the same time empirical and moralistic. In the manner of his school, he divided his exposition into three sections: facts, causes, and cures.

As for facts, he started by pointing out that the contemporary rural unrest was worse in the regions where tenant farming pre-dominated, where rural laborers were more numerous, than in sharecropping country, "where the transition from employee to co-beneficiary is more easily made, and where there is less distance between those who own the land and those for whom their daily labor constitutes nearly their sole resource." Although he felt that the quality of rural housing, diet, and clothing had improved over the years, he was obliged to report a desperate moral situation: the rural family was breaking down, for the children were rejecting all authority. Many respondents had decried the "ravages produced by the cabaret," in particular "alcoholism and socialist activities." Charitable institutions were rare and feeble on the land and the efforts both of individuals and private groups of Christian inspiration were hemmed in by the state.[33]

32. The pattern of Guérin's publications follows the curve of discovery of the social question of many conservative Catholic social thinkers. See his *Victimes populaires de la Révolution* (Paris, 1875), *Le Massacre des otages en 1871* (Paris, 1876), *La Science sociale et l'école de la paix sociale* (Paris, 1883), *L'Evolution sociale* (Paris, 1891).

33. Guérin's 1894 report may be found in the *Bulletin de la Société des agriculteurs de France*, XXV (1894), 235–42 (hereinafter cited as *SAF*). In 1895 Guérin addressed the general assembly once more with what he termed a résumé of the final results of the *enquête*. The second report differed in no substantial way from that of the year before, except that he further frightened his auditors by reading the new agrarian resolution that the Parti Ouvrier Congress at Nantes (1894) had passed. Before warning about the dangers to small proprietors and as a first remedy, he invoked "reviving the belief in God, and with it, public morality" (*SAF*, XXVI (1895), 150–53). The Nantes agrarian

Guérin's list of the causes of these ills began with inheritance laws, which, he argued, so divided up patrimonies that the founding of a stable family was made impossible. Property foreclosure sales, hitherto an urban phenomenon, had begun to take place with increasing frequency in the countryside. Young people, seeking pleasures not found in the country, eager to work at less arduous tasks, and hoping to improve their social position, were leaving the land. The lure of employment in the state bureaucracy was also enticing many away from work in the fields. The military service required of the young men in the village not only removed them from their familiar contexts but also gave them a taste of urban pleasures. And the public education of the secular state resulted in the pupils' learning to scorn the craft of agriculture; it turned them out with a little book learning to find supposedly better jobs in the state bureaucracy. It offered nothing "to develop character."[34]

Finally, he came to the economic causes of rural unrest. Taxes on the agricultural sector were too high. The agricultural crisis had reduced the resources of agriculturalists and this in turn had forced the reduction of the labor force. Farmers had responded by attempting to reduce the extent of labor-intensive farming and, where possible, by introducing machines. Moreover, with the growth of urban industry, cottage industries, especially weaving, had diminished. The countryside had fewer tasks for agricultural laborers and fewer artisanal activities remained for them to supplement their income.

What could be done to solve these problems? Guérin reported the dominant opinions in the responses to his questionnaires. The respondents seemed to despair of any alterations of taxes ("a universal fate"), military conscription, or the "present direction of public edu-

---

program went further along the road taken in Marseille, of assuring the small and even middling peasants of the Socialists' intentions of helping them maintain their lands. Engels wrote of the Parti Ouvrier's peasant programs, "It is not in our interests to win the peasant overnight only to lose him again on the next day, if we cannot keep our promise." He found the parallel revisionist turn of the German Social Democratic Party's agrarian program equally mistaken. Engels wrote his attack in November, 1894, soon after the Nantes Congress closed. It was first published in *Neue Zeit*, I (1894–95), as "Die Bauernfrage in Frankreich und Deutschland." See also, in their private correspondence, Engels' stronger reprimand of Lafargue and the Parti Ouvrier as having traveled too far on the "opportunist path" (Engels to Lafargue, November 22, December 18, 1894, both in Friedrich Engels, Paul and Laura Lafargue, *Correspondance*, ed. Emile Bottigelli (3 vols.; Paris, 1956–59), III, 381, 393).

34. Guérin, 1894 report, *SAF*, XXV (1894), 235–42.

cation." But he could report widespread support from those who responded to his questions for the two great Le Playist remedies for the ills both of the countryside and those of France as a whole: change the inheritance laws and open the way for "the freedom to practice charity."[35]

Policy proposals similar to these go back at least to the Second Empire; despite the fervor of their Catholic proponents, they would not be instituted in the Third Republic. There were too many peasants and members of the elite committed to the proliferation of small landowners—however economically wasteful that practice might be—to readily expect important changes in the practice of equal inheritance for survivors. As for freedom for the exercise of private charity, the restraint came from the rural notables who did not practice such beneficence, not the republican state that prohibited itself from so serious a violation of liberal principles.

In the realm of the practicable, Guérin reported strong commitment to one cure already in place, the tariff. A majority of the respondents wished to supplement the tariff policy with the proliferation of institutions of rural credit. Guérin did not make clear whether improved access to credit was intended as a way of helping discontented peasant laborers become proprietors and/or perhaps simply to shore up property relations on the land. He did urge that ways be found to reduce interest rates.

But above and beyond such remedies, Guérin, and the members of the society who answered his queries, placed their hopes in organization. Perhaps, he reported, the best way to reach agricultural laborers was by means of the syndicats agricoles. Payment of modest dues would help the laborers view the syndicats as their own. "This would be at the same time the way to bring small and large landowners closer together," he argued. The dangers of social division on the land, he warned, were at that moment very real. Not content to propagandize among agricultural laborers in several parts of France, the socialists were also trying to reach the small landowning farmers. "We are deceiving ourselves when we count on their steadfastness," he warned. The socialist agitators do not speak to the landowning peasants of a collectivist vision of the division of property at all. Rather they "seduce" them with visions of removing the heavy tax burdens from their shoulders and transfer-

35. *Ibid.*

ring them to those of the big landowners. He warned that many of the responses to the questionnaire "confirm the success of this tactic with a class we have considered up until now immune to socialist blandishments, a class we considered the rampart of the social order." Guérin concluded by once more proposing the syndicats agricoles as agents of social unity in the countryside and the Société des Agriculteurs de France, because of its concern for the problems of all rural inhabitants, including agricultural laborers, as a true representative to the rest of society of "the agricultural interest."[36]

Preparing the Defenses

Until the early 1890s, the pattern of widespread property holding on the land, traditions of deference, and the shelter from market forces that first poor communications and then tariffs conferred had denied the urban social revolutionaries *their* peasant *levées*. But could these rightist ties bind without an organizational framework? Was Guérin correct about the conservative functions of the syndicats agricoles? By the end of the nineteenth century the French peasantry was probably better organized than the French working class.

Marx, of course, has left us the evocative, but misleading, metaphor relating peasant cohesiveness to potatoes held in a sack. But even as Marx wrote, French peasants related to one another more like grapes in a cluster than potatoes in a sack and displayed their unity by raising against the new tyranny of Napoleon III.[37] To understand the complexities of social organization in the French countryside will require a great deal more research work.[38] Religious societies, clubs, and circles, in the realm of more or less formal organizations, coexisted with communal celebrations of saints' days, village bands, and regular attendance at the same cafe (or at *the* cafe). We have yet to discover how, in important ways, these social patterns, some very

36. *Ibid.*

37. Gordon Wright, *Rural Revolution in France: The Peasantry in the Twentieth Century* (Stanford, 1964), 10; Eugen Weber, *Peasants into Frenchmen: The Modernization of Rural France, 1870–1914* (Stanford, 1976); Margadant, *French Peasants in Revolt.*

38. For just the period of interest here, there are important books by Weber, *Peasants into Frenchmen;* Suzanne Berger, *Peasants Against Politics: Rural Organization in Brittany, 1911–1967* (Cambridge, Mass., 1972); Maurice Agulhon, *La Sociabilité méridionale* (2 vols.; Aix-en-Provence, 1966); Judt, *Socialism in Provence,* 154–77; and Burns, *Rural Society and French Politics.*

old, tied into the modern national political consciousness we seek here to understand. Nevertheless, in this study of French society, which attempts to connect the divergent research traditions of history "as seen from below" and history "from the top down," giving due weight to the social unities of rural life must be placed in balance with an effort to trace those lines of social force which implicate the villages in shifts or, in our case, nonshifts of national power. Tony Judt's insight that the proliferation of rural cooperatives and buying and selling syndicates "helped explain the marked antipathy shown by the peasantry of Provence toward the efforts of the Toulon anarchists to propagate their ideas beyond the city" reveals his awareness of the interpenetration of local and national factors in the life of the countryside—and of the conservatizing role of the syndicats agricoles.[39]

If we look beyond the world of the village, to the founding circumstances and growth of the three major national professional organizations for farmers, we can begin to illuminate the role of the countryside in the new conservative agenda for shaping the sociopolitical order of the Third Republic. In 1867 Drouyn de Lhuys, a nobleman with a distinguished record of state service, became the first president of the newly created Société des Agriculteurs de France. Marcel Faure, in his encyclopedic *Les Paysans dans la société française*, described the society as "regrouping the descendants of the royalists families who had avoided compromising themselves with the 'usurper,'" that is, Napoleon III.[40] We must add that, like the later Bund der Landwirte, the disregard of the crown for the "needs of agriculture" at a depressed moment was probably a more important consideration in the thinking of the founders. The Société des Agriculteurs de France headquartered itself in an elegant building on the rue d'Athènes in Paris. When the "usurper" fell and a republic, not a monarchical restoration, followed, the landed aris-

---

39. Judt, *Socialism in Provence*, 168. Judt argues that the structure and values of village life disposed French peasants to reject the individualist ideals of anarchism. But such a judgment of anarchism seems a rather distorted representation of late-nineteenth-century French anarchism. Not only is this the moment of the formation of the Confédération Générale du Travail, but Spanish anarchists were very successful in reaching peasants in several regions of Spain. Surely it makes more sense to ask *who* exercised ideological hegemony over the co-ops and syndicats in order to explain their role in resisting the radicalization of the countryside.

40. Marcel Faure, *Les Paysans dans la société française* (Paris, 1964), 30–31.

tocracy clung even more fervently to its "society of dukes," as contemporaries soon labeled it.

In 1880, as the republicans struggled to establish their hegemony—
and in the midst of the first wave of tariff agitation—Léon Gambetta
fathered the republican competitor of the Société des Agriculteurs
de France, the Société Nationale d'Encouragement à l'Agriculture.
Although its membership did not grow as rapidly as that of the
Société des Agriculteurs de France, the republican organization came
to dominate such rural credit organizations as developed. Yet because
its members had deeper and more extended roots, the upper-class
group proved better able to create mass organizational connections
in the countryside than its republican rival.

Soon after the 1884 syndicat law went into effect—and just as the
party of Gambetta, Ferry, and Méline had begun to address itself to
the depressed state of farming and to woo the peasantry to the
Republic—a group of aristocratic members of the Société des Agriculteurs de France united seventy-four syndicats agricoles into a
Union Centrale des Syndicats Agricoles de France. Le Trésor de la
Rocque became the first president. If monarchism had lost the
state—hopefully temporarily—its supporters wished to retain (or
reconquer) the countryside. Then too, in a parliamentary republic,
even conservatives had to make their case with masses of votes. In
1892, the year the Parti Ouvrier announced its agrarian program at
Marseille, the Union Centrale moved its offices into the headquar-
ters of the SAF on the rue d'Athènes. The *hobereaux*, the rural gentry,
might now more creditably speak on behalf of "agriculture," that is,
the peasantry.

Let us consider for a moment the success of the new conservative
rural organization. A. Toussaint, probably the leading authority,
estimated that by 1889 the Union Centrale united 260,000 families in
340 syndicats agricoles. A year later 380,000 peasant families had
joined, and by 1894 the number of syndicats reached 533.[41] The
agricultural society controlled by the Opportunists, the Société Na-

41. The data in the Archives Nationales (F[10] 4370–72) are too incomplete to sum-
marize. Toussaint's estimates suggest a growth from 74 syndicats in 1886 to 1000 by
1901 (A. Toussaint, *L'Union centrale des syndicats agricoles* (Paris, 1920), 37–39, 41–43).
The best modern student's estimates are rather different. Faure, *Les Paysans dans la
société française*, 33, offers 648 syndicats with 234,000 members for 1890, and 2069
syndicats with 512,000 members for 1900.

tionale, also tried to reach the peasants. It encouraged the creation of cooperatives and insurance mutuals in the countryside.[42] Its greatest efforts were directed at procuring credit for peasant proprietors, not so that they might acquire new land but that they might better exploit the fields they farmed. Although the data are a bit soft, the two most recent studies of rural organizations agree that by 1893 of 3,640,000 farmers eligible to join a rural syndicat, 1,494,000, or 41 percent, belonged to one affiliated with one or the other national federations. Of 900,236 adherents of all types of syndicats in France in 1893, 353,883 belonged to syndicats agricoles. Two of every five heads of rural families were organized; two of every five Frenchmen belonging to a syndicat were farmers.[43]

The industrial workers, however more disruptive or militant than the peasants, were not well organized. By the period 1895–1905 only 14.8 percent of workers in quarrying had joined a syndicat. For workers in metal trades the percentage was 14.33 percent; leather and hide workers, 16.12 percent; paper, 19.76 percent; and chemicals, 25.54 percent. As we might expect, miners led the list with a unionization rate of 50.95 percent. In the radicalized textile industry of the Nord 1904 statistics reveal a rate of unionization of only 19 percent.[44]

The syndicats of the workers performed, among other functions, as organizations of modern class struggle, while those of rural proprietors were often nothing more than collaborative fertilizer-purchasing ventures. But to dismiss the assessment of the rural organizations as outposts of a new conservatism in the 1890s for that reason would be a grave error.[45] In the Third Republic the agri-

42. But it did not unite under its aegis the co-ops, insurance societies, rural syndicats, and regional rural credit institutions into the Fédération Nationale de la Mutualité et de la Coopération Agricole until the years 1906–10. See Barral, *Les Agrariens français*, 115. Perhaps the tax rebellion of the Midi winegrowers frightened even the republicans of the Société Nationale with its explosive evidence of the growing leftism of the countryside.

43. Gratton, *Les Luttes de classes dans les campagnes*, 403; Louis Prugnard, *Les Etapes du syndicalisme agricole en France* (Paris, 1963), 32–37.

44. Maurice Petticollot, *Les Syndicats ouvriers de l'industrie textile dans l'arrondissement de Lille* (Lille, 1907), 188.

45. Wright, *Rural Revolution in France*, 19, does just this. Communist and socialist trade unions in France and Italy advanced political demands in behalf of their members. But it is very likely that many of these workers joined the unions less out of some conviction to build socialism than the more likely impulse of enhancing their

cultural societies of the conservatives and those of the Opportunists were instruments for integrating the countryside into a new conservative social order, thereby denying the peasantry to socialist politics.[46] Both societies worked to introduce tariffs, and immediately after the passage of the Méline tariff, both joined the Association de l'Industrie Française, which thereby became the Association de l'Industrie et l'Agriculture Française.

A faint echo of the rivalry between the republicans and the clerical-conservatives on the land over religion alone has enriched French literature and film comedy with the figures of the *curé* and the free-thinking school teacher locked in combat over the souls of the children of the village. Indeed, the image is not completely false; sometimes one side or the other did try to enhance its power. The antirepublican propaganda in the countryside of the Assumptionist fathers is a case in point, as was Jules Méline's efforts to make the Chambres consultatives d'agriculture, appointive under Napoleon III, more accessible to republican notables by introducing elections to post in the chambers.

The Chambres consultatives d'Agriculture, created in 1851 by Napoleon III as rural equivalents of the urban chambers of commerce, gathered in imperial appointees who could be trusted. Using the moment of passage of the new law of association, Ferry and Méline proposed reconstituting the rural bodies with elected rather than appointed members. This change would have permitted peasants, their resident farm workers, absentee landowners, and even local veterinarians and teachers to participate in the elections. Migrant workers, of course, were excluded. The effort to make the Chambres consultatives Opportunist strongholds in the countryside foundered on the opposition of rural conservatives who rightly saw it as a way of strengthening republican notables' power in the countryside. Rejected in 1884, the bill was put forward again in 1886, 1889, 1894, and 1900. It did not become law until 1919, when presumably the new postwar fear of the Left united the rural notables of the Right and the Center in spite of themselves. Attempting

---

paychecks and improving their working conditions. So it was with the rural syndicats—except that here the Right was doing the organizing and the representing.

46. That was probably why, despite repeated calls for these societies to function as schools of modern agricultural practice, both the republican and the conservative ones failed to discharge any such function.

before the Ralliement to minimize the strengthening of republican small-town politicians and businessmen into the countryside, the conservatives, in the words of the Marquis Gontram Cornulier (monarchist, Boulangist, antirepublican, and one of the great landowners of Calvados) "preferred that agriculturists alone should name [the body's] members."[47]

But the historical origins of the syndicats and agricultural loan societies, their more mundane roles in rural self-help, and old conservative-republican tensions on the land should not obscure our appreciation of their new function in the 1890s.[48] Increasingly as the decade went on, a great fear overcame the beneficiaries of pacification. Immediately after the socialist victories in the elections of 1893 Emile Cheysson, another Le Playist connected to the Musée Social, rallied the forces of order: "The terrain [of the countryside] is favorable for those mounting the defense. With unity and energy we can dam up this rising flood which has submerged the cities, but from which there is still time to save the countryside."[49] The same year the Comte de Rocquigny, in *Les Syndicats agricoles et le socialisme agraire*, wrote that he was sure that socialist propaganda would yield no returns in the countryside, for the "anti-socialist league formed by our syndicats agricoles will save the peasants from the socialist misleaders." Le Trésor de la Rocque, president of the Union Centrale, echoed his peer's sentiments in the preface to Rocquigny's book.[50]

At the next session of the legislature, in February, 1894, the tariff partners proposed new legislation to hearten the defense. In late February they pushed through both Chambers an increase in the duties on imported wheat and other grain products. The duties on

---

47. The fate of the Ferry-Méline plan may be traced in AN C5344 dossier 91.

48. Ronald H. Hubscher emphasizes the now politically important role assumed by the agricultural organizations in the Pas-de-Calais in the last years of the century in the unprecedented attempt to mobilize rural spirits in behalf of a socially conservative defense (*L'Agriculture et la société rurale dans le Pas-de-Calais: du milieu du XIXᵉ siècle à 1914* (2 vols.; Arras, 1979–80), I, 581, 599).

49. Emile Cheysson, *La Lutte des classes* (Paris, 1893), 23.

50. Robert de Rocquigny, *Les Syndicats agricoles et le socialisme agraire* (Paris, 1893), 55, 334, xii. For a friendly gesture to the free traders—perhaps as a call to a common task—see the reprint of an article by M. H. Blancheville from the *Journal des Chambres de commerce* in *Travail national*, October 15, 1893, pp. 507–508. The piece expresses grave misgivings about the spread of agrarian socialism and looks to the counterrevolutionary potential of the syndicats agricoles.

wheat alone shot up 40 percent per kilogram. Clearly, maintaining farm incomes—and the alliance of growers and industrialists—was more important than any quibbles about the cost of bread to consumers. In addition, that fall Méline himself shepherded a bill through the Chamber that permitted members of a syndicat agricole to form a tax-exempt mutual credit association. Only participants could be shareholders and the return on shares was to be a fixed sum. Thus, to the degree possible, if farmers wished to pool their capital for their mutual benefit and survival, the state of the Opportunist republicans would encourage them.[51]

By 1897, during Méline's premiership and at the height of his political concentration of conservative forces, the ideologists of the syndicats agricoles declared the rural organizations ready to fulfill their mission. The rural anti-socialist party was coming into being, declared René Henri, a Méline supporter in that year of the great debate between Méline and Jaurès over the destiny of the countryside. The land was "permeated with associations": it was "organized and ready to be put into motion." The Catholic theorist of class reconciliation, H. de Gailhard-Bancel, voiced similar sentiments in an address before the Congrès National Catholique, held a few days after the Chamber debate: "You understand as well as I, gentlemen, how gravely our country is suffering at the present hour from divisions of hearts and minds, from the antagonisms, which grow sharper with the passing of each day, between the employers and their workers, between those who possess something and those who have nothing. There's grave danger to our society. By beginning to actualize the reconciliation and rapprochement of classes, if they have not completely conjured away this danger, the syndicats agricoles have at least attenuated it."[52] Most succint was Emil Du-

---

51. Henri Sagnier, *Le Crédit agricole en France: ses origines, son essor, son avenir* (Paris, 1911), 32–40, for which Méline wrote the preface. See also Emile Levasseur, *Histoire du commerce de la France* (2 vols.; Paris, 1911–12), II, 588–601; Auguste Arnauné, *Le Commerce extérieur et les tarifs de douane* (Paris, 1911), 338–42; and Eugene Golob, *The Méline Tariff: French Agriculture and Nationalist Economic Policy* (New York, 1944), 229–47.

52. René Henri, "Le Parti rural organisé et mobilisable," *Revue politique et parlementaire*, XIII (1897), 14–36; Henri de Gailhard-Bancel, *Les Syndicats agricoles et l'union des classes: Discours prononcé à Paris à l'assemblée générale du 1er dec. 1897 du Congrès national Catholique* (Paris, 1897), 10. See also from the flurry of literature of 1897, J. C. Kergall, *Du Rôle social des syndicats agricoles: rapport présenté au 3e Congrès National des Syndicats Agricoles* (Paris, 1897). We owe to Kergall the theory that "all noble [*généreuses*] ideas, all exquisite sentiments, so to speak, are born spontaneously from the manure heap [*l'engrais*]."

port, the great organizer of powerful agricultural associations in the southeast in an address before the members of the Musée Social. He flatly stated that agricultural associations "will save France from the Revolution."[53]

In the early years of the 1890s the defenses of the social order of the Republic were nearly completed. In place was a tariff policy and an ideology of National Production to pacify the working class. In place, too, was a tariff policy and rural organizations uniting both large and small farmers to link the classes in the countryside. But the union of interests around articles on a tariff list could only serve as a marriage of convenience. The alliance partners needed to feel more passion to transform their economic bonds into a union of both spiritual and political depth. The maintenance of social peace—as they understood it—permitted no weaker connection. Let us now see how the Association de l'Industrie Française of the years after 1891 played its part to strengthen the union for social protection. We will look, too, at the timely aid offered by the Church of the Ralliement. Méline's own conservatism was well launched; old conservatives had received his overtures with warm interest.

53. Louis de Vogüé, *Emile Duport, la leçon de ses oeuvres* (Lyon, 1909), 364–65.

V

Conservative Concentration

In the preceding chapters we have seen the upper strata unite around protection from foreign and domestic enemies by means of the new tariff policy of the Republic. The bourgeois-upper class alliances thereby created the first such arrangements in the life of the young Republic, laying the foundations for broader social and political agreements. Growing working-class economic and political resistance, joined by the first stirrings of rural discontent, finally culminated in 1896 in the naming of Jules Méline to head a ministry of pacification. But before the tariff partners could cement together a governmental coalition strong enough to endure the two years of the Méline government, the first tentative collaboration of economic self-interest worked out around the tariff issue had to be built upon. This chapter will examine the next phase in the unification in the ranks of the new conservatives. The expansion of the Association de l'Industrie Française and the initiation of the Ralliement took France a step further toward the coalescing of "the grand reactionary mass" evoked by Engels in 1893.[1] Let us now turn to an examination of how the Association de l'Industrie Française was strengthened after passage of the Méline tariff and how the Ralliement—the conservative concentration encouraged by the pope—grew out of the upper class's concern with creating an industrial society according to conservative principles, and out of the struggle for economic protectionism.

The Association de l'Industrie et de l'Agriculture Française

Even after the 1891 tariff victory, after a decade of successful struggle, the protectionists understood the fragility of their victory. No

1. Engels to Paul Lafargue, January 22, 1895, in Friedrich Engels, Paul and Laura Lafargue, *Correspondance,* ed. Emile Bottigelli (3 vols; Paris, 1956–59), III, 394.

one could guarantee positive results for French tariff policy in the fiercely competitive world of international commerce in the decades of the Great Depression. Nor could anyone be certain that the tariffs would sufficiently increase the earnings of the industrialists so that they might have the wherewithal to pay their workers with higher wages and shorter hours. Finally, the protectionists had to concern themselves with rural discontent, which seemed to be growing and which the socialists were beginning to exploit. Would it quiet down behind the safety of protective barriers? The leaders of the Association de l'Industrie Française understood both the social implications of their tariff policies and the need to strengthen the union of all socially conservative classes in the Republic.

Even while expressing the satisfaction of the members with the passage of the Méline tariff, Paul Aclocque, association president and head of an important iron works in the Ariège, urged the industrialists to turn their attention more systematically to pressing questions of political economy and social policy.[2] The pressure from the Left for state intervention on behalf of the workers would continue; the Association de l'Industrie Française had to array its forces to resist it. It could not be done alone.

Effective resistance required strong allies and a strong alliance. In key moments in the life cycles of individuals and families—births, marriages, and deaths, for example—groups come together as a sign of support and of solidarity. Aclocque died soon after his celebration of the tariff victory at the AIF meeting of February, 1893. We

---

2. *Travail national*, February 28, pp. 71–72, March 6, 1892, pp. 98–99. He singled out workers' accident insurance, child labor, and the length of women's workdays. The response of Aclocque and the Association de l'Industrie Française to these new questions, once they had taken cognizance of them, is another matter. Aclocque led the association into opposing legislation limiting working hours for children, minor girls, and women, in the name of "freedom from restrictions." He fought attempts to remove employers' rights to levy fines. And he rejected attempts to impose health and safety inspections on French industry because such a law "imposed the arbitrary authority of an inspector, whom we do not know." We see here in its full transparency the manufacturers' image of the factory as a part of his home where he does not receive people he does not know socially (*Travail national*, March 12, 1893, pp. 122–23). The views are Aclocque's presidential remarks at the organization's general assembly in 1893. In 1896 Méline characterized pending legislation on work accident insurance, progressive taxes on inheritance, and income taxes, in what was for him an uncharacteristically vicious attack on Léon Bourgeois, the chief proponent of a progressive tax on incomes, as "taking sides against capital" (*Travail national*, January 19, 1896, pp. 33–34).

may catch a glimpse of the solidarity of the French elites by noting the names of the pallbearers at his funeral: General Begin, inspector-general of the naval infantry; Jules Méline; de la Germonière, vice-president of the Association de l'Industrie Française; Baron Reille, deputy president of the Comité des Forges and a Rallié; Teisonnière, vice-president of the Société des Agriculteurs de France; Charles Tambour of the House of Rothschild; Marc de Haut, also of the Société des Agriculteurs de France; General Laffitte de Canson; and Jules Domerque, director of the *Réforme economique*.[3]

On the eve of the 1893 elections, as waves of industrial strikes resurged, woodcutters continued to strike, peasants in the Midi protested the tariffs, and the socialists canvassed the countryside for peasant votes, Méline accepted the presidency of the Association de l'Industrie Française vacated by the death of Aclocque. Immediately he called upon his agrarian friends for even closer cooperation. In June several important regional agricultural societies, as well as the Opportunist-oriented Société Nationale d'Encouragement à l'Agriculture were admitted into the association. The creation of an Association de l'Industrie et de l'Agriculture Française signaled to all the new ties binding the economic leaders of industry and agriculture. It had become the most inclusive and most powerful organization of industrialists and growers in France.[4]

Early in November, after the election results were known, a group of industrialists pooled their resources to purchase for Méline and his organization a daily newspaper, once Léon Gambetta's mouthpiece, the *République française*.[5] The newspaper would serve as the voice of Méline and his friends throughout the rest of the decade, or at least to 1896, when Méline could use the premiership as his platform. The sensationalist Radical and anticlerical newspaper *La Lanterne* printed a series of articles exposing what it called "Les Patrons de M. Méline." But *Lanterne*'s daring exposé fell flat; the majority of the backers of the *République française* turned out to be the usual Lille and Vosges textile and manufacturing entrepreneurs, along with the notorious anti-union employer of Carmaux, Eugène Rességuier, and of course Henri Schneider of Creusot. *La Lanterne* carried one novel revelation: many of the backers of the Opportunist

3. *Travail national*, March 26, 1893.

4. See the appendix for the leading members and their affiliations at various times in its history.

5. *Travail national*, June 18–25, October 8, 1893.

republican newspaper named were indeed neither liberals nor Opportunists, but rather conservatives and clericals—or even former Bonapartists, like Schneider. What *La Lanterne* did not know was that French heavy industry took a corporate interest in the success of Méline's newspaper: by October, 1893, the Comité des Forges had subscribed 11 percent of the paper's capital. Robert Charlie, editor and Méline's spokesman, cheerfully admitted that the paper had been created "specifically to defend the prime interests of national production," for which task men "from all points of the horizon" had come together.[6]

The interests of National Production required the usual special interest legislation that the Association de l'Industrie Française and the growers had been promoting: laws and policies in this direction were to be advocated and reported upon in the pages of the *République française* according to the program published in the first issue under the new owners. The program concluded with the promise to cover the most important factor of all in production, the relation between labor and capital, including in the broadest sense, according to the editors, the social question. The writers of the paper hoped their articles and reports would demonstrate for the benefit of the workers themselves that the "majority of so-called reforms preached by the revolutionary socialist school are impracticable and illusory; [their implementation] would be disastrous for the working class." True to its promise, throughout November the *République française* carried articles on the second national congress of trade unions in the textile industry then meeting at Roubaix, as well as summaries of Jaurès' speeches in the Chamber. This reportage was of course hostile and ironic in tone, but reasonably informative.[7]

On December 9, the anarchist Auguste Vaillant attempted to avenge the execution of Ravachol, a fellow anarchist, by bombing the Chamber of Deputies while it was in session. The labor reporter for *République française*, Edmond Frank, added the voice of the protectionists to the chorus of denunciations in the conservative press. As was common in establishment journalism, he conflated the tiny anarchist movement with the growing socialist one and blackened

6. See the series in *La Lanterne*, January 9, 10, 12, 13, 14, 15, 17, 1897, and the smug rejoinder in *République française*, January 12, 1897, p. 1. See also Claude Bellanger *et al.*, *Histoire générale de la presse française* (3 vols.; Paris, 1972), III, 232–34, 357–58; Etienne Chichet, *Quarante ans de journalisme: feuilles volantes* (Paris, 1935).

7. *République française*, November 4, 1893, p. 1, November 21, 23, 24, 25, 27, 1893.

both in great brushstrokes of rhetoric: "Vaillant had been their [the socialists'] friend, more or less their disciple, their collaborator." An unsigned lead article, written in Méline's style, claimed that there was little difference between socialists and anarchists, except "the conclusion." With a nice nonsequitur the author adduced the example of the recent strike at mines owned by Association de l'Industrie et l'Agriculture Française adherents in the Pas-de-Calais.[8] It had been an ordinary labor dispute over wages and working conditions, he claimed, until "these traveling salesmen of social revolution" intervened to heighten tensions. "Socialists have never protested the dynamitings; their preachments," he concluded, "led to anarchist deeds." The *République française* applauded the immediate response to the bombing by the ministry of Jean Casimir-Perier. It pushed through the Chamber a series of politically repressive laws, the first of which abridged the freedom of press and of assembly.[9] "We are tired of the revolutionary agitation which continues to disturb the work of the nation," fulminated the *République française*, "which paralyzes business activities, which heightens the general *malaise*, and does more harm to the workers than to their employers." Thus spoke the new voice of the defender of "the prime interests of national production."

The Ralliement and National Production

As industrialists and growers closed ranks to protect the social order—and the conservative republic that guaranteed that order—the Church came to their aid. Most French Catholic leaders, both lay and religious, had supported the cause of monarchism in the first decades of the Third Republic. This *parti-pris* isolated them from political influence in the new state and earned them the enmity of republicans such as Léon Gambetta, Jules Ferry, and their liberal followers. Divided regionally, espousing differing economic philosophies, and unresponsive to any party discipline, the liberal republicans welcomed the opportunity to unite around the clerical menace. Largely driven out of education, their religious orders harassed, their priests paid by a secular and hostile state, intelligent Church leaders realized the need to end the Church's isolation from public life and public power.

8. *L'Industrie française*, March 21, 1878, pp. 89–90.
9. *République française*, December 12, 13, 1893. On the "era of attentats," see Jean Maitron, *Le Mouvement anarchiste en France* (2 vols.; Paris, 1975) I, 206.

The year 1890 seemed most opportune to initiate the Church's reconciliation to the Republic. The defeat of Boulangism had discredited the many monarchists who had backed the general and had made others begin to reflect on how best to ensure a conservative order by less radical, and more predictable, means. Labor unrest had occurred in great waves that year, culminating in the first European May Day strikes. And in the Chamber and Senate the protectionists, anticlerical republicans, and Catholic conservatives in the protectionist caucus met to prepare for their almost certain legislative victory. The French domestic scene was set for Cardinal Lavigerie, primate of Africa and archbishop of Algiers and Carthage, to arise from the banquet table at his palace in Algiers to offer his famous toast to the officers of the fleet anchored in the harbor who had dined with him. The military men, most of them convinced monarchists, were taken aback by the cardinal's proposal on the evening of November 12, 1890, that they rally to the Republic whose uniform they bore. Further embarrassment to all was avoided— after Admiral Duperre drank simply to "his Eminence the Cardinal and to the clergy of Algeria"—when the College of St. Eugène's band struck up La Marseillaise, covering over any need or opportunity for further exchanges of toasts.[10]

Lavigerie's action had been approved, indeed inspired, by the pope. Scholars of the Ralliement have generally offered three reasons for Leo XIII's interest in a Church-state rapprochement in France. Leo wished to gain French support—as Napoleon III had supported the papacy—in his still unresolved conflict with the Italian state. The struggle centered on the right of the papacy to secular authority in Italy; the dispute came to be known as the Roman question in the diplomatic language of the nineteenth century. A second motive imputed to Leo was his deep concern for the sad circumstances of

---

10. In the colonies, *La Marseillaise* was accepted simply as the national anthem; it was not associated with *parti pris*. See Alexander Sedgwick, *The Ralliement in French Politics, 1890–1898* (Cambridge, Mass., 1965), 39–73. David Shapiro, "The Ralliement in the Politics of the 1890's," in Shapiro (ed.), *The Right in France, 1890–1919* (Carbondale, Ill., 1962), 13; Adrien Dansette, *Religious History of Modern France* (2 vols.; Edinburgh, 1961), II, 80; J. Dean O'Donnell, Jr., *Lavigerie in Tunisia: The Interplay of Imperialist and Missionary* (Athens, Ga., 1979), 145–47. An English translation of the toast may be found in David Thomson (ed.), *France: Empire and Republic, 1850–1940* (New York, 1968), 245–46. Of course, the *Droite constitutionnelle* was already functioning in the Chamber, but the Chamber of Deputies of the Republic was not the sacred preserve of monarchism that the French Fleet was.

the Church in the secular, anticlerical republic. Making peace with the existing authorities in France might begin the French Church's restoration to dignity and to authority.[11]

Without questioning the accuracy of such a reconstruction of papal thinking, we must nonetheless ask why the pope and his French supporters should expect republican politicians to terminate their hostility to the Church's involvement in politics and education simply because the papacy needed diplomatic support and because Catholics wished to end the assaults on the Church in France. To put the question in this fashion leads us to emphasize the primacy, *in France*, of the third factor in the Ralliement, the desire for social peace. The linchpin of the policy of the Ralliement was the common concern, shared by conservative republicans and conservative Catholics, for order in society, that is, for quieting the discontent of the new working class. Two kinds of evidence might serve to confirm the hypothesis of the paramountcy of social conservatism in the etiology of the Ralliement. There was first what the texts asserted. Second, we must examine the significance of the order of their publication or declaration.

Cardinal Lavigerie's toast merits our first consideration. The theme was certainly reconciliation: "Confronted with a past that is still bleeding, and an ever-menacing future, we are in fact at this moment in supreme need of union." His dinner guests, officers of the French fleet, served the Republic, he was saying; they should bring themselves to support it. He stated, "It would be madness to try to support the columns of a building without going inside the building itself."[12]

But what were the dangers that made endorsing the authority of the Republic the only "way of saving one's country from the disaster that threatens it"? It would seem an excellent strategy on the part of the cardinal to end the resistance of the monarchist officers by reminding them of their duty and moral obligation to protect their homeland against foreign danger. Such seems not to have been his argument.[13]

---

11. See, for example, Sedgwick, *The Ralliement*, 1–12; Dansette, *Religious History*, II, 75–90.

12. All translations of Lavigerie's remarks are from Thomson (ed.), *France: Empire and Republic*, 245–46.

13. *Ibid.*

Lavigerie did speak of the role of the navy in bringing honor to France "wherever the name of France must be maintained," as well as its role in protecting the Christian missions. But France was not involved at that moment in any diplomatic or military situation that could reasonably be called menacing or potentially disastrous. Bismarck had just fallen and the diplomatic house of cards he had erected began to fall almost immediately; in particular, relations between Germany and Russia had begun to deteriorate. Soon, paralleling the newly friendly financial relations between France and czarist Russia, republican leaders would undertake the negotiations of military and diplomatic agreements between the Republic and the Russian Empire. On the contrary, 1890 was a year of great expectations in French foreign relations.[14]

There was, of course, serious internal discord. Perhaps the key phrase in Lavigerie's appeal to the Right—the passage that bathed the whole toast in its light—came in the middle. Indirectly but clearly claiming the support of the pope for his sentiments, the cardinal declared, "Without this resignation and patriotic acceptance, nothing will be possible either to preserve peace and order, save the world from social danger, or to save that very religion of which we are ministers."[15]

While Catholic monarchists and anticlerical republicans wrestled with their consciences over which moral imperatives to follow— those dictated by political loyalties or those mandated by a concern for peace in society—the succeeding months continued to be disquieting. In 1891, workers and their families put on even greater and more militant May Day demonstrations. Especially impressive and violent were the strikes and marches in the cities and industrial centers of Catholic Europe—Spain, Italy, and France.[16] Two weeks after those bloody celebrations (in France, the Fourmies shootings), the pope issued the *Rerum Novarum*, the key social encyclical of the nineteenth century. A number of its salient features bear on French social policy.[17]

First, it is important to remember that *Rerum Novarum* was not the

14. *Ibid.*

15. *Ibid.*

16. Joseph N. Moody, "Leo XIII and the Social Crisis," in Edward T. Gargan (ed.), *Leo XIII and the Modern World* (New York, 1961), 65–86, especially 69.

17. See Etienne Gilson, *The Church Speaks to the Modern World* (Garden City, N.Y., 1957).

first confrontation of Leo XIII with the issue of order in society. Soon after his election in 1878 to replace Pius IX (the pope of the antiliberal and antimodern *Syllabus of Errors*), he had promulgated his first encyclical, *Inscrutabile Dei*, dedicated to defining his position on a number of key questions troubling the faithful. Here he reviewed and delineated the teachings of the Church on Church-state relations, schismatics, marriage and family, Christian education, and papal infallibility, and attacked what he termed the "enemies of public order." In the context employed, contemporaries understood "enemies" to refer to socialists, anarchists, secularists, and Masons; consequently, most observers looking for early signs of the direction the new papacy would follow estimated the conservative spirit of the encyclical's author to be much like that of Pius IX.[18]

In December, 1878, Leo XIII spoke out again on social issues in *Quod apostolici*. This encyclical seemed almost a reedition of the *Syllabus of Errors*, but its salvo was aimed now exclusively at the errors of socialist views on equality, marriage, secularism, and property. Leo XIII reaffirmed the primacy of the supernatural order, of Christian marriage, of the divine origin of all authority, of the rightness of social inequality, of the providential foundation of social class distinctions, and of the basis of private property in natural law. Obedience was "noble"; there was no right to revolution against duly constituted authority. He held up the Church as the defender of public peace and its teachings as the means of killing "at the root, the bad seed of socialism." In more positive fashion, he urged the rich to do their Christian duty to the poor: "who does not see that [in paternalism] lies the best means of appeasing the long-standing conflict which exists between the poor and the rich?" Finally he encouraged the creation of unions of artisans and workmen that, "under the tutelage of religion, may render the members content with their lot and lead to a quiet and tranquil life."[19]

But by 1891 it was clear for all to see that European artisans and workmen were neither content with their lot nor quiet and tranquil. The novelty of *Rerum Novarum*—other than its comprehensiveness—was that after its preliminary condemnation of socialism as

18. Lillian Parker Wallace, *Leo XIII and the Rise of Socialism* (Raleigh, N.C., 1966), 91–92.

19. I have followed the reading of Wallace, *Leo XIII*, 111–112, in my account of the encyclical.

futile and wrong, it addressed itself to the needs of and recourses open to laboring men, and to the role that the state might play in facilitating social reform. In the thirteen years since Leo XIII had issued *Quod apostolici*, the continued intensification of the social crisis seemed to have cooled his hopes that peace would come largely from the efficacy of paternalistic activities of Christian capitalists. Since it was evident that the workers were organizing unions, mutual aid societies, and even political parties all over Europe, why should these organizations not be guided by Christian principles, the encyclical seemed to ask. Moreover, as the text implied, only the state guided by Christian values was powerful enough to bridle the excesses of free market capitalism ("the cruelty of men of greed").

One student of the social encyclicals has argued that because the pope's condemnation of socialism in 1891 was more measured than it had been in 1878 and because he reserved his harshest words to denounce the greed of some capitalists, "obviously he had come a long way since that first encyclical against the socialists."[20] The judgment of Eugène Schneider, Association de l'Industrie et l'Agriculture Française member, Rallié, and one of France's great employers, should contradict any seriously antiestablishment reading of *Rerum Novarum*. When interviewed by the journalist Jules Huret in 1892, Schneider expressed his deep faith in private enterprise and in the message of the new encyclical. When Huret then asked him his views on the eight-hour workday, the theme of the May Day strikes of the past two years, he replied, "Basically, you see, the eight-hour-day is another *dada*, a boulangism. In five or six years people will have forgotten about it; they'll invent something else." Instead, Schneider offered, "The Encyclical! Read the Encyclical! It's all in there."[21]

Rerum Novarum appeared six months after Cardinal Lavigerie offered his toast to launch the Ralliement. That initiative in turn was followed, in February, 1892, by the pope's explicit admonition to French Catholics (*Au Milieu des Sollicitudes*), to accept the Republic as a duly constituted form of civil authority—an authority originating

20. *Ibid.*, 271.
21. Jules Huret, *Enquête sur la question sociale en Europe* (Paris, 1897), 24–35. Huret conducted most of the interviews in 1892. Schneider initiated a company union in his own factory; he ran Creusot, the company and the town, with both extensive paternalism and authoritarianism.

from God—regardless of the nature of the legislation such a government might issue. The welfare of society justified, even made necessary, such a policy, the encyclical asserted. The two encyclicals, the one on the social question and the other exhorting Catholics to accept the Republic, complemented each other. Adrien Dansette suggests that they would have been published together, had not the initial reception to Lavigerie's remarks been so frosty.[22] The one acknowledged the seriousness of the social crisis of capitalist society and proposed means for leading the discontent into the creation of interest groups united by bonds of Christian corporatism. The second opened the way in France for the creation of a new conservative coalition, or if possible even of a party, based on the Catholics' acceptance of the Republic—even if it continued to discriminate against the Church—for the sake of social peace.

The elections of 1893 tested the response of Catholic voters to the policy of the Ralliement. Forty-nine socialists won seats in the Chamber, and the Radicals returned 122. Before the election the Opportunists had been reserved, even suspicious, about the Catholic political initiative. In many places they had contested seats against Rallié candidates, and had usually won.[23] The Ralliés won only 36 places; the Intransigeant monarchists elected 58 deputies. The Opportunists, with 311 mandates, gained an absolute majority. The pope's desires for a great new conservative party in France were disappointed: the Catholic vote, for the moment, was split. Fewer Ralliés had been elected than even socialists. As long as the Opportunists held their majority together—a difficult task in the French parliamentary situation of almost no party loyalty or discipline—they did not need the support of the Ralliés, or independent republicans, as they labeled themselves after 1894. But if Radicals and socialists threatened, in the country or in the Chamber, help from the Ralliés might prove important and easy to accept, since the secular republicans would be the senior partners.

But how might republican politicians so long associated with

22. Dansette, *Religious History*, II, 86–87, 125. Joseph Moody writes in the same vein: "It is remarkable that *Rerum Novarum* appeared between two major steps in his *Ralliement* policy. . . . Even in *Rerum Novarum* his thoughts were never far from France" (Moody, "Leo XIII and the Social Crisis," in Gargan (ed.), *Leo XIII and the Modern World*, 83, n. 15).

23. Sedgwich, *The Ralliement*, 70–73; Shapiro, "The Ralliement in the Politics of the 1890's," in Shapiro (ed.), *The Right in France*, 18.

anticlerical politics come to an understanding with men who had so recently been monarchists and had even rallied to the Republic for ultramontane reasons? Where did the political trust, which had to accompany this political coalition, come from? The answer is that this trust had been incubated in alliances forged in the struggle for tariff protection. To the degree that the Association de l'Industrie Française was an organization of Opportunists and their fellow-travelers we would expect it to operate within the tradition of re-public anticlericalism. But it did not. When the Church attempted to end its political isolation, the Opportunists showed themselves to be receptive. They had become so as a result of a decade of economic preparations for the Ralliement.

Robert Pinot, a Catholic and a spokesman for industrial organiza-tions, who in a few years would lead the Comité des Forges into the leading ranks of the world's organizations of heavy industrialists, captured the new spirit of the growing convergence between tariff collaboration and Catholic-republican cooperation in a telling meta-phor. In his *L'Eglise et l'esprit nouveau*, written in the midst of the Ralliement, he urged the Church to accept the republican state's control of its finances. He suggested that the Church would be "both prudent and well-advised . . . henceforth to place itself behind the state budget for religions as behind a protective tariff, in order to survive and to fulfill the more amply its mission the day the tariff would be lifted."[24] For at least ten years before the passage of the Méline tariff, pro-Republic, Protestant, anticlerical industrialists and politicians collaborated closely with monarchist, Catholic, ultra-montane manufacturers and growers to achieve the overarching goal of tariff protection for French National Labor. In the course of these many years of meeting and planning the protection of their common economic and social interests, Protestant (anticlerical) cot-ton mill owners from the Vosges, like Nicholas Claude of Saulxures, or members of Dietsch Frères of Saint-Dié, made peace with the likes of a marquis de Chevigné, Vice-president of the Agricultural Society of the Bouches-du-Rhône, or the Comte de Saint-Quentin, deputy from Calvados. Two generations of devoutly Catholic Schneiders of Creusot (Henri, the first, a Bonapartist) learned to appreciate the political acumen of the republican Jules Ferry, author of the in-famous laic laws, but also active floor-manager and reporter of the

24. Robert Pinot, *L'Eglise et l'esprit nouveau* (Paris, 1894).

Méline tariff in the Senate. Above all, the economic reconciliation around tariff questions between the Catholic dukes and marquises of the Société des Agriculteurs de France and the largely Opportunist republican leadership of the Association de l'Industrie Française in the eighties created the political coalition of the Ralliement of the mid-nineties. It offered its proponents a model of successful cooperation between Catholics and republicans in behalf of a common interest against a common danger.

We know something of the economic interests of the Ralliés. Certainly all were property owners. Of a composite total of 101 conservative deputies in the Chamber for the years 1889–1898, only 24 were businessmen or bankers. Of that number, 15 were Ralliés, and, as Shapiro points out, they made up nearly half the Ralliés elected. The 9 identifiable Intransigeants had only 2 important industrialists in their ranks: Laroche Joubert, a paper mill owner from Angoulême, and Armand Maille, an iron manufacturer who seemed to devote most of his time to his land in the Maine-et-Loire. The rest either ran small operations or were figureheads in their firms. Thus, modern business enterprise was relatively under-represented in conservative ranks, as we would expect of supporters of Legitimist monarchy; Catholic conservatives, in turn, connected to industry and banking tended to gravitate toward acceptance of the Opportunist Republic.[25]

The Ralliés could count among their number not only the Schneiders, father and son, but also the notorious (at least in the career of Jaurès) Baron René Reille, head of the mines in Carmaux and sometime president of the Association de l'Industrie Française. The Schneiders were of course prominent members of the association, and so was Henri Loyer, a member since 1878, and a Lille cotton mill owner. Comte Melchior de Vogüé, an ambassador under MacMahon, landowner in Beny, active in the direction of the Suez Company and of Saint-Gobain, and soon to be chosen to lead the Société des Agriculteurs de France, served as one of the liaisons between the society and the Association de l'Industrie Française, although he did not accept a formal office in Méline's organization until some years later.

Also adhering to the new course were Prince d'Arenberg, a direc-

25. Shapiro, "The Ralliement in the Politics of the 1890's," in Shapiro (ed.), *The Right in France*, 26–28.

tor of Anzin; Stephen Pichon with interests in the Béthune mines, which had experienced much labor trouble in 1893; Louis-Ernest Brincard and Baron Robert Eugène des Rotours, both important sugar manufacturers; and Paul Le Gavrien, owner of a Lille machinery firm. These men were all major figures in industries adhering to the coalition brought together in the Association de l'Industrie Française.[26]

A look at the regions of Rallié strength suggests another interesting pattern. As a consequence of the elections of 1893, the only two major industrial areas of France still strongly Catholic politically, the Nord and the Pas-de-Calais, elected nine of the then thirty Ralliés, but only one of the fifty-six Intransigeants. In the relatively underdeveloped West, thirty-nine Intransigeants gained seats, but only six Ralliés managed to get elected. Thus the connection between Ralliement and industry, especially persons and regions of *protection-seeking* industry, was close.[27]

Finally, there are the voting patterns in the Chamber to consider. Here economic interest so overwhelmed any other considerations that we should not expect to find Ralliés and Intransigeants voting at cross purposes on tariffs, for example. The vote on the 1881 tariff reveals little about the relations of protectionists and future Ralliés because industry and agriculture were still split. Méline and his friends worked for the next ten years to put together the successful agricultural-industrial coalition of 1891. When finally in 1891 the Méline tariff was voted, all the conservatives who would become Ralliés voted for it.[28] The vote in 1894 to increase the minimum duties on imported wheat by seven francs also found all the Ralliés lined up on the protectionist side.[29]

26. On the members and participants at Association de l'Industrie Française and Association de l'Industrie et l'Agriculture Française meetings, see the appendix of this work. On de Vogüé, see Pierre Barral, *Les Agrariens français de Méline à. Pisani* (Paris, 1968), 78–90.

27. Shapiro, "The Ralliement in the Politics of the 1890's," in Shapiro (ed.), *The Right in France*, 31.

28. Michael S. Smith, *Tariff Reform in France, 1860–1900: The Politics of Economic Interest* (Ithaca, N.Y., 1980), 181. Several important Ralliés went off on their summer vacations (Reille, Schneider, DeMackau) once the passage of the tariff was a foregone conclusion, and seven Ralliés had not yet been elected to the Chamber. The seventeen Ralliés voting yes were Desjardins, Delafosse, Paulmier, Dufaure, Balsan, Bourlon de Rouvre, Le Gavrien, de Rotours, De Montalembert, Pichon, Achille Adam, Tailliander, Achille Fould, de Monfort, Brincard, Dupuytren. *Journal Officiel*, Chambre des députés, Débats, July 18, 1891, p. 1870 (hereinafter cited as *JO*).

29. *JO*, Chambre des députés, Débats, February 21, 1894, Annexe, pp. 320–23.

But the Intransigeants also voted yes to both the Méline tariff and to the duty increase of 1894. Thus the issue of tariffs did not divide Ralliés from Intransigeants. It is reasonable to surmise that, to the degree the Intransigeants saw protectionism as a necessary buttress in support of the value of their landed estates, they refused to allow their displeasure with the Republic to cheat them out of the practical benefits of Opportunist policies. Then, too, they may have been far-sighted enough to discern the dampening effects on the class struggle flowing from protectionism. Thus, although not all Catholic conservatives were willing to work with the Opportunist republicans in parliament—and indeed, the majority would not—even the Intransigeants appreciated the convergences of economic interests.

The electoral successes of the Left in 1893 and the relatively poor (that is, nonthreatening) showing of the Ralliés, induced the Opportunist government of Casimir-Periér to yield *politically* to the Catholics' wooings.[30] They were not immediately needed for a parliamentary majority; the elections had returned an absolute majority of pro-Republic Opportunist deputies. Rather, a new conservative consensus for the maintenance of privilege was taking form. In the Chamber, the government's minister of instruction, fine arts, and cultes, Eugène Spuller, who had been a close friend of the anticlerical Gambetta, announced the new conservative republicans' attitude towards the Ralliés. In March, 1894, he rose in the Chamber to make his famous speech that repudiated old sectarian attitudes and promised a "new spirit" in Church-state relations; while outside the parliament Méline's associates were more specific about the purpose of the new spirit. As an editorial in the *République française* put it, "the heroic period of the Third Republic may now be adjudged closed. We are in an era of organization. It is time to embark on a new path, to put aside our party-political quarrels—and even our religious ones." At the terminus of the new path, the editors announced, was "the *Defense of National Labor* in all its forms."[31]

Some members of the loosely knit Opportunist majority could not stomach Casimir-Periér's courtship with the Right. Their defection cost the government votes, although the Ralliés made up most of the deficit.[32] Some of the Opportunist defectors, incensed by the

30. *Travail national*, September 10, 1893, p. 445; Sedgwick, *The Ralliement*, 131.

31. *JO*, Chambre des députés, Débats, March 3, 1894, pp. 486–92; *République française*, November 4, 1894, p. 1.

32. Sedgwick, *The Ralliement*, 133–34.

new spirit, joined with the Radicals to elect Henri Brisson, rather than Méline, president of the Chamber in December, 1894. When Casimir-Periér failed to keep a majority behind him in the Chamber, he resigned. Ribot's government of January, 1895, continued the Opportunist leadership in the Chamber, but at the price of having to name two Radical ministers.

When in late September in Limoges various organizations of labor united to create the Confédération Générale du Travail and a month later Léon Bourgeois managed to form the first all-Radical ministry, a national shift to the Left seemed in the offing.[33] To be sure, the threat of the Confédération Générale du Travail in 1895 was more potential than actual, but the organization represented an additional rejection—along with the spread of socialism in the cities and on the land—of the social order of the bourgeoisie's *belle epoque*.

It was true, also, that Bourgeois' politics were at least as hostile to syndicalism and socialism as Méline's. He too sought to create coalitions at that dangerous moment, a moment Daniel Halévy judged as the great conjuncture of political polarization of the nation between Left and Right.[34] Bourgeois wooed the left wing of the Opportunists and tried also to curb government-inspired excesses of anticlericalism. But he did see the need, for the sake of financing a modern state whose usual revenues had been cut by depression, to dip a bit deeper into the pockets of the rich by means of a progressive tax on incomes. Radicals, socialists, and a few breakaway Opportunists pooled their votes to squeeze the bill through the Chamber. Most Opportunists and Catholics (both Ralliés and Intransigeants) voted against it. The more conservative Senate rejected the new tax on April 21, 1896. Bourgeois and his ministry had to resign. The long depression had engendered the fiscal crisis that forced the contemplation of the new tax on income and at the same time unified the enemies of social equity into a sometimes effective political force.

The tariffs did not divide the Catholic deputies, therefore, but rather encouraged the more modern industrialist elements, especially from the North, to consider wider collaboration with the Opportunists.[35] Those who owned factories, employed labor, or other-

33. Daniel Halévy, *La République des comités: essai d'histoire contemporaine* (Paris, 1934), 34.

34. Judith Stone, *The Search for Social Peace: Reform Legislation in France, 1890–1914* (Albany, 1985), 26–36.

35. See David Landes, "Religion and Enterprise: The Case of the French Textile

wise had to function daily in the market economy understood better than their more removed coreligionists the need to close ranks with other capitalists before the growing pretensions of organized labor. Albert de Mun, the Catholic conservative most aware of the suffering and impatience of the working class, voted for tariffs and championed a new republican conservatism.[36]

There was another arena in which republicans and Catholic conservatives could associate to their mutual advantage. A valuable lesson taught the industrialists by the depression was the potential importance of the markets of France's growing colonial empire. In a France growing yearly more pagan and irreligious that same empire afforded the opportunity for the renewal of French Christianity and with it French conservatism. The Empire provided both a cause and a place—not republican France but the historic France that was the motherland of *all* the French—where supporters of the new regime and followers of the old could forget metropolitan antagonisms for mutual benefit. The next chapter will analyze these mutual benefits of empire.

Industry," in Edward C. Carter II, Robert Forster, and Joseph N. Moody (eds.), *Enterprise and Entrepreneurs in Nineteenth and Twentieth Century France* (Baltimore, 1976), 69–82, on the Catholic industrialists of Roubaix (a center of protectionist sentiment); and Jean Lambert, "Quelques familles du patronat textile de Lille-Armentières, 1789–1914" (Dissertation, University of Lille, 1954), 751–52 on the opportunism in matters of politics of the textile manufacturers of the Nord.

36. Benjamin F. Martin, *Count Albert de Mun* (Chapel Hill, N.C., 1978), 86–128, 300–301; Xavier de Montclos, *Le Toast d'Alger: Documents, 1890–1891* (Paris, 1967).

VI

The Quest for Colonial Markets and Christian Souls

In the late nineteenth century, ruling elites in Germany, Italy, and France looked to the instrumentalities of nationalism and imperialism to weld together societies embarked on the process of national formation or transformation. The enthusiasms of nationalism were suited to gaining and holding the loyalties of the urban working class via ideologies on the order of the French appeal to National Labor.[1] The spirit of imperialism, at least in France, aided in the creation of the new republican conservatism. Having examined the workings of nationalist economics, let us now look at how the colonial empire reconciled the strata at the top of French society.

Late in the century the accumulation of overseas possessions and the development of spheres of influence promised both adventure and responsibilities to underemployed aristocrats.[2] It promised churchmen renewal of the faith by means of the saving of the souls of Asians and Africans. Soldiers and naval officers could hope to avoid rusting, and perhaps gain advancement, by fighting skirmishes with tribesmen or pirates. The high yields, albeit through limited and risky opportunities, tempted bankers to float colonial ventures. And in the depths of the Great Depression of industrial prices, the colonial empire promised both new markets for national production and the industrial truce conferred by propitiated workers.

Yet, to make all their plans, hopes, and dreams of the rewards of empire possible diverse groups had to work together. Silk manufacturers and bankers in Lyon, although committed to free trade, nev-

1. Or, for example, the German Kaiser's statement on the outbreak of war in 1914 that he did not recognize divisions among his people, only Germans.
2. Even if Schumpeter's thesis on the atavistic nature of imperialism is seriously flawed, the visibility of aristocrats in colonial adventures and administration cannot be gainsaid. Joseph Schumpeter, *Imperialism and Social Classes* (New York, 1955).

ertheless had to accept the diplomatic and military help of the pro-tectionist republic. Conservative prelates, in order to protect and further their missions, had to gain the support of the political allies of Jules Ferry, the father of lay schools in France. Politicians repre-senting Vosges and Norman textile manufacturers had to encourage the civilizing mission of the Church so that the nakedness of the savages might be covered with French cotton goods. Priests, sol-diers, and millowners were all mindful of the opportunity to forge a national unity, that is, a conservative social order, offered by the new colonial possessions.[3] The colonial empire, like the tariffs, en-hanced the unity of the metropolitan elite. For the Opportunist politicians who led the forces of colonial annexations in the 1880s, empire meant markets above all. They extended their hands to all who would collaborate to achieve this goal. To men of the military and of the Church, colonies promised revitalization of threatened traditions and institutions. To the merchants and shippers of Bor-deaux, Marseille, and Lyon they meant a valuable concession for their commerce in a nation armored against foreign trade. If the conservatives of the eighties could be recruited—or at least not arrayed against them—republican politicians, in turn, would not allow monarchist phantoms to frighten them away from a mutually beneficial enterprise. If the defeated free trade interests could em-ploy the economic opportunities offered by the empire to cut their losses due to the depression and the consequences of protectionism, they too might be reconciled to the economic priorities of the re-founded republic.

The question we must address, then, is not who benefited from the new conquests and seizures of territories but how the overseas possessions served the cause of domestic social reconciliation.[4] To

3. The resistance to empire by Radicals of the cut of Georges Clemenceau disap-peared once they took on the burdens of social conservation. With the heating up of imperialist conflicts among the major powers, nationalists among the former oppo-nents to the Opportunists' empire even championed it. See Christopher Andrew and A. S. Kanya-Forstner, *France Overseas: The Great War and the Climax of French Imperial Expansion* (London, 1981), 30.

4. But even if we were to ask the accountant's question, "who benefited from the colonial empire," Henri Brunschwig's answer of "profiteers," a few businessmen, careerist officials, and stifled and brave soldiers must be judged inadequate. See his *French Colonialism: Myths and Realities* (New York, 1966), 152–55. This translation is a revision of *Mythes et réalités de l'impérialisme colonial français, 1871–1914* (Paris, 1960). J. Dean O'Donnell, Jr., links the consolidation of the colonial empire with the Rallie-

do so, we shall first render the hopes of protectionist industrialists for greater sales in the colonies. Then we should look at the vision of social peace that many colonial advocates offered in defense of the empire. Finally, we shall say something about the Church's quest for more Christians in the areas where the businessmen were searching for new clients.

The Promise of the Colonial Market

The successful expansion of British industry in the nineteenth century was in no small measure a result of its possession of a colonial empire, especially India. In the first half of the nineteenth century only Britain had access to guaranteed markets large enough to permit a vast expansion of productive capacity. Cotton textiles were at the heart of the colonial nexus: Indian peasants supplied some of the cotton for Britain's ravenous mills and, increasingly, much of the clientele. The manufacture of cotton goods continued to occupy more British workers to the eve of World War I than any other single industry. It remained, too, the premier export commodity. We may discern the countercyclical functioning of the textile trade—especially that of the Indian market—well into the twentieth century.[5]

In late-nineteenth-century France, Britain's good fortune in the uses of its colonial possessions did not go unnoticed. Eugène Etienne, animating spirit of the forces pressing for development and expansion of a great French colonial empire, proposed an antidote to business depression. He stated, "Our colonies supplying cotton to French industry, French industry furnishing the cotton goods needs of our colonies: those are the two faces of a solution to all our present and future economic crises." But the French possessions did not become significant sources of raw materials for the textile industry; attempts to spread cotton culture in Indochina yielded only modest results. The United States, a major commercial rival, continued to supply the bulk of the cotton processed by French manufacturers. However, metropolitan sales in the French colonial empire, especially sales of cotton goods, grew rapidly. These outlets for metro-

---

ment in both the mind and the work of Cardinal Lavigerie. See his *Lavigerie in Tunisia: The Interplay of Imperialist and Missionary* (Athens, Ga., 1979), 129–47.

5. Eric Hobsbawm, *Industry and Empire: An Economic History of Britain Since 1750* (London, 1968), 110–26.

politan-produced goods served the cause of social peace as much as the new tariffs that accompanied the growth of the colonial annexations.[6]

It will be recalled that, although certain agricultural products—wheat and cattle—were protected with higher duties in the mideighties, industrial products remained subject to the vagaries of international price fluctuations. Many protectionists deemed even the 1892 duties inadequate to completely defend the domestic market. Both Jules Ferry, the champion of the new colonial empire, and Jules Méline, proponent of protectionism, were from the important cotton mill region of the Vosges Mountains; each was connected by personal ties and ties of economic interest to that region's main industry.

The idea of employing overseas possessions to absorb gluts in products of metropolitan manufacture was not new in France. Such ideas had surfaced in the depressed years preceding the revolution of 1848.[7] And during the industrial crisis of 1857, Pouyer-Quertier liked to remind his audiences, the economic wounds to cotton manufacture in Normandy were nearly fatal. He credited the growth of sales in Algeria in the 1850s, continuing into the 1860s, for the survival of what was indeed the most backward region of French textile production. Later and less partisan assessments confirm his judg-

6. Raoul Vimard, *La Situation économique et l'avenir de l'industrie cotonnière en France* (Paris, 1905), 234; Jacques Guérin, "Les Colonies cotonnières" (Thesis, University of Paris, 1907), 132. See John Laffey's study of the attempts of the French to create a plantation economy in the new protectorate of Tonkin, where as early as 1883 the *Journal des Chambres de commerce françaises* envisioned crops of rice, sugarcane, cotton, tobacco, vegetables for oil, coffee, and coca ("Land, Labor, and Law in Colonial Tonkin Before 1914," *Historical Reflections/Réflections historiques*, II (1975), 223–63). Although *colons* had managed to gain possession of substantial tracts of land, it is clear that by 1914 the uncooperativeness, indeed, resistance, of the local peasants had made a failure of the French agricultural effort.

7. Charles-Robert Ageron, *France coloniale ou parti colonial* (Paris, 1978), 86–87, writes of this interest on the part of economic writers in the use of colonies as markets, in the manner of Great Britain, as far back as 1847 to refute a reading of the renewed interest in empire in the late nineteenth century as originating in economically countercyclical concerns. But 1847 was a depressed year in France, indeed a part of the "hungry forties," which had sent Britain searching after markets abroad and imperial expansion. As in the instance of tariffs, which have existed in the French past, so with the hopes that colonial markets would serve countercyclical functions. On the British domestic uses of empire in the forties, see John Foster, *Class Struggle and the Industrial Revolution: Early Industrial Capitalism in Three English Towns* (New York, 1974).

ment. Claude Fohlen, historian of the French textile industry, agrees that "Algeria [in the fifties and sixties] became the last refuge, and the only hope, of the Norman cotton mill owners."[8] But between the tariff years of 1881 and 1885, the combined index of industrial prices declined by 10 percent, the greatest drop in any five-year period of the Great Depression.

Algeria was not the only region of French predominance that served as an outlet for French manufacturers. In 1883 and 1884, as Jules Ferry tightened and extended French control in Indochina, his undersecretary of state for the navy and colonies, Félix Faure, sent off to the presidents of the chambers of commerce and of arts and manufactures a letter calling their attention to the possibilities of the new colonial market. Since the indigenous population of Indochina was poor and lived simply, he wrote, France could sell them neither shelter nor food. "There remains clothing: that's a branch of commerce which it behooves us especially to develop." Today, the natives of Indochina wear cotton clothes of English manufacture. When French Indochina is enclosed in the French tariff system, "our spinners and cloth makers could compete successfully against their English competitors." *Le Travail national* commented, "The English have taught us that, although the army conquers territories, it is commerce which makes of them colonies."[9]

Delegates to the general meeting of the Association de l'Industrie Française in December, 1884, voted to demand of the government "a privileged position" for French business in the colonies and for the protection of French business enterprises against the commerce of foreigners. The obliging Opportunist ministry of Jules Ferry accordingly covered Algeria with the tariff of metropolitan France later that month, and in 1885 Réunion, Guadeloupe, and Martinique were similarly brought under the provisions of the metropolitan tariff legislation.[10] It remained for the association to press its friends in the government to cordon off for the sake of metropolitan interests the populous French possessions and protectorates in Indochina.

Only after his fall from power in March, 1885, did Ferry offer his

8. Claude Fohlen, *L'Industrie textile au temps du Second Empire* (Paris, 1965), 154.
9. *Travail national*, September 14, 1884, pp. 122, 123. *Travail national* commented as well that Tonkin was not the only colonial area suitable for commercial penetration, and reported another memorandum from Faure on the commercial possibilities of the southern provinces of China (pp. 127–28).
10. *Travail national*, December 21, 1884, pp. 298–99, February 1, 1885, pp. 54–55.

fellow deputies a systematic justification for what he considered his "system of colonial policy." Addressing the Chamber in late July, 1885—during the depths of the great five-year slide of industrial prices—he defended his colonial acquisitions, especially that of Tonkin, on the grounds of France's civilizing mission and rivalries with other nations of both political and military sorts, as well as a means of bringing within reach of French businessmen millions of potential consumers whose purchases would counteract the grave depression. He even hinted at a social imperialist justification for colonies when, during his speech, he was interrupted with the challenge that colonies benefited only the capitalists. His response: "I agree . . . the capitalists. Is it a matter of no concern to you . . . that the total capital of this country should increase as a result of intelligent investment? Is it not in the interests of labor that there should be plentiful capital in this country?"[11]

The argument of this study does not require us to sort out Ferry's prime motives; much less are we obliged to advance a general analysis of the causes of French colonialism. Rather, given that colonies existed or were in the process of being annexed, we are concerned with how they functioned to further the new conservatism. Two observations will suffice to this end.

First, that French colonial expansion and exploitation were promoted by coalitions of the ruling strata—like the tariffs, the Ralliement, and social pacification—should not surprise the reader. To be sure, different partners heard different arguments. Expectations and intentions are more important here than are outcomes.

Second, we must take seriously any argument in behalf of colonial annexation and development put forth in the Third Republic that was realized in state policy. The successful efforts in 1887 of leading members of the Association de l'Industrie Française in the Chamber to bring duties on foreign goods entering France's Indochinese possessions up to metropolitan rates serves as evidence on this topic.[12]

The inclusion of these Asian territories within the metropolitan commercial wall immediately, if unevenly, improved the market for

11. Ferry gave his speech in the session of July 28, 1885. *JO*, Chambre des députés, Débats, reprinted in Paul Robiquet (ed.), *Discours et opinions de Jules Ferry* (7 vols.; Paris, 1893–98,), V, 187–220.

12. *Travail national*, February 2, 13, 1887, pp. 73, 82–83.

French manufacturers. As a hedge against the future, the new markets appeared to be promising.[13] Yet improved colonial sales were not sufficient in the short term to replace the deficit in domestic sales, nor to stop the roller coaster swings of industrial prices and of the associated industrial strikes. French producers were a long way away from forcing foreign competitors out of their colonial market, even with the help of the 1882 tariff and the inclusion of Indochina under its provisions in 1887.[14]

Therefore, it is in the context of the beginning of another cyclical descent (1889–1890) and a peaking of labor troubles that we should understand Ferry's further elaboration of his economic justification for the colonial empire. In the 1890 preface to his and Léon Sentupéry's *Le Tonkin et la mère-patrie*, Ferry pointedly linked his advocacy of empire with the twin evolving social policies of Opportunist politicians and their allies: tariffs and social pacification. He wrote in part,

> The protective system is like a steam engine without a safety valve, if it has not healthy, genuine colonial policy as a corrective and auxiliary. The plethora of capital invested in industry tends not only to diminish the profits from capital, but to halt the rise in wages. . . . In the industrial age of humanity, social peace is a question of outlets. The economic crisis which has weighed so heavily on working Europe since 1876 and 1877, the resulting malaise, of which long frequent strikes, often ill-advised but always significant, are the most painful symptom, has coincided in France, Germany, and even England, with a notable and persistent reduction in export figures. Europe can be compared to a commercial firm which has seen its business decreasing over a number of years. The European consumer market is saturated. New layers of consumers must be brought in from other parts of the globe.[15]

13. *Ibid.*, October 6, 1889, pp. 465–67, October 13, p. 485, October 27, 1889, pp. 501–502.

14. For the celebrations and laments, *ibid.*, December 9, 1888, pp. 601–608, April 21, 1889, pp. 134, 218, June 21, 1889, pp. 285–86, May 11, 1890, pp. 231–32.

15. Ferry's and Sentupéry's *Tonkin et la mère-patrie* was published in Paris in 1890. The preface is reprinted in Robiquet (ed.), *Discours et opinions de Jules Ferry,* V, 557–59. For my quotation I have followed the translation of David Thomson (ed.), *France: Empire and Republic, 1850–1940* (New York, 1968), 309–310. See also Thomas F. Powers, Jr., *Jules Ferry and the Renaissance of French Imperialism* (1944; rpr. New York, 1966). J. Ganiage, in *L'Expansion coloniale de la France sous la Troisième République, 1871–1914* (Paris, 1968), rejects economic factors in general as "the principal motor of imperialist growth" (p. 415). Charles-Robert Ageron, "Jules Ferry et la colonisation," in François Furet (ed.), *Jules Ferry, fondateur de la République* (Paris, 1985), 191–206, has presented a strong case against the economic interpretation of Ferry's empire-build-

Eugène Etienne shared Ferry's position. From the start of his activities in behalf of the colonial empire, and especially in the late eighties, he focused on the colonies as the last available new market for French goods in a world of competing industrial societies suffering from crises of overproduction.[16] But many French businessmen in the colonies saw the question differently. As exporters of raw materials, and importers eager to buy commodities from the cheapest source, they would have preferred a freer commercial policy than the assimilationist one being legislated from Paris.[17] After the inclusion of Indochina within the French tariff system, *colon* businessmen and even officials resisted metropolitan measures to put the new rules in operation.[18] In June, 1887, Méline, for example, was compelled to call upon the new undersecretary for colonies, Eugène Etienne, to prompt the official to use his authority to gain the cooperation of M. Filippini, the governor of Cochinchina, in the enforcement of tariff regulations.[19]

---

ing motives. That the motives impelling policy makers—or indeed churchmen and soldiers—to promote colonial possessions may be subtle, complex, and indeed spiritual is doubtless true. However, to deny that important support for empire in the 1880s arose as a contribution to a strategy for overcoming the socioeconomic ravages of the Great Depression, especially in France, borders on assuming an ideological *parti-pris* in behalf of the exclusive role of the noneconomic factors in French imperialism. See Brunschwig, *French Colonialism*, Chap. 6: "The Protectionist Legend," 82–96.

16. Herward Sieberg, *Eugène Etienne und die französische Kolonialpolitik, 1887–1904* (Cologne, 1968), 77–90, 149.

17. Andrew and Kanya-Forstner, *France Overseas*, 16–17. In the showdown in 1910 between the colonial party, which desired free trade for the purposes of developing the *colon* economy of the empire, and the Association de l'Industrie et l'Agriculture Française which they correctly label "the main [metropolitan] employers' federation," over the proposal to raise the duties which had come into force in 1892 still higher, the protectionist elite of the mother country prevailed. See also Andrew and Kanya-Forstner, "The French 'Colonial Party': Its Composition, Aims, and Influence, 1885–1914," *Historical Journal*, XIV (1971), 99–128; "The *Groupe Colonial* in the French Chamber of Deputies, 1892–1932," *Historical Journal*, XVII (1974), 837–66; Andrew, P. Grupp, and Kanya-Forstner, "Le Mouvement colonial français et ses principales personalités, 1890–1914," *Revue française d'histoire d'outre-mer*, LXII (1975), 640–73.

18. Ironically, not only did the colonial party come into conflict with metropolitan protectionist, but the colonial advocates in the mère-patrie were appalled by the narrow vision, crudity, and even xenophobia of the *colons* and came into conflict with them over substantial matters of colonial policy. See Laffey, "Land, Labor, and Law in Colonial Tonkin," 249.

19. *Travail national*, June 26, 1887, p. 305. Etienne, himself an Opportunist, tried to walk a fine line on this issue. Originally a free trader, in 1885 he came over to

The passage of the Méline duties further disquieted the colonial businessmen of Saigon and Haiphong. Jules Ferry, who had piloted the new tariff through the Senate, tried to bring these overseas Frenchmen to their senses with his analysis of the place of tariffs in the colonial policy he had energetically championed.

In his open letter to the citizens of Tonkin, published simultaneously in the colony and the *Travail national*, Ferry synthesized a decade of Opportunist domestic and commercial policy. The importance of this statement goes beyond the immediate occasion of its composition, for in it he underscored a fact that the colonial free-traders perhaps had not fully appreciated: that the pro-empire [*tonkinois*] majorities of both the Chamber and the Senate "are at the same time for both colonial expansion and protectionist. The two ideas are closely associated in their thinking. An active colonial policy is in their eyes, the necessary counterpart of the policy of protection for national labor." France's great industries, encouraged by the tariff policies of the Republic, were selling appreciable and ever-growing volumes of merchandise to buyers in Indochina. He continued, "It is for the laboring masses who only knew about Tonkin from the ill they have heard spoken of it, it is for French capital, so uninformed and so timid, a lesson of things which make tangible and vital the colonial policy which we have so successfully pursued. It is natural that French industry views our colonial policy above all else, as a search for market outlets."[20]

Two future foreign ministers shared Ferry's hopes for converting the colonies into pressure-releasing markets. In a speech to the Senate in 1893, on the eve of his appointment to the newly created post of minister of colonies, Théophile Delcassé held up the colonial markets as France's surest outlets; once France had expanded into these markets, he assured the senators, she would become one of the leading commercial nations in the world. Soon afterward the Opportunist government separated the office for colonies from the

---

protectionism out of a belief that protective duties would benefit the colonies. He supported the Méline tariff, although ten years after its passage he expressed regrets that it was not more accommodating to the special needs of the colonies. He retained an old-fashioned mercantilist concern, which in view of the strength of the protectionist forces in the metropole and his need not to offend them showed intelligent trimming, that no colonial industry should compete with one in the mother country. See Sieberg, *Eugène Etienne*, 77–78, 87.

20. *Travail national*, March 27, 1892, pp. 156–57.

ministry of commerce, elevating it to the rank of a full ministry. Delcassé became its head.[21]

As a consequence of the passage of the 1892 tariff, it was the charge of the young diplomat Gabriel Hanotaux to negotiate future treaties of commerce that conformed to the maximum-minimum boundaries of the new law. In his 1926 obituary for his friend Méline he recalled, "The bases for the negotiation of the commercial treaties were the new tariffs and the colonial achievements which naturally complemented them. With [the creation of the colonial empire] we hoped to extend and develop in the new lands both fields of raw materials and markets opened to French products. Such was the object of my daily labors as it was at that time the constant preoccupation of the initiator of the tariffs."[22] Méline made Hanotaux foreign minister in his government of 1896–1898, which in its two years' existence carved out a powerful French sphere of influence in China and joined Algeria and Tunisia to the newer French possessions of Senegal, Fouta-Djalon, the Ivory Coast, the Sudan, and the Congo to make France a major power in Africa.[23]

By a law passed soon after the passage of the Méline tariff, the millions of potential consumers of Indochina were in their turn ushered behind the wall of protection of the mother country. The passage of the tariff and the inclusion of the Asian possessions perched on the edge of yet another dip in both industrial and agricultural prices. Using 1880 as the base year (100), the index of industrial prices in 1892 had fallen to 91. By 1896, when Méline formed his ministry, it had tumbled to a low of 85.

The chorus of proponents for developing the colonial markets, especially Méline's collaborators, grew larger and louder. Throughout the summer and fall of 1896 Henry Sagnier devoted a series of articles, at the same time both warning and exhortatory, in *La Répub-*

21. Reprinted *ibid.*, May 7, 1893, pp. 238. An undersecretariat for colonies in the Ministry of Commerce already existed when in March, 1894, the Ministry of Colonies was created. Its first head, Ernest Boulanger, served only ten days. Delcassé then took the post and gave it the shape it would retain in subsequent years.

22. Gabriel Hanotaux, "Jules Méline," *Revue des deux mondes*, 7th ser., XXXI (January, 1926), 447–48.

23. Georges Lachapelle, *Le Ministère Méline* (Paris, 1928), 76–77, 83–84. Of Hanotaux's work with Méline, Lachapelle wrote that Hanotaux and Méline continued the work of Ferry and in the process conferred "an imposing character" upon the French colonial empire (p. 87).

lique française, noting the early successes of French cloth exports to Indochina and the need to redouble the efforts. In pieces written during the winter he added the exports of French sugar (the industry toward which Méline had such fatherly feelings) to cheer on.[24] Charles Georgeot in the same newspaper expressed hopes that the colonies would supply France with cocoa and coffee and open new market outlets. But like some of the followers of Le Play, he envisioned the empire also as beckoning to French settlers. The new possessions, he warned, should not continue to weigh on the mother country as a financial burden.[25] In the same vein Robert Charlie, Méline's editor of *La République française,* wrote of the possibilities for, and necessity of, expanding sales of French textiles on the west coast of Africa.[26]

Did the colonial empire serve the great commercial functions its supporters laid out for it? That the empire was a valuable source of raw materials or investments is doubtful. The hopes aroused in the pages of *La République française* for the profits that could be realized from what the newspaper reported to be the rich deposits of coal, copper, lead, and iron in the mines of Tonkin and other parts of Indochina did not become reality. Nor did the expectations it encouraged for riches for France from the ivory, rubber, rosewood, ebony, and rich delta soil come to pass.[27] And, as the next chapter will discuss, French investment tended to flow toward the less developed nations of Europe rather than toward more primitive regions unable to assimilate large infusions of capital. Finally, if we focus for a moment on the national government independently of the social groups that employed it to their profit and protection, we have to agree with the commentators who judged that any gains

24. Henri Sagnier, "Les tissus français en Cochinchine," May 31, 1896, "Le mouvement des industries textiles," July 29, 1896, "Les tissus Français en Cochinchine," July 21, 1896, "L'exportation française," August 28, 1896, "Les tissus français en Cochinchine," September 30, October 26, November 16, 1896, January 26, 1897, all in *La République française.* The last article was in part devoted to sugar sales increases. Sagnier normally wrote the agricultural articles in *La République française.*

25. Charles Georgeot, "Les dépenses coloniales," December 4, 1896, "L'avenir économique de nos colonies," December 9, 1896, both in *La République française.* Above all else, French colonial policy should be *"une politique commerciale"* (his italics). See also Georgeot's "La colonisation," in *Travail national,* March 28, 1897, pp. 178–81.

26. *République française,* "Notre politique coloniale," October 9, 1897.

27. See, for example, *République française,* June 29, October 2, 1880.

from the empire—in this case, colonial sales—were far inferior in value to the costs of the colonies to the French state.[28]

What of the empire as market outlet? One estimate suggests that from 1882 to 1913 the portion of French exports to the colonies, expressed as a percentage of total exports, rose from about 7 to roughly 11 percent. Although a net increase of 4 percent scarcely qualifies as impressive, the industries involved and the key role colonial markets played in their export sales are. On the eve of World War I, sales to the colonial empire represented 67.6 percent of the total of overseas sales of the sugar industry, 21.6 percent of those of the iron industry, 29.6 percent of machine tools, 41.4 percent of French metallurgical exports, and 33.1 percent of the exports of the cotton industry.[29] Moreover, although in 1905 France's colonial possessions (including Algeria) were only the fourth most important recipients of French commerce, the colonies ranked that low only because the neighboring advanced industrial nations, Britain, Belgium, and Germany, occupied the first three positions.[30] In 1905 Vimard discerned that "it was our protected colonies alone which consume our products, that is, those upon whom we can impose them by force."[31]

28. *Ibid.* See further the standard for such calculations in Brunschwig, *French Colonialism*, 135–51.

29. Ganiage, *L'Expansion coloniale*, 415–17; Jacques Thobie, René Girault, and Jean Bouvier, *La France impériale, 1880–1914* (Paris, 1982), 68. These were the relatively modern and heavily capitalized industries for whom the colonial market constituted a substitute for unavailable outlets in advanced nations. The colonial market was as well the last hope of the French hide, candle, and soap industries. See also Jacques Marseille, "Les Relations commerciales entre la France et son empire colonial de 1880 à 1913," *Relations internationales*, VI (1976), 146–60.

30. In 1906 the colonial exports passed briefly to third place because of the temporary but substantial decline of Belgian imports from France. See "Commerce de la France avec les principaux pays de provenance ou de destination," *Annuaire du commerce extérieur, 1908* (Paris, 1908), 63.

31. Vimard, *La Situation économique et l'avenir*, 113. The role of the French colonial empire matched that played by India for Britain as consumer of metropolitan-made products: in both cases approximately two-thirds of the imports came from the metropole. Largely via tariffs that restricted colonial purchases from nations other than France, more so than the average for the other colonial powers, the overseas possessions were captive markets. See the instructive Table VII, "The Relative Share of the Metropole in the Total Imports of Selected Colonies in 1913," in Paul Bairoch, "La place de la France sur les marchés internationaux," in Maurice Lévy-Leboyer (ed.), *La Position internationale de la France: aspects économiques et financiers XIXᵉ–XXᵉ siècles* (Paris, 1977), 45–46.

Cotton textiles, France's biggest industry and the greatest source of industrial employment, is typical of how important the colonies were as markets for certain important French industries. In this respect the insight of Jacques Marseille, the most recent student of the role of the cotton industry in French colonial imperialism, is telling: as French cotton manufacturers proved unable to compete with their trading rivals, "colonial sales constituted not simply an essential outlet but to all intents and purposes an exclusive one up to the moment of decolonization." After Algeria, Indochina was the principal client of the cotton textile firms of the Vosges and Normandy on the eve of World War I. In the prewar decades, sales to the colonies averaged 34 percent of total sales for the industry, and as France lost one contest after another with competitors, it attained 90 percent of sales by the outbreak of World War II.[32]

Peace Both Social and Christian

Yet, there were other, perhaps less tangible, benefits from the empire. A number of its chief proponents hoped that it might reconcile differences between groups at the summit of society and between strata at the top and bottom. Lyon may serve as an example of the first case. The bourgeoisie of this silk and banking center had long been interested in French involvement in Asia and the Middle East. Interest in foreign missions at the beginning of the century was soon supplemented by the search for new sources of raw silk. In 1852 the quest was spurred on by the outbreak of pebrine, an epidemic disease of silkworms. By 1888 two-thirds of Chinese raw silk exports found their way to Lyon.[33]

In 1895, eager to extend economic contacts with China, the Lyon chamber of commerce organized a two-year-long commercial study expedition to Indochina and southern and western China. The

---

32. Jacques Marseille, "L'Industrie cotonnière française et l'impérialisme colonial," *Revue d'histoire économique et sociale*, LIII (1975), 392–93; Marseille, *Empire colonial et capitalisme français: histoire d'un divorce* (Paris, 1984), 35–57; Ganiage, *L'Expansion coloniale*, 388–89. With decolonization, of course, came the collapse of the industry in the metropole.

33. John Laffey, "Roots of French Imperialism in the Nineteenth Century: The Case of Lyon," *French Historical Studies*, VI (1969), 78–92. On Lyon in the Far East, see Laffey, "Lyonnais Imperialism in the Far East, 1900–1938," *Modern Asian Studies*, X (1976), 225–48.

chambers of commerce of the protectionist cities of Lille and Roubaix, as well as those of the free trade bastions of Bordeaux and Marseille, agreed to participate. The expedition gained the backing and financial support of the Opportunist government. Soon after the expedition's return with encouraging news, the Compagnie Lyonnaise Indo-chinoise was founded (1898) with Ulysse Pila, the leading ideologue of colonialism on the Lyon chamber of commerce, as its president. Also founded in that year was the Société Cotonnière de l'Indochine. The Compagnie Lyonnaise had the exclusive right to sell the cotton of the Société Cotonnière. Thus the protectionist Nord and the free-trading Lyon found ways to collaborate in France abroad despite deep differences over domestic commercial policy.[34]

But even Lyonnais businessmen broke ranks on the issue of tariffs soon after the Méline tariff went into effect. As importers of raw materials and exporters of finished silks, the Lyonnais retained a proclivity for free trade. However, as the antiquated Lyonnaise industry lost ground to that of their more mechanized German and Swiss competitors, and the Swiss even began to undersell them in the home market, a number of the silk merchants abandoned the free trade position of the chamber of commerce's majority and joined the protectionist forces.[35] The chamber, whether because of the pressure exerted by this faction or from a collaborative spirit like that which guided the Far East expedition, by the turn of the century included among its contributions to various colonial societies an annual subsidy to the Association Cotonnière Coloniale.[36] By 1898 a Lyonnais silk manufacturer, Ennemond-Richard, had been elected to the executive committee of the Association de l'Industrie et de l'Agriculture Française. The next membership roll we have, that of the annual meeting of 1909, lists as members of the executive committee alone four Lyonnais: Ennemond-Richard; Albert Esnault-Pelterie, president of the Association Cotonnière Coloniale; Genin,

---

34. Laffey, "Roots of French Imperialism," 90–91. A cement firm also was founded, the Société des Ciments Portland artificiels de l'Indochine.

35. John Laffey, "Municipal Imperialism in France: The Lyon Chamber of Commerce, 1900–1914," *Proceedings of the American Philosophical Society*, CXIX (1975), 8–9.

36. *Ibid.*, 10–11. The subsidy was between three hundred and five hundred francs, on the order of what it contributed to the important Comité de l'Asie Française.

president of the Association de la Soierie Lyonnaise; and Paul Guéneau, silk manufacturer.[37]

The Méline duties were not prohibitive; the protectionists did not wish to drive the industries that needed international commerce to the wall. In this sense the legislation itself functioned to permit an understanding between different segments of the French business community.[38] The instance of Lyon merchant interests making their peace with the protectionists may serve as a microcosm of parallel accommodations on the highest levels of French business by means of the colonial empire. Collaboration, the onetime free traders expected, would boost the economic circumstances of industries that had lost business to foreign competitors or to the dampening effects on foreign commerce of the tariffs. France's colonial empire functioned, among other ways, as an economic cushion for injured free trade industries and the fortunes of the regional bourgeois that lived from them. Moreover, some protectionists claimed to see in the tariffs a means of reducing tensions between workers and employers. Could the colonies aid in social reconciliation across class lines too?

The persistence of the social peace argument as employed by industry spokesmen to protect their *positions acquises*—in this instance their domination of a locked-up colonial market—is remarkable. Ageron finds that the safety valve argument was already in wide circulation in the earlier part of the century. In the wake of the Commune advocates of colonial expansion like Ernest Renan saw the beneficial social consequences of empire as an especially valuable way to avoid the dangers of socialism.[39] In the mid-eighties, at least one speaker before the important Société Française de Colonisation emphasized the curative properties of colonial expansion for both the depression and the social question. We get a sense of its pervasiveness and its status as something approaching a canon in discussions about colonies during the depression era from a passage in Joseph Chailley's entry "colonie" in the 1891 edition of the *Nouveau*

37. *Travail national*, March 6, 1898 (report of the Annual General Assembly held March 2), April 11, 1909.

38. This is Michael S. Smith's main point. See his *Tariff Reform in France, 1860–1900: The Politics of Economic Interest* (Ithaca, N.Y., 1980), 196.

39. Ageron, *France coloniale ou parti colonial*, 44, 52. He questions its validity for earlier periods as well as for the heyday of French colonial expansion at the end of the century.

dictionnaire d'économie politique. It states in a matter-of-fact manner that "in respect to the metropole the colonies play the role of safety valves."[40]

Even Eugène Etienne, for whom the pacification of the workers was not the first consideration, thought it wise to invoke this concern from time to time to gain support for French imperialism. In 1895 he wrote, "We forget too easily that the improvement of the lot of the workers depends on the solution of the economic problem confronting us, and is intimately tied to the prosperity of our national industry: the more capital finds markets, the more profits it realizes, the better it can improve the workers' lives."[41] Again in 1904 he suggested the valuable role the colonies might play as safety valves to the discontents of industrial society. Large numbers of new consumers for French-made goods in the colonies, he predicted, would "protect the workers of the Old World from [another] potentially long spell of unemployment and the train of social miseries which is inseparable from unemployment." Whether or not their expectations came to fruition, or indeed whether the truth of such a proposition can even be tested by the historian, we must take the expectations of historical actors seriously. Jacques Marseille's phrase, "the blackmail of unemployment," serves well to sum up both the industrialists' arguments for protection and those urging the exploitation of colonial markets for imperialist reasons.[42]

A noneconomic interest in the colonial empire, indeed a spiritual one, was also important both for the establishment of the empire and for the creation of the new elite strata of the Republic. Just as the Reformation prompted Catholic rulers and prelates to launch numerous missionary projects to the New World—to make up with native converts the losses inflicted by the religious rebels—so in the nineteenth century the ravages of paganism and acquisition of new colonies impelled yet another campaign. Appropriately, as the

40. M. Froger, *La Question sociale et la colonisation* (Paris, 1886).

41. Foreword to F. Laurens, *Les Réformes commerciales* (Algiers, 1895), cited in Sieberg, *Eugène Etienne*, 88.

42. Sieberg, *Eugène Etienne*, 408. In 1913, for example, the millowners of Bolbec not far from Rouen collected a long list of names of workers professing themselves opposed to lowering the tariffs of Madagascar. See also Marseille's account of the concern for the workers manifested by the Epinal chamber of commerce in 1932 should the colonial market not continue to be available to the French cotton industry (*Empire colonial et capitalisme français*, 193–94).

Catholic land where godlessness was most advanced, especially in the cities, France led the way in missionary work. Missionaries were sent abroad with the blessings and the subsidies of the local bourgeoisie. In this effort Lyon's Oeuvre de la Propagation de la Foi was especially active. In the course of the century it became the French center of "colonizers of souls." The triumph of the anticlerical republic, if anything, intensified both internal and overseas missionary efforts.[43]

The Catholic social reformers assembled around Le Play applauded the colonial ventures and adventures of the republicans, however unhappy they remained with the anticlerical state. A. Delaire, writing in the *Réforme sociale* in 1882, for example, accepted *economic* justifications for colonial expansion. But more typical of the followers of Le Play was the piece by A. Noguès, a retired naval officer, that applauded the colonial movement as a "precious outlet" less for goods than for both the "adventuresome types" who often caused trouble at home and the offspring of the "root families" whose proliferation was central to Le Play's prescriptions for contemporary troubles.[44]

The internal concern was matched by external efforts. In 1885 when Ferry sought additional funding from the Chamber to finance the French military efforts in Indochina, only one deputy of the parliamentary Right dared at that juncture to publicly support a republican initiative with his vote. This principled imperialist was Monsignor Freppel, Bishop of Angers, and the Assumptionist paper *La Croix* warmly supported him. Nevertheless, Ferry's expansionist venture in Tonkin had significant support among Catholic conserva-

---

43. Joseph N. Moody, "The Dechristianization of the French Working Class," *Review of Politics,* XX (1958), 46–69; Raoul Girardet, *L'Idée coloniale en France de 1871 à 1962* (Paris, 1972), 13–14; John Laffey, "The Lyon Chamber of Commerce and Indochina During the Third Republic," *Canadian Journal of History,* X (1975), 325–48; Laffey, "Roots of French Imperialism," 78–80. For the proportions of religious belief and disbelief in the population see the excellent overview by Jean-Marie Mayeur, *Les Débuts de la Troisième République, 1871–1898* (Paris, 1973), 135–53.

44. A. Delaire, "La France et la colonisation," *Réforme sociale,* IV (1882), 71–75. The rest of Noguès' proposals showed the usual concern of L'École de la paix sociale for curbing both the morcellation of farm property and the practice of birth control, corrections of which, he believed, would facilitate France's colonial enterprises greatly. The French original, *"famille-souche,"* evokes rootedness and nurturing at the same time.

tives outside the Chamber.[45] The French Church was actively en-
gaged in missionary work in the new French possessions. Indeed,
by the late nineteenth century two-thirds of the missionaries active
in nonwestern lands were French.[46]

Thus we should see the 1890 toast of Ralliement offered to the
officers of the Mediterranean Fleet by Cardinal Lavigerie, who in
addition to his other titles and achievements was the founder of the
important missionary order the White Fathers, as in part a celebration of domestic unity *through* the colonial empire. Could the naval
officers deep in their hearts accuse the Mélines—and even the Ferrys—of any less patriotism or concern for French grandeur than
monarchist military men and missionary-priests?[47] When in 1892 a
colonial group emerged in the Chamber it was chaired by Eugène
Etienne, deputy from North Africa and a collaborator of both Ferry
and Méline. Prince d'Arenberg, an ardent Catholic conservative and
Rallié of the first hour, served as its vice-chairman. Two-thirds (sixty-
one of ninety-one) of the group acknowledged allegiance to some
version of the Progressiste-Modéré-Opportuniste party. The next
largest cluster of pro-colonial deputies was the Catholic Right, both
monarchists and Ralliés. We have seen how the Right supported
protectionism in 1892. In these pivotal depression years the colonial
party, in both the Chamber and the Senate, was indeed enthusiasti-
cally aligned to the pro-tariff alliance, as Ferry had claimed.[48]

In their turn iron manufacturers, shippers, and cotton mill own-

45. Judson Mather, "The Assumptionist Response to Secularization, 1870–1900,"
in Robert J. Bezucha (ed.), *Modern European Social History* (Lexington, Mass., 1972), 70–
71. The Assumptionists exempted the colonialist and imperialist ventures of the
Republic from their condemnation of it and its works. On the early division among
Catholics over support for the Republic's empire and the prevailing of the Right
imperialists, see Charles Alfred Perkins, "French Catholic Opinion and Imperial
Expansion, 1880–1886" (Ph.D. dissertation, Harvard University, 1964), 172–246.

46. Some 70,114 in all, of which only 17,184 were men (Mayeur, *Les Débuts de la
Troisième République*, 135–36).

47. See *Lettre ouverte à nos hommes d'état* (Paris, 1915) by Monsignor F. Charmetant,
a disciple of Lavigerie and secretary-general of the Oeuvre des Ecoles d'Orient, a
society notable both for its patriotism and its enthusiasm to spread the Catholic faith
in the colonies.

48. Brunschwig, *French Colonialism*, 106–34; Stuart M. Persell, "The French Colonial
Lobby, 1899–1914" (Ph.D. dissertation, Stanford University, 1969), 83–84. The strong
rejection by the colonial businessmen of assimilation under the French economy
comes only some ten years later (see pp. 84–85).

ers, encouraged by their organic intellectuals, expected that in these captive colonial markets they would realize enough sales to replace the depressed markets at home and the ones closed to them in Europe.[49] The colonial empire fulfilled the yearnings of churchmen to add new souls to a faith that at home was shrinking. It gave the chance for honor and promotion to military men who were willing to abridge their monarchist principles in the service of a French *présence* in Haiphong or Algiers. Rather than as the aberration of an unbridled nationalism, the French colonial empire should be seen, at least in its early days, as a way of continuing in life social institutions, social power, and social peace that seemed to be slipping away at home in the last quarter of the nineteenth century. The loyal colonial soldiers, dressed in uniforms of metropolitan manufacture, carrying French weapons, who took communion before battle in World War I, gave a depopulated and socially divided land the edge that brought victory in that bloody war. Indeed, only the nations of Europe without important colonial empires to assist their war efforts suffered intense social conflict, revolution, or dissolution at the expiration of the struggle: Italy, Germany, Austria-Hungary, and Russia.

However important the understandings among the diverse interests forged in the colonial sphere were, the new conservatism aimed to bring order to metropolitan France. By the spring of 1896 the scene was set for a last great effort to confront the growing forces of disorder with a new Right dedicated to both capitalism and traditional hierarchies, to a conservative Republic, and above all to social pacification. After the fall of the Radical government of Léon Bourgeois, when its attempt to legislate a graduated income tax was defeated, President Faure asked Jules Méline to form a ministry. France's consummate conservative coalition builder was now put in a position to complete the work started in the tariff alliances.

49. Etienne, for one, realized that the colonial market would not necessarily profit France as a whole immediately. As he said in the Chamber, "The colonial effort we have undertaken is a work of the future. We do not labor solely for the present, we labor above all for tomorrow" (*JO*, Chambre des députés, Débat, November 22, 1894, p. 394).

VII

The Ministry of Social Pacification

The Méline Ministry, 1896–1898

From the vantage point of the highest political post of the Republic, Méline undertook a work no less ambitious than the pacification of French society. To appreciate his efforts, and his successes, we have to follow three distinct but interlocking stories. First, we must look at his intentions and efforts on behalf of French agriculture, the key sector for the depressed economy as well as for the cause of social peace. Second, from the examination of rural credit, we must trace the contributions of French overseas investment bankers to peace at home and international social stability. Finally, the efforts of the Méline ministry to institute domestic social reforms, especially those touching the workers, complete the history of his initiatives on behalf of social and economic protectionism. Tracing the lines connecting the socialist hopes for successes in the countryside, the issue of rural credit, and French foreign investments will give us a sense of the accommodation of the financial interests to the forma-tion of the French new conservative alliance.

Méline's most important opportunity to contribute to the project of creating social peace arrived with his assumption of the premier-ship in April, 1896. He devoted his two years' ministry to completing the work started with the protective legislation of the past decade and a half. The new tariffs alone had not ended the agricultural depression, if we take as a measure the continued fall of land values and ground rents. Nor had they stilled the discontent of many French industrial workers, if the strike activity and the growth of workers' organizations in the early nineties can be taken as the index. The depression, and its baleful social workings, continued. As a consequence, Méline, together with other conservative re-publicans, intensified the promotion of policies that would strengthen the bonds linking the conservative strata and, at the same time, tame working class discontent. Failing that, the socioeconomic order of France would at least be buffered against future disorders. However, we must keep in mind that it was the tariffs that laid the foundations of work of social pacification of the late 1890s.[1]

On the eve of Méline's ministerial declaration, Henri Colson, writing for *La République française*, offered an explanation as to why the relatively (for French politics) unambitious Vosgien had consented to form a ministry: "To have refused to take office, would perhaps have delivered up more followers to revolutionary socialism." In his opening statement to the Chamber the next day, Méline announced his famous intent to pursue "a work of pacification," to "bar the road to revolutionary doctrines by remaining faithful to the ideals of justice and of solidarity which are the traditions of the republican party." His government would reform the taxes on alcoholic drinks and on inheritance, he declared. To unburden "the small taxpayers," he proposed to lower direct taxes, taking into account especially the economic burdens of the family and the pressures on agriculture. Of course, he promised to do all that he could for agriculture. He declared the moment right, finally, to create a colonial army. And all this he would accomplish within a balanced budget. "Messieurs," he concluded, "the France which works is weary of agitation; she has a thirst for peace and tranquillity. She adjures us to think of her, to terminate the dissensions which weaken her."[2]

1. The Société des Amis de Jules Méline at Remiremont does not possess any of Méline's papers, nor does the Archives Nationales. I was therefore forced to employ for this period his statements in the Chamber and in his various publishing outlets, the testimony of his coworkers, and the evidence of contemporaries. Both Georges Lachapelle, *Le Ministère Méline* (Paris, 1928), and Gabriel Hanotaux, "Jules Méline," *Revue des deux mondes*, 7th ser., XXXI (January, 1926), 440–42, worked with him, the former on his newspaper, the latter as his foreign minister.

2. Henri Colson, "Le Cabinet de M. Méline," *République française*, April 29, 1896, p. 1; Méline, "La déclaration du Gouvernement," *Journal Officiel*, Chambre des députés, Débats, April 30, 1896, pp. 751–52 (hereinafter cited as *JO*). Méline's ministry had at justice, Darlan; foreign affairs, Hanotaux; interior, Barthou; finance, Cochery; war, General Billot; navy, Vice-Admiral, Besnard; public instruction, Rambaud; colonies, André Lebon; public works, Turrel; commerce, Henri Boucher; and at agriculture, as well as president of the council, Méline. Méline of course resigned as head of the Association de l'Industrie et l'Agriculture Française. The renewed focus by Méline and his friends on questions relating to the agricultural population is evidenced

Radicals who were angry with Méline's reactionary posture and the socialists, who shared Millerand's pithy political characterization that Méline was "the protégé of the Right," moved several votes of no confidence. Méline, despite some defections from the ranks of the Opportunists, and the discrete abstentions of some of his partners on the Right, won every test with a comfortable margin of votes.[3] The next day, May Day, the socialists in the Chamber issued a manifesto denouncing the Méline ministry, which they castigated as "the predominance of the retrograde Senate, and the humiliation and defeat of universal suffrage." The manifesto concluded, "War on the Senate and shame to the traitors! Long live the Socialist Republic!"

The *République française*, naturally, praised Méline's declaration of his intentions of following a policy of "order, work, and progress." This would be the perfect remedy for the depression: "the business stagnation," the paper offered hopefully, "perhaps does not have a cause more profound than uncertainty and fear of tomorrow."[4]

But how might the new government restore to producers the optimism needed to revive investment? Soon after taking office, the

---

further by the selection of M. Sebline, the former vice-president of the agricultural side of the association, as the group's new president. Guy P. Palmade points out that not Méline's but Maurice Rouvier's cabinet of 1887 was the first all Opportunist government supported by the monarchist Right (*Capitalisme et capitalistes français au XIXe siècle* (Paris, 1961), 208). However, the situation of 1896 was different in several ways. Méline had the firm support of the Ralliés and the toleration of the monarchist Right for over two years against nearly fifty newly elected socialists. Rouvier's brief policy of concentration was directed at the apparently radical threat, offered by General Boulanger, but fell apart in a few months at the outbreak of the Wilson Scandal. Both coalitions did however operate under a common sign: conservative unity in the face of revolutionary menace. See also François Goguel, *Géographie des élections françaises de 1870 à 1951* (Paris, 1951), 24.

3. *JO*, Chambre des députés, Débats, April 30, 1896, p. 765; Goguel, *Géographie des élections*, 30.

4. Lachapelle, *Le Ministère Méline*, 31–32; *République française*, May 1, 1896, p. 1. For the remainder of the spring and summer the *République française* conducted an intense antisocialist, anticollectivist crusade in its pages. In one week in April five of seven lead articles attacked socialists and socialism. Because of the initial successes of the socialists and the excesses of the anarchists, virtual obsession with the menace of the left had seized bourgeois society. Pierre Sorlin was struck by the intense fears of socialism that dominated French political life in the years in the last decade of the century and, more precisely, between the municipal elections of 1892 and the legislative elections of 1898 (*Waldeck-Rousseau* (Paris, 1966), 358).

new premier traveled to Soissons, the heart of the sugar-beet-pro-
ducing region of the Paris Basin, to address an agricultural fair. In
several addresses Méline repeatedly assured the sugar beet farmers
(who were thoroughly capitalist large growers) that they had a
friend in him. He promised to restore "the hands to capital and the
brains to the land." He labeled this task "the great social mission," *la
grande oeuvre sociale,* "the question which dominates all the others,
which is the key to all the others." The current social malaise, he
argued, originated neither from some alleged maldistribution of the
fruits of labor nor as a consequence of low wages. Those explana-
tions, put forth by revolutionaries, he rejected. Rather, he argued,
the problem lay in the disequilibrium between industrial production
and agricultural output. Once again hammering on the theme just
outlined in 1892, he conjured up the image of vast hordes of unemployed peasants who, fleeing a crisis-struck agriculture, were
swarming into the cities of France (see Table 6). The peasants' immi-
gration intensified an already gravely serious problem, for it was in
the cities—especially the industrial centers of the provinces—that
the social question was posed in its most acute form. Once again,
now as the head of a ministry, Méline insisted on the necessity of
dealing with the agrarian crisis as the key move in solving the socioeconomic crisis. "That is the illness that we have to cure, if truly
we wish to do something for the workers," he concluded.[5]

In actuality the depression had slowed the flight from the countryside, however much it increased rural and urban misery. City
jobs were not growing, and staying on the farm with relatives was
still the safest protection against the hardships of unemployment.
But the force of the ideological dismay at the rural exodus more than
kept the idea afloat that the cities were filling with rootless peasants
even when the data in a given period did not support such an
ominous conclusion.

Strengthening the conservative institutions of the countryside for
the sake of labor peace in the cities would be the theme of the Méline
ministry. More precisely, Méline intended to strengthen the forces
of social order on the land and perhaps to increase the prosperity of
all classes of the agricultural population. Thus he hoped both to
inhibit the penetration of the radical workers' ideology into the
countryside and at the same time brake the movement of peasants to

5. *République française,* June 30, 1896, pp. 1–2.

TABLE 6

Population Growth of Selected Cities (in thousands of inhabitants)

	1872	1886	percent increase
Marseille	312.9	376.1	20.2
Saint-Etienne	110.8	117.9	6.4
Lille	158.1	188.3	19.1
Roubaix	76.0	100.3	32.0
Tourcoing	43.3	58.0	34.0
Nancy	73.2	79.0	7.9

Source: André Armengaud, "Le Rôle de la démographie," *Histoire économique et sociale de la France,* vol. III, pt. 1, p. 231, copyright © 1979 Presses Universitaires de France. Reprinted with permission of the publisher.

the cities, where unscrupulous socialist agitators could exploit their social restment. And as a consequence, little by little, the alliance for social order could throttle the radicalism of socialist workers in the industrial cities, while at the same time the tender new shoots of rural revolt would wither in the fields. Paul Louis' echo of Jaurés' charge voiced the apprehension of the socialists at Méline's ultimate goals: "M. Méline . . . is trying to set the peasant against the worker, to arm one against the other so that these two mounting rages against social inequity consume one another. But for all the stratagems they have tried thus far the protectionists have managed neither to deepen the differences between the two proletariats, nor to arouse them to civil war against one another."[6]

6. Paul Louis, "Les résultats du système Méline," *La Revue socialiste,* August 24, 1896, pp. 129–69. The lines I quote concluded a sustained statistical denunciation of the misfortunes that the *Système Méline* had conferred upon France. Robert Charlie, editor of *République française,* wrote the refutation for the Méline camp: "Socialisme et libre échange," August 27, 1896, p. 1. Although he attempted to confound all the arguments Louis had advanced about the decline of France's commercial position, the closing of markets to French products, the ruination of important French industries, the injuries to certain French ports, the weakening of the merchant marine, the fall in prices, and many more, he did not specifically deny the allegations of Louis' closing charge, that Méline was trying to set the peasants against the workers.

Historians of France have questioned whether the Third Republic had anything that might be called an agricultural policy.[7] If we ask whether the social coalition that Méline was fashioning of elements of the industrial bourgeoisie, the aristocracy that had rallied to the Republic, and the more profit-oriented rural notables had an agricultural policy, the answer must be in the affirmative. But, in a liberal age, the state could not be their only instrument, nor the improvement of the welfare of the country people their only goal.

Rural Prosperity and Rural Credit

The second and most delicate phase of Méline's strategy for stability depended on the cooperation of the banking elite. Méline aimed at obtaining the acquiescence of as large a part of French finance as could be won over to the new conservative coalition. In particular during his ministry he worked to create if not a unity at least a parallelism of interests between the comfortable and prosperous part of the peasantry and rural notables with investment portfolios on the one side and French finance capitalists on the other. To this end he undertook to improve the flow of short-term capital into the countryside while at the same time he tried to ensure that nothing constricted the stream of rural savings on their way to the bankers and financiers. In turn these would find safe, profitable, long-term uses for the savings entrusted to them. Having placated some workers with tariffs, and benefited many growers and industrialists at the same time, Méline now sought to mobilize the men of finance to perceive that their interests coincided with maintaining the countryside both economically healthy and socially stable. The rest of this chapter will be devoted to tracing the ways Méline and his political allies found of linking stability on the land, pacification in the industrial cities, and opportunities for safe and profitable investments for French investors and bankers.

After the disturbing election results of 1893 were known, Méline revived a draft law (which had died in the last legislature) for the creation of local banks to provide credit for farmers and small businessmen, including, he expected, ambitious workers. And in his statement of justification Méline emphasized that the institution

7. Gordon Wright, *Rural Revolution in France: The Peasantry in the Twentieth Century* (Stanford, 1964), 16.

would not just serve the rural population but also help intelligent workers elevate themselves to the ranks of small owners, if all they lacked was access to credit. The Marquis de Dampierre, president of the Société des Agriculteurs de France, immediately proffered his praise: "M. Méline assures us that *le crédit agricole et populaire* would be a most powerful instrument of social pacification, perhaps the only means of effecting that reconciliation of labor and capital we so desire."[8] In the Chamber debate, the draft law, now proposing only a rural credit institution, was strongly attacked by Jaurès.[9] Méline accused Jaurès of displaying such animosity because the socialist appreciated what a powerful weapon these rural banks provided for the struggle against the spread of socialism among the peasants. "Indeed," Méline admitted, "it is one of the numerous means by which we hope to confound agrarian socialism," adding, "We are well aware of the seductive promises you are making the inhabitants of the land." The editors of *Le Travail national* commented, "We shall see that with our new agrarian organization we will have, with the Germans, the best and most democratically divided rural land-holding."[10] The bill passed the Opportunist-dominated Chamber by an overwhelming margin.

A few weeks after his exchange with Jaurès, Méline went to Rouen to inaugurate the monument erected to honor the godfather of Third Republic protectionists, Pouyer-Quertier. He praised Pouyer-Quertier, who was after all an industrialist and not a grower, for his perspicacity in realizing that, at that time of economic crisis, the revival of French agriculture was paramount for the recovery of the rest of the economy. Then, in the clichéd expression of concern for the severity of the agricultural depression, he illuminated the consciousness of the classes for which he had made himself spokesman. He did not retell the tale of the immiseration of the poorer peasants, or the struggles of farmers to pay their debts, or even the shrinkage of demand for

8. Henri Sagnier, *Le Crédit agricole en France: ses origines, son essor, son avenir* (Paris, 1911), 27–28; *Bulletin de la Société des agriculteurs de France,* XXV (1894), 19.

9. Sagnier blamed the opposition of the Conseil Supérieur du Travail in the Ministry of Commerce and Industry (therefore, business opposition), for scuttling the extension of special credit to urban workmen (Sagnier, *Crédit agricole,* 29).

10. Debate cited in *Travail national,* October 28, 1894, pp. 561–62; the original exchange was on October 27. The editors of the *Travail national* well understood the international nature of the movement for crédit agricole, citing parallel legislation in Belgium, Austria-Hungary, Denmark, Sweden, and especially the German Empire.

products of industry. He drove home the enormity of the agricultural crisis by offering his audience the estimate that in just a few years land values had fallen as much as 40 percent.[11] The index of suffering for him was the fall in value of ground rents (see Table 4). But how could the tariffs help raise land values and rents?

We have seen the role the tariffs of the 1880s and 1892 played in uniting the ruling elites while at the same time functioning to placate the urban working class. We have also examined the pacifying role the tariffs were intended to play among the peasantry. However, lest we falsely paint Méline as a kind of sociologist-in-politics, we must emphasize that his prime goal was to reverse the fall in land values. Social peace, to be sure, would come about as a highly desirable consequence of the lifesaving efforts for the fortunes of the rich. The tariffs functioned to protect the farm rents of the big growers— often to increase their incomes. Higher prices for domestic agricultural products permitted both greater direct profits for large and small growers, as well as greater rent income (or less of a decline in the bad years) for landlords involved in various tenancy and share-cropping arrangements. France's peasant farmers were not known for their zeal for capital investments. Some of the poorer cultivators who sold what they produced might have benefited from tariff protection against foreign grains and meats, while the larger and often more efficient ones stood to make great profits, or perhaps get out of debt, when the tariffs began to do their work. But because the new tariffs gave growers a protected market in which to function, they made investments in agricultural improvements less pressing. And because they inhibited growth in agriculture, they made purchases of land intended as good investments less attractive.

Moreover, the rural tug-of-war over land accumulation that had gone on since the Revolution had so stalemated the wealthy proprietors that both large and small parcels of land did not come on the market very often, thereby further restricting opportunities for good rural investments. In the depression years, low rents and poor land prices combined to make investments in farmland unattractive for individuals with wealth to invest and an appreciable risk for small farmers who could scarcely make ends meet with their current holdings. When land did change hands, a financial institution typically

---

11. Jules Méline, *Discours et inauguration du monument de Pouyer-Quertier à Rouen le dimanche 17 nov. 1894* (Evreux, 1895), 10.

had to provide a mortgage. Here too, the more valuable the land, the more profitable the mortgage-granting business was.

Since neither large nor small cultivators could reinvest in the land, they had to look outside of agriculture to place their profits and savings. Therefore, the very insufficiency and stagnation of French agriculture provided French financial institutions with a portion of their loan capital.

In the last quarter of the century foreign stocks and bonds began to appear with increasing frequency in wills and family investment portfolios. With rare exceptions this had not been the case before the depression years.[12] Although our picture of who in France purchased foreign emissions is far from complete, we know that in the last decades of the century certain departments exceeded the national average in the retention of foreign holdings. We would expect the Seine to lead the rest of France. But the relatively poor peasant region of the Haute Savoie, the agricultural department of l'Orne and Lozère, and the mixed industrial-agricultural Rhône (Lyon and its rich countryside) were also highest among the areas of France where individuals held foreign stocks and bonds or willed them to their heirs. At the turn of the century even in agricultural Vaucluse in the South and Caen in Normandy, foreign issues can be counted—in modest proportions, to be sure—in farmers' fortunes.[13] As we have seen, in the period of the Great Depression foreign investments were much more attractive, or more available, than domestic ones.[14] The urban rentiers and rural investors who placed their savings in foreign ventures were only following the lead of some of the banks who often managed their portfolios for them. In 1896, for example, the Bank of France held portfolios for its depositors in which foreign stocks and bonds comprised 38 percent of the capital

12. A. Daumard, "Diffusion et nature des placements à l'étranger dans les patrimoines des Français au XIXe siècle," in Maurice Lévy-Leboyer (ed.), *La Position internationale de la France* (Paris, 1977), 431, 432. The chief exception was of course Lyon, for reasons of its special religious and economic inclinations toward the world abroad (see Chap. VI herein). In the first three-quarters of the century, on average, over 20 percent of the value of legacies and investment portfolios in Lyon took the form of foreign investments.

13. C. Mesliand, "La fortune paysanne dans le Vaucluse, 1900–1938," *Annales: économies, sociétés, civilisations,* XII (1967), 123–28; Daumard, "Diffusion," 433.

14. They offered steady and high returns, compared both to French emissions and investments in lands; otherwise investors would not have bought them. See Daumard, "Diffusion," 441.

value of the total.[15] Moreover, a significant and growing portion of the foreign certificates was Russian. Let us now turn to the first tentative association of French financial institutions with the Méline project of social pacification.[16]

Cybele and Mercury

A few months after he was named premier, Méline's government initiated the process of renewal of the monopoly privilege of issuing bank notes retained by the Bank of France. This legislation was in principle a routine matter. The bank, created under the consulate of Napoleon in 1800, received its special status and exclusive note-issuing privilege in 1848. Napoleon III reconfirmed its status in 1857 for the remaining years of its original fifty-year term. Therefore, the legislature had to act by the end of 1897.[17]

The appropriate bill was put on the table late in October, 1896. Referred to the finance committee of the Chamber, the bill was reported out by Maurice Lebon in late January, 1897. The Chamber debated the draft on May 25 and 31, and on June 1, 3, 10, 14, 15, 17, 21, 22, 24, 28, and 29 before adopting it virtually unaltered on July 1. The Senate, however, passed the bill without much debate on November 5.[18] Normally, so routine a piece of legislation should arouse no curiosity, for states need central banks to issue their paper currency.

But the renewal of the privilege of the Bank of France was exceptional in two important respects. Linked to it was a provision that the bank set aside a loan fund of forty million francs, to be supplemented by an additional two million per annum, so that farmers might procure low interest loans. Moreover, the long debate over renewal—taking up much of the June legislative session—offered Jean Jaurès the incitement to lay out his analysis of the socioeco-

15. A. Daumard, "La fortune mobilière en France selon les milieux sociaux, XIXe– XXe siècles," *Revue d'histoire économique et sociale*, XLIV (1966), 386.

16. See Rudolf Hilferding, *Das Finanzkapital* (1910; rpr. Vienna, 1923), 433–39, on the benefits customs duties heap upon financial institutions.

17. A history of the Banque de France may be found in Alex Synckers, *La Reichsbank et la Banque de France: leur politique* (Paris, 1908), 1–5. See also Gabriel Ramon, *Histoire de la banque de France d'après les sources* (Paris, 1929).

18. *JO*, Chambre des députés, Débats, May and June, 1897, pp. 1288, 1342, 1375, 1436, 1499, 1524, 1540, 1596, 1613, 1635, 1702, 1725, 1748. The text of the law may be found in the *JO* for 1897, p. 7072.

nomic position of the French peasantry and of Méline's pacification strategy.

The rural banks created in 1894 were mutual credit associations; they used the members' pooled money for loans. However, the peasants' money seemed to remain either in the famous wool sock or was placed in some safer long-term investment, such as Russian bonds. Thus, Méline sought to infuse additional outside capital into the countryside by requiring the Bank of France to set aside a sum for low-interest loans for terms of up to ninety days for this purpose. As Jean Codet, reporter of the committee created by the Chamber to examine the renewal, commented, "We should take advantage of the present circumstance [the renewal] to encourage the Bank to offer terms even more favorable to agricultural paper than to that of industry."[19]

In committee and on the Chamber floor Radicals and socialists attacked the renewal of the privilege. Still a private institution, the bank's general assembly seated only two hundred stockholders. Each member held a minimum of sixty shares of bank stock. If the threshold of membership were lowered to twenty shares, one (unnamed) critic proposed in committee, the participants in decision making might be expanded tenfold; the charge that a tiny rich clique ran the bank's affairs would be disarmed. "Too unwieldy," responded the bank's governor, Joseph Magnin, former industrialist, Opportunist politician, and friend of Méline. The sources do not reveal whether the minister of finance, Georges Cochery, pressed the governor of the bank on this matter, but we do know that no proposals to change the size of the general assembly reached the Chamber floor. In the 1930s, this omitted reform was to haunt the ruling class in the myth of the two hundred families whose financial hegemony allowed them to rule France.[20]

19. Proceedings of the Commission of the Chamber charged with examining the law on the renewal were recorded, as was usual for parliamentary committees, in a *cahier*. It may be found in the AN C5545 dos. 286, no. 2, séance du déc. 4 1896. Codet was another of the many friends of agriculture we have encountered in this study whose real life activities had little connection with farming. Codet started in the prefectoral administration but soon moved into the paper industry. He was elected *président honoraire* of l'Union des Fabriques Françaises. He ran for the Chamber as an Opportunist, professing to admire the philosophy of Léon Bourgeois. He did sit for many years on the Conseil Supérieur de l'Agriculture (Jean Jolly, *et al.*, *Dictionnaire des parlementaires français 1889–1940* (8 vols.; Paris, 1960–77), III, 1088–89).

20. AN C5545 dos. 286, no. 2. See R. D. Anderson, *France, 1870–1914: Politics and Society* (London, 1977), 24.

For some of the socialists in the Chamber, the renewal bill offered the opportunity to press for the creation of a true national bank, one that would "not enrich private capitalists," in the words of René Viviani. Camille Pelletan, one of the Radicals' spokesmen, proposed that the Bank of France put aside not forty million francs for loans to agriculture but one hundred million. Pressures for transforming the bank into a national bank (or creating a new national bank) and increasing the special loan fund for cultivators were easily resisted by the alliance of conservative forces in the Chamber.[21]

However, when Jaurès rose to present his analysis of the agrarian question in France—even though in the end the bank bill was not in the least altered—Paul Deschanel, the Opportunists' best parliamentary intellectual, and the prime minister himself both had to actively counterattack the powerful arguments of the socialist orator.

Various commentators have viewed Jaurès' speech primarily as another example of his courtship of the small peasant proprietors. Yet, Jaurès delivered his views on the prospects of French peasant agriculture on the occasion of the renewal of the special monopoly of the Bank of France. He chose that moment to address the debate over the adequacy of rural credit.[22]

The theme of Jaurès' great three-day parliamentary discourse was the same insight, and reproach, he had hurled at Méline and his allies back in 1893: they wished "to use the rural democracy like a sturdy tree trunk to support themselves in resisting the upward thrust of the workers." But now, he argued, the tactic was doomed to failure for at least three reasons.[23]

21. *JO*, Chambre des députés, Débats, May 25, 1897, pp. 1288–96, 1342–56, 1359–91, June 24, 1897, pp. 1643–46.

22. Harvey Goldberg, *The Life of Jean Jaurès*, (Madison, Wisc., 1962), 188–94; Goldberg, "The Myth of the French Peasant," *American Journal of Economics and Sociology*, XIII (July, 1954), 353–79; Pierre Barral, *Les Agrariens français de Méline à Pisani* (Paris, 1968), 157–64.

23. *JO*, Chambre des députés, Débats, June 19, 1897, pp. 1589ff. The disappearance of the precapitalist peasantry and the hopes of its revival was being debated all over Europe at this conjuncture. It was one of the fundamental issues of the debate over the need to revise Marx in the German Social Democracy. It figured as well as in the dispute over the future social complexion of German society among conservative social scientists. On this latter issue see Herman Lebovics, "'Agrarians' versus 'Industrializers': Social Conservative Resistance to Industrialism and Capitalism in Late Nineteenth Century Germany," *International Review of Social History*, XII (1967), 31–65. In contemporary Russia the Narodniks were asserting that the peasants had not yet come into the capitalist orbit and could therefore become the supporters of a peasant

Jaurès took as his major premise that the French peasantry had already entered the capitalist system and the capitalist age. They paid capitalist rents and ran their farms for a profit. Those who did not, or could not, had to hire themselves out as laborers to survive. He offered as example the case of the woodcutters of the Cher and the Nièvre. Moreover, extensive regions of the French countryside produced for the market—in some cases, the world market. Thus the peasants of France could not be depended upon to resist the anomic disintegration that the Right and the Opportunists claimed to witness taking place in the industrial cities. How could the Right expect the peasants to resist the appeals of socialism when their lot was ever more approximating that of the urban workers?[24]

Jaurès attempted to confound the new conservatives with a second argument demonstrating the disappearance of the independent small and middle peasants. He used the 1882 census (the one of 1892 had not yet been released) to demonstrate that half the peasants owned little or no land. Those who did were often crushed under unfavorable rental or sharecropping arrangements, or simply deeply mortgaged. Moreover, over three million French peasants suffered brutal proletarianization as live-in farm workers or day laborers. Where, in effect, he questioned, are these peasants who will serve as a counterweight to the revolutionary movement of the propertyless of the cities?[25]

Finally, he struck at what seemed to him the heart of Méline's pacification strategy. He denied the possibility of building a conservative rural party. He admitted that by retaining ownership of extensive property in the countryside, the big landowners had managed to "prolong in the present the forces of the past." Further, he charged the ruling classes of the Old Regime with harboring the hope of "main-

socialism based on the village community. Even in Britain Jesse Collins agitated for giving the poor a few acres and a cow.

24. *JO*, Chambre des députés, Débats, June 26, 1897, 1693.

25. *Ibid.*, 1694–96. Here Jaurès thrust himself into the contemporary debate as to whether peasant property was giving out before large holdings. Since the issue was intensely ideological and French statistical data make conclusions difficult to draw—especially from one ten-year census to the next—we need not settle the issue. Here, we may treat it as a kind of litmus paper test of a political posture. For the best literature and actual arguments of the era see Michel Augé-Laribé, *Grande ou petite propriété: histoire des doctrines en France sur la répartition du sol et la transformation industrielle de l'agriculture* (Montpellier, 1902), 133–40.

taining this base of landed property so that one day they might reconstitute their political power." But a true farmers' party was not possible anymore. Even in Germany, the Junkers (Jaurès used the French term *hobereaux*) had not managed to create a real agrarian party. The majority of the so-called agrarian party there "are ruined stock exchange speculators who, unable to pay their debts, have withdrawn to the country." They are not at all enemies of finance, but like their French counterparts, they "have thrown themselves into peasant politics simply to recuperate, much like worn-out rakes who retire for rest in the country."[26]

Nor was the class of English landlords any longer the same one that had existed a half century ago, in Jaurès's view. Involvement in business and intermarriage with the American aristocracy of money had stripped them of any title to spokesmanship for the landed interest. As for France, he stated that "as a consequence of their other investments the great land owners became ever more real capitalists; they may be found more often seated on the boards of directors of industrial companies than in the local agricultural societies." Méline interrupted, "You are taking the exception for the rule." Jaurès continued, "They are like a coin, Cybele on one side, Mercury on the other, but Mercury stands out in higher relief," for the god of commerce now dominated the goddess of nature.[27]

Although Deschanel's elaborate refutation of Jaurès is the more famous, Méline's supplies us with more insight into the grand strategy of his coalition. He could not easily refute Jaurès' charge that the French peasants were not inside the capitalist system; for Méline, that would surely have been a positive condition. But armed with the now (suddenly) available 1892 census results, the premier could claim that great holdings were not increasing and that the smallest ones of one hectare or less, "democratic property *par excellence*," had increased from 2,167,000 to 2,235,000, a rise of 68,000 holdings.[28]

The premier did not reply to Jaurès's charge that the Opportunists and the Ralliés were attempting to create a great agrarian party, for Jaurès had hit the mark. Yet, the concentration Méline was constructing did not pretend to be solely a farmers' party. It was more

26. *Ibid.*, 1592.

27. *Ibid.*

28. *JO*, Chambre des députés, Débats, November 13, 20, 1897, reprinted in *République française*, November 15, 22, 1897.

complex than that: it attempted to unite—much like a great, geologically layered rock formation—different ages of French economic life to contain and to stabilize radical upheaval in the land. The fervor of Jaurès' and his socialist friends' attacks suggests that they feared Méline was indeed succeeding.

The parliamentary socialists dreaded, too, the conservative consequences of Méline's courtship of the peasantry. They believed that, as had happened in 1871, Méline's measures might just succeed in thwarting the victory of the urban working class by mobilizing the conservative spirits in the peasantry. As Méline himself freely admitted at the conclusion of his rebuttal of Jaurès, when the remainder of his agrarian legislation was passed and functioning, he felt certain the rural exodus would reverse. Then the agitated workers who still followed the absolutist politics of the prophets of social revolution would discover that their brethren in the country "have emancipated themselves, and that they have resolved the social problem in a better fashion than you [socialists] can ever hope to do."[29]

His fellow socialists reprinted Jaurès' speech as a pamphlet, but the Chamber voted Méline's the rare honor of having it officially posted in public places. The monopoly of the Bank of France was renewed as proposed by the government, with the sum of forty million francs set aside for agricultural credits, as envisioned.

Students of the question disagree widely on the precise nature of the impact made by the credit arrangement with the Bank of France. Marcillac suggested that between 1900 and 1909 the bank loaned or discounted bills of agriculturists to the value of 576 million francs. The more skeptical Augé-Laribé estimated a total of agricultural credit from all sources not exceeding 200 million francs. What was certain was that between 1897 and 1910 the bank was legally obliged to make 66 million available but in fact put up larger amounts annually, for a total of 106 million according to Henri Sagnier. It seems safe to say that the bank loaned more money to agriculture than it was obliged to by law, and that its credit facilities were the most important (to 1910) of short-term credit arrangements farmers had available.[30]

29. *Ibid.*
30. Marquis de Marcillac, *Les Syndicats agricoles: leur action économique et sociale* (Paris, 1913), 128; Michel Augé-Laribé, *L'Evolution de la France agricole* (Paris, 1912), 182; Sagnier, *Crédit agricole*, 124. See also Eugene Golob, *The Méline Tariff: French Agriculture and Nationalist Economic Policy* (New York, 1944), 229–31. The records of the 1897

We must still puzzle over why great financial institutions such as the Bank of France agreed to such unusual arrangements. In the late nineteenth century, making loans to French cultivators or syndicats agricoles was surely not as lucrative as colonial investments nor as safe, it was believed, as Imperial Russian bonds.

Despite their generally good record of taking the initiative, French venture capitalists had suffered in the crisis decade of the 1880s.[31] Defaults, forced conversions, bankruptcies, and various local difficulties that lamed their activities caused French venture capitalists to defer making new investments on the scale of past years in the Latin countries of Europe and the Austro-Hungarian Empire. In the case of Germany, Italy, and Austria-Hungary, diplomatic tensions compounded concerns arising from the bad business climate to further discourage French investors. French bankers even stopped investing in Egypt and the Ottoman Empire for a time. Certainly the depressed incomes and profits that plagued growers and industrialists also played an important role in slowing the rate and volume of French investment abroad. The Great Depression, then, proved punishing to French international banking as well; the net result was a marked decline in French foreign investment in the decade after 1882.

Accordingly, when French bankers and investors regained confidence and, after 1890, proposed new offerings of European issues they were inclined to search out the much safer forms of government or railway and mortgage bonds of fixed returns in preference to riskier undertakings. The developing Russian Empire became the special choice of new French investment. In the period between 1882 and 1914 Russia became the chief recipient of French foreign investments.[32] In the course of these years the Russian Empire also be-

---

renewal of the privilege in the Archives Nationales are curiously silent about the forty million francs (AN C5545 dos. 286, no. 2, pp. 5437–5438).

31. Rando Cameron, *France and the Economic Development of Europe, 1800–1914: Conquests of Peace and Seeds of War* (Princeton, 1961), 504.

32. *Ibid.*, 485–487, 504. In a direct way Russia's turning away from reliance on German sources of capital and the new interest in French capital are part of the tariff history of Europe. In 1884 Germany was by far (60 percent of total) the biggest foreign investor in Russia. Bismarck's giving in to the Bund der Landwirte, which desired tariff protection to aid the recovery from agricultural depression, injured Russian agriculture as the profits from grain exports were Russia's chief source of foreign earnings. Moreover, the new Russian industry and that of neighboring Germany

came the chief military ally of the French Republic. The requirement for safe outlets for investment thus dovetailed nicely with the diplomatic and defense needs of the Opportunist republic. This new international unholy alliance also served the cause of domestic neoconservatism within the Republic.[33]

A pattern of Russian borrowing in republican France began with the 4 percent gold loans of 1889–1890, which in four issues totaled 1.2 billion francs. Further issues of government bonds, guaranteed bonds, and municipal issues in the years 1891, 1893, 1894, 1896, 1901, 1906, 1909, and up to the eve of the war amounted to a French investment in the Russian public sector of 10.5 billion francs. French investments in Russian joint-stock companies added another 1.75 billion. French investors held a steady 30 percent of the total debt Russia owed abroad in the period 1888–1914. On the French side, while in 1888 Russian certificates made up only 9.5 percent of the value of foreign issues in French portfolios, by 1914 the Russian share had reached 25 percent.[34]

Private investment made up only approximately 17 percent of French involvement in Russia. The names of some of the important French industrialists who participated in Russian enterprises are familiar to us. In what is probably an early example of the runaway shop, four Roubaix textile firms set up operations in Russian Poland. Three had a member of the Motte clan in the management. In 1890 the Mottes participated in founding a wool-spinning factory in Lodz. Eugène Motte headed the cotton-spinning company in Czenstochowa that was incorporated as La Czenstochovienne at Roubaix in 1899. The next year the firm of Motte, Meillassoux et Coulliez set up

---

were rivals in a way that the depressed French industry could not be. Tariff war led to diplomatic tensions, to nonrenewal of the German-Russian reinsurance treaty, and soon to closer French-Russian economic relations and the diplomatic-military rapprochement. See René Girault, *Emprunts russes et investissements français en Russie, 1887–1914* (Paris, 1973), 140–41, for the fascinating story of the change in partners.

33. Girault sees only a parallel "concordance" between the development of the financial and diplomatic rapprochement between France and Russia. He discovered no important economic factors at work in the conclusion of the *entente;* the decision, he argues, rested primarily on political calculations (*Emprunts russes,* 220, 580–81). This, of course, is not to say there were no social reasons for the convergence.

34. Olga Crisp, "Russian Public Funds in France, 1888–1914," René Girault, "Investissements et placements français en Russie, 1880–1914," both in Lévy-Leboyer (ed.), *La Position internationale de la France,* 264, 251. See also the cautionary piece by Fred V. Carstensen, "The Numbers and Reality: A Critique of Foreign Investment Estimates in Tsarist Russia," *ibid.,* 275–83.

another woolen mill in Czenstochowa. The Mottes put together a consortium of fifty industrialist-investors from the Nord to found one of their textile firms in Russian Poland. In all, by 1910 French firms employed ten thousand people in Poland. These enterprising efforts of Association de l'Industrie et l'Agriculture Française members abroad should also be booked as part of the industrialists' strategies against the losses from depression and from the breaches of industrial peace in France.[35]

However, two-thirds of the French private capital went into the Russian iron industry. Robert de Nervo served both as president of the Société des hauts fourneaux, forges and aciéries of Denain-Anzin and as a director of the Russian iron works of Krivoi-Rog. The Schneider family and Paulin Talabot, son of the protectionist iron industrialist and manager of the Paris-Lyon-Marseille Railroad, helped organize the iron works at Volga-Vichera in 1896. Le Creusot, the Companie des forges de Châtillon et Commentry, and de Wendel participated in prospecting ventures in the Urals in search of new mining ventures. The Société des études, which directed the explorations and planning, was headed by Pierre Darcy, son of a director of Châtillon-Commentry.[36]

Whereas in France the relations between business and the banks were not close, Russian commercial investments resulted in good collaborations. French banks participated in every one of the joint French-Russian industrial ventures. Krivoi-Rog was heavily funded by the Société Générale, the bank in which Talabot and Schneider played an important role, as well as by the Crédit Mobilier, Banque de Brabant of Brussels, and the Lyon money market. The Volga-Vichera metallurgical firm received its capital from the Banque Internationale de Paris and the Banque d'Escompte et de Prêts. Henri Schneider frequently turned to the Banque de Paris et Pays-Bas (Paribas) to finance banking ventures in Russia. As in the case of the colonial empire, the French elite found ways of collaborating abroad to open the way to cooperation at home. In both cases, too, the Opportunist Republic took on the role of intermediary or protector.[37]

The Opportunists were eager to see Russia become the outlet for

35. Girault, *Emprunts russes*, 262; John P. MacKay, *Pioneers for Profit: Foreign Entrepreneurship and Russian Industrialization, 1885–1913* (Chicago, 1970), 49.

36. MacKay, *Pioneers for Profit*, 63–64; Girault, *Emprunts russes*, 283–90. See also J. B. Silly, "Capitaux français et sidérurgie russe," *Revue d'histoire de la sidérurgie*, VI (1965), 28–53.

37. Girault, *Emprunts russes*, 296.

depressed French industrial production. Girault tells of Gabriel Hanotaux, during both the Ribot and the Méline ministries, frequently urging Russian purchases of French industrial goods in conversations with the Danish banker Hoskier, who represented the Russian embassy in Paris in financial transactions, with Arthur Raffalovitch, the Russian financial agent in Paris, and with Baron Mohrenheim, the ambassador in Paris. He even wrote directly to Count Sergei Witte, the tsar's minister of finance, to argue the French case. In each of these interviews his theme was that, since the French market was the sole outlet for Russian bonds, the French deserved something in return. In a letter to Witte, Raffalovitch reported an interview with Hanotaux in May, 1898, in which the Frenchman again emphasized the need to increase French sales in Russia. He quoted Hanotaux as stressing "the orders . . . for locomotives, machines, dredges, and naval vessels, so that we could say to our worker-voters in the regions where there are factories which produce these goods: 'Look here, thanks to the government of the Republic you have a well-paid job, for it has procured these orders from its friend the Russian government.' Your Excellency remembers my reference to these same kinds of conversations in the letters I wrote you at various times in 1897," Raffalovitch concluded.[38]

This intervention bore fruit. A month later the Russian government ordered from French firms fifty locomotives with tenders and two tug boats. It did so at prices 15 percent higher than those at which the items were available from other countries. Raffalovitch booked the transaction as a business expense in the larger enterprise of cementing good relations between France and Russia.

But this sale was an uncommon instance of the successful use of political influence. In 1896 Le Creusot had refused a Russian order for ten locomotives with tenders because the firm could not deliver at the price offered by the Russians. Nor was the Russian consumer as philosophical as representatives of the government; most French goods came upon the Russian market at prices too high to find many buyers. In the end, it was Russian state bonds that comprised the overwhelming monetary value of the transactions between the two nations.

Dealing in these bonds brought the French banks great and

38. Letter from Raffalovitch to Sergei Witte, May 17, 1898, translated and quoted *ibid.*, 309–10.

steady revenues. For although the fees for handling the bond transactions were not high, the sums at issue were so vast that the banks made their profits on the volume. By just placing the Russian treasury bonds of 1904 the Crédit Lyonnais, the Paribas, and Hottinguer earned four million francs each. In addition the banks received a commission for servicing the loans. Finally, and most importantly for our concerns, on the basis of a convention signed with the Russians in 1895, the Bank of France assumed a special position as a depository of Russian bearer bonds. This agreement, and the status it granted to the Bank of France, put the French government, at least in the eyes of many investors, behind the Russian state loans.[39]

In the midst of the strikes and labor unrest of 1891, the Freycinet ministry energetically pursued simultaneously both secret negotiations with imperial Russia for a military entente and domestic negotiations with growers and manufacturers for the passage of the tariff. Guided by the same sense of orderly government, it refused to intervene in the miners' strike in the Pas-de-Calais. Subsequent Opportunist ministries followed Freycinet's lead in domestic and in foreign policy. As we have seen, they encouraged the parallel economic rapport with the Russian Empire.[40] The banks received governmental, political, and diplomatic support for their foreign loans. As a result these loans were safe profitable medicine for the investors' ills of the previous years. On the level of domestic politics, the banks (in particular, the Bank of France) were helping to build safety abroad and pacification at home by manifesting special interest for the needs of agricultural credit and accepting special state interest in their dealings in Russian stocks and bonds.

Gabriel Hanotaux, when foreign minister of the Méline ministry, worked hard to expand the Russian alliance beyond its military dimensions. In his obituary for Méline he praised the former premier's heavy emphasis on friendship with Russia and his simultane-

39. Crisp, "Russian Public Funds in France," 272–73.
40. As usual, Beau de Loménie sensed an arrangement. He judged that the conclusion of the Russian alliance and the passage of tariff reform were both dominated in the parliament by the concern to protect at the same time great industrial and financial interests. It is possible that he is right, for it is true that the financial community, normally free trade in orientation, did nothing to oppose the new tariff policy of the 1880s and 1892. We need research in the bank archives to answer this question, since arguments from nonaction, such as Beau de Loménie's, do not persuade. See his *Les Responsibilités des dynasties bourgeoises* (3 vols.; Paris, 1947), II, 231–33.

ous efforts to create a domestic peace, "a truce which anticipated, long before the fact, the *union sacrée* of World War I."[41]

On the occasion of the czar's visit when Méline was premier, the Left was vociferous in its hostility. Robert Charlie, of *La République française*, chided the socialists for receiving delegates of the German Social Democratic party at their recent congress at Lille and then opposing the visit of the Russian ruler: "Isn't it evident—if we admit of the existence of a formal alliance between France and Russia— that this alliance should have, among other outcomes, that of preventing the revolution, 'the final upheaval' dreamt of and prepared for by the French collectivists under the peremptory direction of the German collectivists?"[42]

The foreign policy of the Opportunist republic mirrored the internal policy of social pacification. Both the economic protectionism erected against the menace of German economic power and the threat of an international socialist movement made concluding an alliance with czarist Russia easier for Opportunist politicians to undertake. The bankers, in turn, were nervous enough about the dangers of financial setbacks to welcome the support and encouragement of the state, while the Opportunist governments—Méline's chief among them—knew how to manage them to obtain from them the toleration of a protectionist commercial policy and of the new conservative alliance to protect the social order.[43]

Reform

Creating and intensifying the conservative concentration was, of course, a means rather than an end in itself. Georges Lachapelle,

---

41. Hanotaux, "Jules Méline," 448–50.

42. Robert Charlie, "Les socialistes et le Tsar," *République française,* August 25, 1896. Italics mine.

43. The banks were willing to do their share for social peace but not at the price of subsidizing debtors. The movement for bimetallism that the Société des Agriculteurs endorsed every year from the passage of the 1892 tariff to the start of the Méline ministry, which the business interests united in the Association de l'Industrie et de l'Agriculture Française also supported, could not move France off the gold standard. The Ligue Bimétallique Nationale, formed in 1895 by the leaders of the two national agricultural societies and the Association de l'Industrie et de l'Agriculture Française, and warmly supported by Méline while in office, could not achieve the inflationary monetization of silver alongside gold that the promoters hoped for.

Méline's old collaborator, attributed at least thirty measures of reform to the two-year ministry. Reform, however, is a rubber-sack concept that can be expanded to fit whatever we may be interested in stuffing into it. Thus, some of Méline's reforms for the benefit of agriculture simply aided his friends. For example, the government granted tax relief to the big alcohol distillers (from as high as 37.5 francs to as low as 3 francs per hectoliter) and subsidized exports of the sugar-beet growers in their international and very costly price war. Other measures perpetuated the ideology of an "agricultural interest," such as the laws controlling the alcohol content of wines, that reducing the sales tax on "hygenic drinks" (wine, beer, and cider) and measures seeking to discipline the middlemen and inhibit fraud in the sale of goods to farmers (fertilizers, chemicals). The law indemnifying cattle and dairy farmers whose tubercular animals had to be destroyed was a gracious gift to relatively prosperous farmers, for it worked to reward them in proportion to the number of diseased animals they raised. The law providing for agricultural warrants benefited middling and larger growers by allowing them to borrow money against crops stored in their barns, so that they did not have to sell outright at a moment of low prices.[44]

A further agricultural reform was a direct consequence of the 1897 debate with Jaurès. Although Méline had included reduction of the tax burden on agriculture in his ministerial declaration, he did not initiate any reforms in that direction until Jaurès challenged his commitment to the small farmer. The publication of the agricultural census of 1892 fueled the passions kindled by the parliamentary debate; were small cultivators—the heroes of the peasant republic—dying out? In 1898 Méline sent through the Chamber a measure reducing the land tax on unimproved property of small size, offering small peasant-proprietors a tax reduction totaling an estimated twenty-five million francs. This was certainly a stout blow in the duel with agrarian socialism.

Of course, so that he would have free use of what had become his prized weapon in his class war for social peace, Méline got the parliament to pass the law of *Cadenas* in 1897. This legislation empowered the premier to alter tariff levels by decree without need to suffer the inevitable delays of parliamentary debate and votes.

44. Lachapelle, *Le Ministère Méline*, 35ff; Augé-Laribé, *L'Evolution de la France agricole*, 166–67.

Méline had to use his new powers late in the summer of 1898. The short wheat harvest sent prices up. Just before the May elections, the price of wheat reached an unprecedented thirty-four francs per quintal. Although the powerful agricultural societies from the wheat-growing regions (for example, the Seine-Inférieure and the Sud-Est) urged the government not to touch the current levels of tariffs on foreign wheat, even more vehement protests poured in from the urban centers. The Paris Municipal Council formally requested relief, and socialist and radical journals escalated their campaign against the premier with the old charge, "Méline The Starver." With the elections set for May 8, Méline suspended the seven franc duty on imported wheat until July 1. Appeasing the urban workers and radicalized peasant consumers might require certain sacrifices from the coalition partners. Maintaining political power in troubled times had to come before the narrow interests of one group of the coalition.[45]

Other than reducing the price of bread for the elections, the Méline ministry's record of labor legislation was unimpressive. It is true that legislation that facilitated employers maintaining accident insurance for their workers, as well as a measure granting a modicum of state support for mutual aid societies, passed both chambers. But the Opportunist ministry also tried to change the 1892 law that had limited women's and children's labor in industrial establishments to ten hours and had left men's labor limit at eleven to a uniform eleven hours for all. The differing workday limits had disturbed production, especially in the textile industry. Only its opponents' successful tactic of tacking on amendments that extended the measure to the food industries, thus offending the small shopkeepers, caused the government to abandon this labor reform.[46]

The one solid achievement of Méline's administration in the field of labor relations was one for which it never took credit. In 1898 the railroad workers, increasingly influenced by the Confédération Générale du Travail, began to threaten a system-wide strike. We now know that at the same moment Adolphe Turrel, the minister of public works, aided by General Billot, minister of war, had devised a

45. *République française*, May 5, September 15, 1897; René Girault, "Place et rôle des échanges extérieurs," in Fernand Braudel and Ernest Labrousse (eds.), *Histoire économique et sociale de la France* (8 vols.; Paris, 1977–82), vol. IV, pt. 1, p. 221.
46. *République française*, April 15, 1898; Lachapelle, *Le Ministère Méline*, 356.

new, elaborate, and streamlined plan for the rapid deployment of troops throughout the rail network in the event of labor troubles. The armed soldiers would protect equipment against sabotage, while engineering troops would be deployed to keep the system running. The government's plans seem to have been well thought-out, but since the strike had not occurred by mid-June, when the Méline government resigned, it could not be tested. When the railway workers walked out in October, the planning inherited from the Opportunist ministry was immediately set into motion, bringing the strike to an early and miserable end.[47]

Drawing the balance of the Méline ministry in 1898, *La République française* chose to make resistance to the socialist menace the key to two years of legislative activity. The premier had unmasked their "dream of general plundering," it recorded triumphantly. To the socialists' propaganda Méline had replied not simply with yet another program, according to the newspaper, "but with facts, *i.e.*, with a series of thirty or so laws which exist and which no one can deny." *La République française* predicted that in the coming years the efficacy of Méline's legislation would become increasingly apparent. The government itself, however, expired in June, 1898; this government of moderation—not to say tedium—could not endure the passions of the Dreyfus affair.[48]

47. For this little-known and fascinating contribution to labor peace—via the army—of the Méline government, see Arthur Fryar Calhoun, "The Politics of Internal Order: French Government and Revolutionary Labor, 1898–1914" (Ph.D. dissertation, Princeton University, 1973), 186. Turrel's correspondence on the strike threat may be found in AN F[7] 12774.

48. *République française*, April 17, 1898.

Epilogue

The memorial statue erected by his friends at Rouen shows Pouyer-Quertier gazing off into the distance from atop a pedestal, while Industry and Agriculture, symbolized by two strong women surrounded by plows, sickles, and great cogwheels, strike admiring poses. At the dedication on November 17, 1894, Jules Méline, the principal speaker, exhorted the young industrialists who might pass the statue in future times to remember Pouyer-Quertier's efforts on behalf of the workers, his strivings to keep jobs for them. Méline could find no greater praise than to call him "the most dedicated defender of French labor."[1]

Although the new social conservatism that had been forged in the depression years was sorely tested in subsequent decades, it held French society—at least up to the Popular front—in its cushioned restraints. Pouyer-Quertier, Jules Ferry, and Jules Méline, along with their Opportunist republican friends and Conservative allies, had forged a socially conservative sociopolitical coalition that not even the travail of the Dreyfus case could tear apart.

By January, 1898, the Méline ministry had flourished for the unusually long term of twenty-one months. Its work of social conservation had gone well; now all that remained was to integrate the monarchists-turned-republicans into reliable coalition partners so that parliamentary politics strengthened and reinforced that which had been forged socially. But in January, 1898, the troubling irregularities posed by the conviction of Captain Dreyfus for treason (in peacetime) exploded across the pages of *L'Aurore* with Emile Zola's publication of *J'accuse*. In the course of that winter Colonel Henry, an intelligence officer who had played a central role in supplying the documents proving Dreyfus' guilt, admitted that he had forged a

---

1. Speech of Jules Méline, *Discours et inauguration du monument de Pouyer-Quertier à Rouen le dimanche 17 nov. 1894* (Evreux, 1895), 13.

key piece of the incriminating evidence. He was arrested, but before he could be interrogated he committed suicide in his cell. As a consequence, General de Boisdeffre, chief of the general staff, was moved to resign his post. Events had passed from the lonely belief of Dreyfus' family in his innocence to the conversion of republican intellectuals like Zola to the cause of Dreyfus.

Radical deputies in the Chamber interpellated the premier about the Dreyfus "affair." Méline's meager answer, "There is no Dreyfus Affair," aimed to protect the threatened republican-Catholic coalition and stave off another Radical ministry. Even more to be feared than the loss of reputation of the conservative-dominated general staff was the graduated income tax sponsored by the Radicals. Méline threw himself into the May elections. When in midterm some of his Remiremont constituents had charged him with deferring to the clerical Right, he had responded that on the contrary the Right had begun to follow his principles, "or rather, it does not vote with us, it votes against social revolution." Now in the electoral campaign he took credit for having moved the Right to accept the Republic and thereby further to isolate the socialist revolutionaries to the distant edge of the political spectrum.[2]

The results of the election were gratifying for the Opportunists, although not decisive. The Radicals slipped from 128 seats to 104. The Intransigeant monarchists lost 8 seats (53 to 45), while the Ralliés added 8 (30 to 38). However, despite the losses of Jaurès and Guesde, the socialists increased their numbers (52 to 57), as did their sometime parliamentary allies the Radical-Socialists (68 to 74). And although candidates labeling themselves "republican" returned four members stronger (increasing from 250 to 254), the failure of the Méline ministry to deal deftly with what was now clearly an "affair" cost it its parliamentary life. Méline was replaced by the Radical Henri Brisson, who could not last the winter of 1898–1899. Charles Dupuy, a seasoned Opportunist politician and a former premier, tried to calm the Chamber by creating a ministry of "republican concentration" that tried not to rely on the Ralliés for voting support. The religious and political passions of the Dreyfus affair had become so entwined that, in the face of the attacks from the clerical Right, many left republicans feared for the life of the new Republic.

But the left republicans, especially the socialists, also saw the

2. Georges Lachapelle, *Le Ministère Méline* (Paris, 1928), 120; *Travail national*, May 24, 1898.

opportunity offered them by the political fissures opened by conflict over Dreyfus' guilt. The socialists in the Chamber initially took no sides. That was the position their Manifesto to the Proletariat of mid-January, 1898, announced. But even that apparent declaration of neutrality, signed by thirty socialist deputies including Guesde, Jaurès, Millerand, Vaillant, Viviani, and Walter, implied the strategy which would finally bring them into the struggle as Dreyfusards. They asked,

> Why has the Dreyfus Affair taken on such vast proportions? Because it has become the battleground of two rival factions of the bourgeois class, the two bourgeois clans: the Opportunists and the Clericals. Both Opportunists and Clericals are in accord in their desire to dupe or checkmate democracy. They are in accord in their desire to maintain the people in tutelage, to crush the trade unions, to prolong by all and any means the capitalist order and the wage system, to permit their privileged class the continued unbridled exploitation of both labor and the budget of the state.
>
> But they quarrel about the division of profits in the society and about who has the right to exploit the Republic and the people much like those barbarian clans which join forces to pillage and then brawl over the booty.

The socialist deputies urged the proletariat to stay out of this "ignominious melee." They advised, "Do not deliver yourselves up to the propertied classes, who are sometimes rivals, but always allies in privilege. They are like heavy drinking and gluttonous dinner guests who fall quarrelling at the banquet, but who the morning after make peace and together turn on you if you try to force the door of their banquet hall."[3]

But by October, the early Dreyfusards among the socialist factions—primarily Jaurès—had persuaded the Left that the clerical Right aimed at nothing less than the overthrow of the Republic, now defined by Jaurès as the Republic of the proletariat. As such it had to be defended.[4] In the 1890s, in the Chamber and at political meetings Jaurès had repeatedly spoken against the danger from the Right to the new working class of the Republic. He had attacked Opportunist

---

3. R. Kedward, *The Dreyfus Affair* (London, 1965), 100–101. Translated by the author.

4. Jean Jaurès, "Les Preuves," *La Petite république*, 1898, p. 11. On October 16, 1898, a socialist mass meeting in Paris voted to defend the Republic against its enemies.

governments for accepting the friendship of the Ralliés: "You cannot destroy the Republic," he admonished Charles Dupuy in 1893, "but you are inviting its old enemies into power and authority."[5] Now in 1898 the army, the Church, the Leagues, the parliamentary Right— Intransigeants and Ralliés alike—had set upon the Republic, Jaurès warned.

Few in numbers and politically weak, the sympathetic Radicals and socialists seized upon the Dreyfus affair as the hoped-for opportunity to explode the Opportunist-Rallié concentration. The dangers of conservative coalition of which Engels had warned Lafargue in 1893, the wording of the socialist manifesto on the affair, and the nature of Jaurès attacks on the conservative coalition as it took form all attest to the Left's strategy during the affair: it sought to set the conservative banquet participants at each others' throats so that they might not unite against the Left. Even the most reactionary Opportunist republican would not dare dishonor the labors of decades by giving in to a clerical assault on the Republic. Might not the cries of clerical and military danger cause Opportunists to pull back the hand of friendship held out to the Right as Dupuy had done in his ministry of 1898–1899? Or failing that, might the Mélines not lose credibility in the camp of the parliamentary republicans?

By early 1899 the political tide turned toward the Dreyfusards. One of the first acts of the new ministry of René Waldeck-Rousseau in September was to prevail upon President Loubet to pardon Dreyfus. There followed a spasm of anticlerical legislation that circumscribed and limited the role of the Church, especially of the religious orders that had fought to confirm Dreyfus' guilt. In December, 1905, Church and state were separated formally and legally; the Concordat of 1801 was thereby abrogated. The Ralliement was struck a heavy blow by the outcome of the affair.

The work of "republican concentration," as Waldeck-Rousseau himself called it, continued. Although he could not stop the anticlerical campaign in the affair's aftermath, he carried on other aspects of the work Méline had begun. Author of the 1884 law legalizing workers' organizations, a disciple of Gambetta and Ferry, his career as a lawyer for big Association de l'Industrie Française firms had sensitized him to the need for social pacification. Méline broke with him in 1899 and would not support his government when

5. Jaurès, *Journal Officiel*, Chambre des députés, Débats, Nov. 21, 1893.

Waldeck-Rousseau appointed one of the leaders of the socialists in the Chamber, Alexandre Millerand, minister of commerce. To bring the army and its conservative supporters back into conservative union, he appointed General Gallifet, the so-called Butcher of the Commune, minister of war. His cabinet of republican defense calmed much of the anger of the affair and reinforced the conservative coalition needed to isolate revolutionaries and members of the far-right Leagues. His opponents recognized his achievement by labeling his government simply "the bloc."[6]

Had the Republic been in danger from the clerical Right? It is very difficult to marshall conclusive evidence to prove that Dreyfusard thesis. A president of the Republic was insulted; the army tried to close ranks against an outsider and then to protect itself from exposure for its duplicity; intemperate Assumptionist Fathers unleashed viciously anti-Semitic attacks on Dreyfus, his defenders, and the republican social system that tolerated such a traitor; small numbers of intellectuals centered mainly in Paris formed right-radical organizations to continue the struggles the affair had started and, for their own reasons, to spoil the moderate-right coalition. But at no point did either the Church or the army *act* to overthrow the Republic. On the contrary, the affair erupted at a delicate moment in the Church's attempt to make its peace with a moderate Republic. The French army, through all the changes of regimes in the nineteenth century, had played no independent political role. The decisive failure of General Boulanger is perhaps the most striking example of that truth. The aristocrat-filled officer corps of the mid-nineties devoted itself above all to the defense of its corporate honor; the moves of the military elite, from picking Dreyfus as their culprit, to falsifying evidence, to Dreyfus' second conviction at Rennes, were all defensive.

The old Right suffered serious defeats in the Dreyfus affair. The hopes for the Ralliement, as Leo XIII had envisioned it, were ruined; it brought the Catholic Right into disrepute. It split the conservative republicans; in 1899 Raymond Poincaré led a small group of defectors from Méline's party, charging that the Republic had to be de-

6. Alexandre Zévaès, *Sur l'écran politique* (Paris, 1928) 273; Joseph Caillaux, *Mes Mémoires* (3 vols.; Paris, 1942–47), I, 119; Malcolm O. Partin, *Waldeck-Rousseau, Combes, and the Church: The Politics of Anti-clericalism, 1899–1905* (Durham, N.C., 1969), 3–19.

fended against the reactionary Right.[7] Jaurès' brilliant stratagem, if a deliberate stratagem it was, for dividing his enemies and uniting his friends worked admirably. But did it destroy the new conservative socioeconomic coalition? Méline's career in the Chamber ended, and his party was in disarray. Did the new republican Right lose power with him?

The answer is complicated, for it must be given for two levels of inquiry. For the life of the Republic, that is, to 1940, in the circus of French party politics, nothing like the Opportunist majorities of the 1890s were ever again achieved. However, in 1903 the loose union of the republican Right for the first time took on unified political form. On November 19, at the hall of the Société des Agriculteurs on the rue d'Athènes, the three main tendencies of the Opportunist cause, including that led by Jules Méline, united under the leadership of Eugène Motte, the Roubaix industrialist and deputy, to create the Republican Federation.[8] Motte, other than bearing the distinguished name of one of the important industrialist families in the Nord, had earned his political eminence by twice defeating Jules Guesde in contests for a parliamentary seat for Roubaix.[9] Despite later defections, the Republican Federation remained a force in parliamentary politics in the years before World War I. In the interwar years under the leadership of Louis Marin, it grew in eminence. In the 1930s perhaps 100 deputies of the 600 sitting in the Chamber belonged to the party. Marin's lifelong friend and fellow deputy from Meurthe-et-Moselle, François de Wendel, secretary-general of the Comité des

7. René Rémond, *L'Anticléricalisme en France de 1815 à nos jours* (Paris, 1976), 198; Malcolm Anderson, *Conservative Politics in France* (London, 1974), 36; P. Miquel, *Poincaré* (Paris, 1961), 171; William D. Irvine, *French Conservatism in Crisis: The Republican Federation of France in the 1930s* (Baton Rouge, 1979), 2.

8. The meeting and the talks were extensively reported in the *Journal des débats*, November 20, 1903. The three Opportunist groups that merged that evening were Méline's Républicains Progressistes, the parliamentary group of senators and deputies of the new Right persuasion; the Union Libérale Républicaine, founded during the Boulanger affair to better represent the interests of the anti-Boulanger grand bourgeoisie; and Ferry's own organization, the Association Nationale Républicaine (Irvine, *French Conservatism in Crisis*, 3).

9. The main ideological emphasis of Motte's speech at the meeting was the need, and the possibility, to close ranks against the socialists. He believed that it was possible to defeat them even where they were strong if like-minded men worked together, and he exhorted his listeners to look at the good results at Roubaix (*Journal des débats*, November 20, 1903).

Forges, exemplified the continuity of family and political interest in the ranks of the respectable right of the Third Republic.[10]

However, the moderate conservatism of the Opportunist heritage could not master the labor and political problems of the 1930s.[11] To stop the growth of the Left both at home and abroad the Republican Federation proved willing to establish good relations with the right-radical leagues and even abandoned its tradition of anti-German nationalism to support appeasement. The majority of its members welcomed Vichy.[12] The system of republican conservatism their spiritual and familial ancestors had created, and which had endured decades after the Opportunists and their successors lost control of the Chamber, broke down under the social stresses of the last years of the Republic.

However, on the level not of parliamentary politics but of socioeconomic power, with the possible exception of the government of the Popular Front, it is difficult to see where the preeminence of the republican Right was curbed or diminished during the life of the Third Republic. So formidable an alliance had the Opportunists fashioned, so powerful were the *positions acquises* by the sections of the republican Right that, like Méline, prominent neoconservatives could leave parliamentary politics and know that they could block actions or policies they did not want while entrusting the burden of government to a lower strata of new men.[13]

The republican order crafted in the late eighties and early nineties would ensure that the politicians would perpetrate no mischief upon the social hierarchy or the economy, however self-indulgently the Radicals harassed the Church. The outcome of the Dreyfus affair

10. Not only were the deputies of the Republican Federation drawn from the social and economic elite of France, in many cases they were from the same families—often aristocratic families—mentioned in earlier chapters of this study. See Irvine, *French Conservatism in Crisis*, 19–26, especially 19 n. 26.

11. André Siegfried, whose own family played a role in the fashioning of conservative republicanism, saw the Republican Federation as the fusion of what he termed the "industrial feudality," intransigent nationalism, and Catholic social defense (*Tableau des partis en France* (Paris, 1930), 182).

12. See Irvine, *French Conservatism in Crisis*, 98–126, 159–203, 204–30. For an example of a more direct line of connection to the radical right of the 1930s see Robert Soucy, *French Fascism: The First Wave, 1924–33* (New Haven, 1986), 96–104. Soucy has identified one of the principal financial supporters of Georges Valois' *Faisceau* as Eugène Mathon, president of the Association of Textile Manufacturers of Roubaix-Tourcoing.

13. Nicos Poulantzas, *Political Power and Social Classes* (London, 1978), 173–80.

confirmed the passing over of governing authority to the Radicals; and although it sorely tried the newly wrought republican conservatism, it did not destroy the ethos of conservative concentration. Having constructed the armature of republican social conservatism, the Opportunist republicans and their allies among the conservative notables passed on the governance of republican France to others. The Clemenceaus, the Briands, the Poincarés saw to it that in subsequent decades the conservative republic created by the older generation did not become the social republic of Jaurès' eloquent orations.

It was both the end of the Great Depression in 1896 and the completion of the new Right coalition with the Méline ministry that persuaded labor leaders and many socialist politicians that the social republic would not issue forth from the Chamber of Deputies. Thus, in the end, the Left's attempts to break out of the conservative circle during the Dreyfus struggle failed. Jaurès prevailed upon the working class to accept the Republic as its own, but the Opportunist-fashioned Republic made no place for the growing industrial working class. Escalating revolutionary rhetoric and labor militancy after 1900 were the workers' responses to the checkmate of reform and to their growing awareness of political isolation.

Whenever Georges Clemenceau needed the support of Catholic conservatives or parliamentary *Progressistes* for his hard line on labor, he could depend on them. Briand, too, could count on New Right toleration, and they in turn could depend on him. For in 1910 it was the Briand government that piloted through the Chamber sharply raised commercial duties. The new tariffs signaled as much as any public act could the adhesion of Radicals and Radical-Socialists to the new conservative union.

Poincaré, who in 1899 had broken with the Méline faction of the Opportunists because Méline's circle had gone too far toward clerical conservatism, in 1913 was pleased to accept the votes of these same clerical reactionaries in his successful bid for the presidency of the Republic. The patriotic coalition of the Union Sacrée called for by Poincaré to unite France in war should be understood as a continuation of the tradition of social pacification. Three socialist deputies broke their party's rule not to participate in bourgeois governments and took their places in the wartime coalition alongside old *Progressiste* politicians like Ribot and Jules Méline, who returned to head the ministry of agriculture for the last time.

Victory in 1918 strengthened the republican Right immensely. On the eve of the elections of November, 1919, the Opportunists overcame their hesitations to unite with the rest of the forces of social order and nationalism in the *Bloc National*. The resounding conservative triumph that yielded the *Chambre bleu horizon* continued to echo in the Republic's social policies of the interwar decades. The burden of leadership had passed from Ferry, de Mun, and Piou, first to Clemenceau, then to Millerand, Leygue, Briand, and Poincaré. But the conservative republic the "refounders" had created remained. Not until the Popular Front of 1936, and another great depression, did the Left threaten that conservatism.

But what the Opportunist republicans created persisted for the existence of the Third Republic and—it can be argued—into the early postwar years. In the work of these somber provincials from the North, the Vosges, and Lorraine, in the negotiations over duties on iron, cotton thread, and wheat, in the pious self-serving concern for the people on the land voiced at meetings of the Société des Agriculteurs de France, and in their general worries about the social question, we have observed individuals in the throes of creating a new social stratum. The evidence of their success is the inability of later governments—be it that of the Popular Front, Vichy, or François Mitterrand—to completely overthrow their work.

Appendix

The growth in the power and inclusiveness of the Association de l'Industrie Française and the expanded Association de l'Industrie et l'Agriculture Française may be seen in the lists of members of the executive committees at selected moments. The years 1878, 1892, 1893, 1898, 1909, and 1913 offer samples of the association's leadership. What follows are the names and affiliations of members of the executive committee who attended the general assembly in Paris in the years selected as reported in *L'Industrie française* and *Le Travail national*. The 1878 membership list was printed in *L'Industrie française*, March 21, 1878. Membership lists for 1892, 1893, 1898, 1909, and 1913 were printed in *Le Travail national*, February 28-March 6, 1892; June 18-23, 1893; March 6, 1898; April 11, 1909; May 25-June 15, 1913.

The officers and executive committee in 1878

PRESIDENT
> Alexandre Jullien, chairman of the board and director, Société des forges et fonderies de Terrenoire, la Voulte et Bessèges

VICE-PRESIDENTS
> Adolph Japy, Japy Frères, Baucourt, hardware, clockmakers
> Arthur Joly de Bammeville, spinner and weaver; director, Houillères de l'Aveyron
> J.-B. Martelet, managing director, Forges de Denain et d'Anzin
> J. Mignon, director, Société de constructions navales du Havre
> Félix Moreaux, managing director, Compagnie de Fives-Lilles
> Arthur Petitdidier, Société d'armements maritimes
> Charles Saint, Saint Frères, cloth manufacturers
> Emile Vuillemin, chairman, Comité de houillères du Nord et du Pas-de-Calais

SECRETARIES

Sampson Jordan, director, Compagnie des hauts-fourneaux de Marseille

Paul Schneider, director, Houillères de l'Aveyron

Emile Widmer, director, silk floss spinning mills at Essonnes and Amilly

TREASURER

Trouillier, David, Trouillier et Adhemar, Epinal and Saint-Quentin

MEMBERS OF THE EXECUTIVE COMMITTEE

Paul Aclocque, former deputy; managing director, Société des forges de l'Ariège

Bichon, shipbuilder, Lormont-Bordeaux

Maurice Blin, cloth manufacturer, Elbeuf

Anselme-Henri Bocquet, jute spinner, Bocuet, Carmichael, Dewailly et Cie, Ailly-sur-Somme

Amédée Burat, engineer, Compagnie des mines de Blanzy

Cabrol, spinner and weaver, Flers

Albert Courant, spinner and weaver, Le Havre

Paul-Ferdinand Delaville le Roulx, managing director, Compagnie des mines de Grand-Combe

Alfred Desalle, spinner, Madeleine-lès-Lille

Alfred Dupont, former deputy; vice-chairman, Comité des Houillères du Nord et du Pas-de-Calais

Augustin Farcot, machine builder, Saint-Ouen

Jules Favre, spinner, Epinal

Alphonse Fould, Dupont et Fould, maîtres de forges, Pompey, Meurthe-et-Moselle

Gargan, president, Chambre syndicale des mécaniciens, chaudronniers et fondeurs de Paris

Alphonse Grimault, Mignon, Rouart, et Delinières, iron pipe, Paris

Emile Japy, Japy-Marti-Roux, clockmakers

Charles Laedrich, spinner, Epinal

Emile Magnier, Comptoir de l'industrie linière, Paris and Lille

François Marral, Marral Frères, maîtres de forges, Rive-de-Gier

Alfred Ponnier, Vincent Ponnier et Cie, Senones, Vosges

Honoré Reverchon, former deputy; director, Companie des forges d'Audincourt

Henri Schneider, manager-director, Usines du Creusot

Sessevalle, director, Société anonyme de Commentry-Four-chambault

Jean Vignal, chairman of the board, Société des Chargeurs réunis

*Members of the executive committee who attended
the general assembly held on February 25, 1892*

PRESIDENT
Paul Aclocque

VICE-PRESIDENT
de la Germonière, vice-president, Société des Agriculteurs de France

EXECUTIVE SECRETARY
Armand Pihoret

MEMBERS OF THE EXECUTIVE COMMITTEE PRESENT
Cabrol, spinner and weaver, Flers
Carmichaël, spinner and weaver of jute
Deblock, linen manufacturer, Lille
Ed. Faucheur, president of the Comité linier, Lille
Jordan, engineer; professor at the Ecole centrale
Laederich, spinner and weaver; member, Epinal chamber of commerce
E. Lahaye, Comptoir métallurgique de Longwy
Ernest Manchon, manufacturer; secretary, Rouen chamber of commerce
Ponnier, spinner and weaver
René Jourdain, director, Saint-Quentin à Guise Railroad
Reverchon, former deputy; president, Syndicat des maîtres de forges de Comté
Simon, engineer
Thiriez, president, Comité cotonnier du Nord
Tréves, manufacturer
Widmer, silk floss spinner
Marc de Haut and Boucher d'Argis, sitting with the executive committee as representatives of the Société des Agriculteurs de France

*Members of the executive committee who attended the extraordinary
general assembly held on June 14, 1893, upon the death of Paul Aclocque
and the elevation of Jules Méline to the presidency of the association*

PRESIDENT
  Jules Méline
VICE-PRESIDENTS
  Julien Le Blan, president, Lille chamber of commerce
  de la Germonière, vice-president, Société des Agriculteurs de
    France
  Charles Saint, Saint Frères, cloth manufacturers
  Sébline, senator
SECRETARY
  Widmer, Feray and Cie of Essonnes
TREASURER
  Trouillier, David, Trouillier, et Adhémar
EXECUTIVE SECRETARY
  Euverte
MEMBERS OF THE EXECUTIVE COMMITTEE
  Philippe Bazin, spinner, Condé-sur-Noireau
  Comte Lionel de Bondy, president, Société anonyme des chan-
    tiers et ateliers de la Gironde
  Carmichaël, spinner and weaver of jute
  Cocquel, manufacturer, Amiens
  Deblock, linen manufacturer, Lille
  Gustave Denis, spinner; president, Syndicat cotonnier du Sud-
    Ouest
  Ed. Faucheur, linen spinner; president, Comité linier de Lille
  A. Grimault, Chambre syndicale des mécaniciens, chaudron-
    niers, fondeurs
  E. Lahaye, Comptoir métallurgique de Longwy in Paris
  Magnier, Comptoir de l'industrie de linière at Paris
  Ernest Manchon, manufacturer; vice-president, Rouen chamber
    of commerce
  Baron Robert de Nervo, president, Société anonyme des forges et
    aciéries de Denain et d'Anzin
  Auguste Pinel, spinner, Petit-Quévilly-les-Rouen
  Alfred Ponnier, Vincent, Ponnier et Cie, spinners and weavers,
    Senones
  Baron Reille, president, Comité des Forges de France
  René Jourdain, managing director, Saint-Quentin à Guise Railroad
  Simon, engineer, Paris
  Augustin Thouroude, businessman; president, Comité commer-
    cial et industriel de la Seine-Inférieure et de l'Eure

E. Touron, spinner, Saint-Quentin

Albert Trèves, manufacturer of embroidery

Yver, manager, Société anonyme des filateurs et tissages Pouyer-Quertier, Rouen

ALSO SITTING WITH THE MEMBERS OF THE EXECUTIVE COMMITTEE

Jules Domergue, editor, *Réforme économique*

Charles Georgeot, secretary to the executive committee

Members of the executive committee of the Association de l'Industrie et de l'Agriculture Française who attended the general assembly on March 2, 1898

PRESIDENT

M. Sébline, senator from the Aisne (absent because of indisposition)

VICE-PRESIDENT

Comte de Saint-Quentin, deputy from Calvados; president of the section agricole of the executive committee (presiding)

EXECUTIVE SECRETARY

Emile Joubert

TREASURER

Ponnier, Vincent, Ponnier et Cie, Senones

EXECUTIVE COMMITTEE

Gustave Denis, senator

Fourgeirol, senator

Ancel-Seitz, manufacturer, Granges, Vosges

Comte Lionel de Bondy, president, Société anonyme des chantiers et ateliers de la Gironde

J. Bénard, president, Société d'agriculture de Meaux

Carmichaël, spinner and weaver of jute

Cocquel, manufacturer, Amiens

Deblock, linen manufacturer, Lille

Faucheur, president, Comité linier; vice-president, Lille chamber of commerce

Gautreau, president, Chambre syndicale des constructeurs d'appeils de machines agricoles

Hélot, member, Cambrai chamber of commerce

René Jourdain, managing director, Saint-Quentin à Guise Railroad; departmental inspector of technical education

de Lagorsse, secretary-general, Société Nationale d'Encouragement à l'Agriculture

Jouët-Pastre, president, Société anonyme des forges et Chantiers de la Méditerranée.

Keittinger, member, Rouen chamber of commerce

Georges Lemaître, Albert Manchon, Lemaître et Cie, spinners, Bolbec

Lôthelain, president, comice agricole de Reims

Muret, Société des Agriculteurs de France

Petit, president, comice agricole de Seine-et-Oise

Edmond-Richard, silk manufacturer of Lyon

Henry Sagnier, Conseil Supérieur de l'Agriculture

Tétard, president, Syndicat des fabricants de sucre

Tréves, manufacturer

Touron, member, Saint-Quentin chamber of commerce

Widmer, former manufacturer, Paris

Yver, manager, Société anonyme des filateurs et tissages Pouyer-Quertier, Rouen

Paul Pion, president, Elbeuf chamber of commerce

etc. [*sic*]

*Members of the executive committee of the Association de l'Industrie
et de l'Agriculture Française who attended the general assembly
on March 10, 1909, held on the eve of the passage of the elevated
tariffs of 1910*

PRESIDENT

Jules Méline, senator; former president of the council of ministers and minister of agriculture

VICE-PRESIDENT

J. Bénard, grower; regent of the Bank of France

Comte de Saint-Quentin, senator

Carmichaël

TREASURER

Henri Ponnier

SECRETARY

P. Ancel-Seitiz, former deputy, manufacturer

EXECUTIVE SECRETARY

Charles Renard

ON THE PLATFORM

Touron, senator

Richard Waddington, senator

Gustave Denis, former senator

Faucheur, president, Lille chamber of commerce

EXECUTIVE COMMITTEE

E. Bechmann, manufacturer, Blamont

Casimir Berger, president, Syndicat général de l'industrie cotonnière française

Bessonneau, père; manufacturer, Angers

A. Bouchon, sugar manufacturer, Nassandres

J. Cabrol, spinner, Flers

A. Dauphin, manufacturer, Amiens

J. Domergue, editor, *La Réforme économique*

Dreux, director, Aciéries de Longwy

A. Duhem, manufacturer, Lille

Albert Esnault-Pelterie, president, Association cotonnière coloniale

Léon Fremaux, president, Armentières chamber of commerce

Genin, president, Association de la soierie lyonnaise

Prosper Gervais, vice-president, Société des Viticulteurs de France

P. Guéneau, silk manufacturer, Lyon

Louis Guérin, manager, Comptoir de l'industrie linière, Lille

Guillain, deputy; president, Comité des Forges de France

Jules Hélot, sugar manufacturer; vice-president, Cambrai chamber of commerce

Juillard-Hartmann, president, Syndicat cotonnier de l'Est, Epinal

Paul Labbé, maitre de forges, Gorcy

René Laederich, manufacturer, Epinal

Julien Le Blan, president, Syndicat des filateurs et retordeurs de coton de Lille

Georges Lemaître, president, Bolbec chamber of commerce

Maurice Lemarchand, manufacturer, Rouen

Georges Leverdier, vice-president, Rouen chamber of commerce

Charles Marteau, manager, Société des tissus de laine des Vosges à Reims

Henri Petit, president, Syndicat agricole de Seine-et-Oise

Ed. Pinot, manufacturer, Rupt-sur-Moselle

Robert Pinot, secretary-general, Union des Industries métallurgique et minières, Paris

Alfred Ponnier, honorary treasurer of the association

Léopold Pralon, chairman of the board, Société anonyme des hauts fourneaux, forges et aciéries de Denain et Anzin

Edmond-Richard, silk manufacturer, Lyon

Henry Sagnier, editor, *Journal de l'agriculture*; secretary of the Association

Albert Treves, manufacturer, Paris; secretary of the Association

Arthur Waddington, president, Syndicat Normand du tissage de coton, Rouen

Joseph Wibaux, chairman of the board, Wibaux-Florin, Roubaix

Charles Georgeot, editor, *Le Travail national*; secretary to the executive committee

Members of the executive committee of the Association de l'Industrie et de l'Agriculture Française who attended the general assembly on May 19, 1913

PRESIDENT

Eugène Touron, vice-president of the Senate

FORMER PRESIDENT

Jules Méline

WITH THEM ON THE PLATFORM

A. Dreux and L. Pralon, vice-presidents, Comité des Forges

R.S. Carmichaël, president, Union Textile

J. Bénard and R. Laederich, regents of the Bank of France

H. Ponnier, treasurer of the association

E. Faucheur, president, Lille chamber of commerce

Gustave Denis, former senator; president, Laval chamber of commerce

C. Berger, president, Syndicat général cotonnier

A. Esnault-Pelterie, president, Association cotonnière coloniale

Juillard-Hartmann, president, Syndicat cotonnier de l'Est

Charles Grosclaude, administrative secretary of the Association

EXECUTIVE COMMITTEE

P. Ancel-Seitz, former deputy; president, Caisse d'assurance accident de l'industrie textile

R. Barbet-Massin, manufacturer, Paris

D. Chedville, honorary vice-president, Elbeuf chamber of commerce

A. Dauphin, manufacturer, Amiens

Digonnet, former president, Association de la soierie lyonnaise, Lyon

Domergue, editor, *La Réforme économique*

Marcel Dubois, professor at the Sorbonne

A. Duhem, vice-president, Lille chamber of commerce

Léon Frémaux, president, Armentières chamber of commerce

P. Fraenckel, president, Elbeuf chamber of commerce

H. Génin, silk manufacturer, Lyon

Louis Guérin, manager, Comptoir de l'industrie linière, Lille

De Lagorsse, secretary-general, Société d'Encouragement à l'Agriculture, Paris

E. Lahaye, engineer, Paris

Jules Legas, sugar manufacturer, Besny and Loizy

Georges Lemaître, president, Bolbec chamber of commerce

Maurice Lemarchand, president, Syndicat Normand du tissage de coton, Rouen

Georges Leverdier, vice-president, Rouen chamber of commerce

Charles Marteau, chairman of the board, Société des tissus de laine des Vosges, Reims

Baron Léon de Nervo, chairman of the board, Compagnie de Mokta-el-Hadid, Paris

Robert Pinot, secretary-general, Comité des Forges

Edouard Pinot, spinner, Rupt-sur-Moselle, Vosges

Henry Sagnier, editor, *L'Agriculture pratique*

Albert Trèves, manufacturer, Paris

Comte de Vogüé, vice-president, Société des Agriculteurs de France

Arthur Waddington, manufacturer, Lille

Maurice Wallaert, manufacturer, Lille

Joseph Wibaux, chairman of the board, Etablissement Wibaux-Florin, Roubaix

Henri Widmer, director, electrical sector of the Place Clichy

Bibliographical Note

Because this study has focused on the worries, fears, hopes, and unspoken arrangements of strata of the French elite in the last decades of the nineteenth century, the problem of sources loomed large. I consulted what archives, memoir literature, government inquiries, correspondence, newspapers, organizational publications, and contemporary fiction promised to supply for evidence on the arguments I advanced. The notes to the chapters contain specific references. In this essay I shall review the major sources used in the writing of this book in the course of commenting on a number of the historiographical issues raised herein. The note is organized into three sections. The first is a comment on the issue of the fragility of societies at moments of major political transformation and the beginnings of new conservatisms. The second is a discussion of the role of tariffs as occasions and as means for societies to define themselves in the present and for the future. The third section reviews those aspects of the historiography of the Third Republic appropriate to this inquiry into the *problématique* of creating a ruling authority in one of the new political entities arising in late-nineteenth-century Europe.

Theoretical Works on Conservatism

This study has explored the analytical fissure between those theorists who follow in the tradition of Thomas Hobbes in posing as their first question, how do societies hold together? and those, who, in the manner of Marx, stipulate a degree of (coerced) social order but ask how social change occurs. By examining the coming to life of a new sociopolitical order in a concrete historical setting, this study has attempted to clarify some of the issues of a great, and too often rather abstract, debate. The search for a new order in the Third

Republic engendered some of the divisive social tensions the new leaders of the state so feared, while at the same time that fear of disorder from below assisted their efforts to forge a viable governing system. We have observed how an aspiring new conservative leadership fashioned strategies of republican defense in late-nineteenth-century France. And we have seen something of how a coalition of classes and remnants of classes—for France, a new ruling stratum—made itself.

Because fear of social disorder is so deeply rooted in the conservative world view, conservative analysts of social relations have written most usefully on the fragility of social structures in transition. W. W. Rostow's *The Stages of Economic Growth: A Non-Communist Manifesto* (London, 1960), despite its flaws, was quite astute in focusing on those moments of transition in the economic development of nations when their political order is most at risk. Samuel Huntington, *Political Order in Changing Societies* (New Haven, 1968) has contemplated the risks to order from social change in a more sophisticated manner than Rostow. That these are not merely academic questions may be evidenced by the fact that in the 1960s the insights of both authors informed American foreign policy in interventions in the internal politics of developing nations. For an attempt to take a middling way, I recommend Barrington Moore, Jr., *The Social Origins of Dictatorship and Democracy: Lord and Peasant in the Making of the Modern World* (Boston, 1966), the great modern work of American liberal sociology addressing itself to the issues of persistence and change in political structures. Moore, however, is overly deterministic about the long-range effects of the French Revolution; France underwent many deep changes in the nineteenth century not predetermined by the events of the Revolution. On the left, Nicos Poulantzas, *Political Power and Social Classes* (London, 1978) offers an Althusserian formulation of the question of the origin of stability in Western societies. Although his brief remarks on France are erroneous and unhistorical, his adaptation of the Gramscian idea of a power bloc has illuminated this study.

This power bloc was nothing less than a new republican conservatism. A major argument of this study has been how important the formation of the new Right ruling bloc was for the stabilization of the republican political order. In this I differ from both the masterful synthesis Stanley Hoffmann contributed to *In Search of France*, "Paradoxes of the French Political Community," (New York, 1963), 1–117, and the argument of Michel Crozier in *La Société bloquée* (Paris, 1970). Hoffmann focuses on the cumulative effects of *positions acquises* in immobilizing the society of the Third Republic and excluding the working class from public life. Crozier faults the French style of bureaucratic management for creating the stalemate, or "stalled society." I have argued in this book that much of the stalemate was a consequence of the deliberate efforts of Opportunist republicans and former monarchists to craft a new conservative coalition devised to structure a society safe for rank, wealth, and aristocratic family heritage. René Rémond, *Les Droites en France* (4th ed.; Paris, 1982), neglects this most durable of French conservatisms. See the fine studies collected in David Shapiro (ed.), *The Right in France, 1890–1919* (London, 1962), especially Shapiro's essay on the sociology of the Ralliement. For a useful theoretical work on the persistence of aristocratic influence in the so-called bourgeois era, see Karl Brinkmann, "Die Aristokratie im kapitalistischen Zeitalter," *Grundriss der Sozialökonomik*, IX (1926).

My debt to the socioeconomic historians of imperial Germany should be clear from what I have said in this essay and from the notes to the preface and introduction. The school around Hans Rosenberg and Hans-Ulrich Wehler has gone farthest toward integrating the findings of sociopolitical history with those of economic history. Their work on the political consequences of the Great Depression of 1873–1896 has been extremely helpful. Basic to any study of the Great Depression's workings on the internal politics of a European nation is Hans Rosenberg, *Grosse Depression und Bismarckzeit: Wirtschaftsablauf, Gesellschaft und Politik in Mitteleuropa* (Berlin, 1967). Rosenberg has influenced a whole generation of German historians who found valuable his systematic analysis of the depression as a means of making sense of an extremely complex era. Joseph Schumpeter's rich and idiosyncratic *Business Cycles* (2 vols.; New York, 1939) began the modern study of the interconnection of economic cycles and the sociopolitical life of a nation. He influenced Rosenberg and his school greatly and, as a technically proficient economist, managed to avoid the economic determinism that blemishes some of the work done in the Rosenberg tradition. I have adopted with great profit aspects of the Schumpeter-Rosenberg-Wehler approach to the study of France in the same period.

We do not have anything comparable for France in the years of the Great Depression. In the section of Chapter I on the economics of the Great Depression, I have offered the information and theory necesssary for this study, but these few pages are at best just a prolegomenon to a larger effort in the future. We have the beginnings in Jacques Néré, "La Crise industrielle de 1882 et le mouvement boulangiste" (Dissertation, University of Paris, 1959); Néré, *Le Boulangisme et la presse* (Paris, 1964); and Néré, "The French Republic," Chapter XI of the *New Cambridge Modern History*, XI (Cambridge, England, 1962). Our current state of knowledge is pulled together in the appropriate volumes of the excellent *Histoire économique et sociale de la France* under the general editorship of Fernand Braudel and Ernest Labrousse (8 vols.; Paris, 1977–82). Volumes III and IV were most helpful for this study.

Finally, the discipline Rudolf Goldscheid named "*Sozialökomik*" in the last years of the Weimar Republic very much bears on this investigation. Goldscheid was concerned with investigating the social-power implications of state fiscal policies. See, for example, his *Steuerwendung und Interessenpolitik* (Munich, 1928). My concern has been the sociopolitical function of struggles over tariffs and the social implications of the outcomes. When they debated free trade versus protectionism, French intellectuals, politicians, and businessmen were in a sense debating what sort of society they desired and who should head it. German intellectuals and policy makers passionately debated the merits and the dangers of the development of an *Industriestaat* versus continuing as an *Agrarstaat* on the occasion of the struggle over the passage of the Bülow tariff in 1903, just as the French were in the tariff debates of the 1880s and those culminating in the passage of the Méline tariff. See my study of the German case in "'Agrarians' versus 'Industrializers': Social Conservative Resistance to Industrialism and Capitalism in Late Nineteenth Century Germany," *International Review of Social History*, XII (1967), 31–65. Of course, the question of who should rule Germany in the face of economic dangers and a growing social democratic movement was decidedly a parallel of the French debate, too.

The Role of Tariffs in French History

For France we are fortunate to have two good studies of the wider meaning of tariff debates and policies late in the century: Eugene Golob, *The Méline Tariff* (New York, 1944) and Michael S. Smith, *Tariff Reform in France, 1860–1900: The Politics of Economic Interest* (Ithaca, 1980). Whereas Golob subscribes to the simplistic idea that agrarian nostalgia fueled the pro-tariff struggles in the late century—and neglects the prime role of the most modern of the industries and industrialists—Smith concentrates almost completely on the struggle between protectionist and free trade industrialists over future commercial policy. I have indicated in my text and footnotes the ways I differ from Smith, but I am most grateful for the work he has done to define the economic interests with respect to the tariffs. Smith's book is now the best recourse for the reader interested in detailed information on the stand of various business interests on the tariffs. I concur with his argument that one sees here a new governing arrangement for the Republic emerging from the struggles over what seems simply commercial policy. Jürgen Hilsheimer, "Interessengruppen und Zollpolitik in Frankreich: Die Auseinandersetzungen um die Aufstellung des Zolltarifs von 1892" (Dissertation, University of Heidelberg, 1973), adds little new to previous work, and his work suffers from attempting to apply an American-style pressure-group scheme to the story of more weighty events than such a theory can support.

Not directly pertinent to tariffs in the narrow sense but directly touching the socioeconomic arguments of my study is William M. Reddy, *The Rise of Market Culture: The French Textile Trade and French Society, 1750–1900* (Cambridge, England, 1984), 248–50, which Reddy offers as a study in reinterpreting French labor radicalism as a non-accommodation, indeed rejection, of the "rules of the market game" (p. 252). Reddy is correct in emphasizing that we must understand that the factory and the mill town are much more than market places for a reified commodity labeled "labor." However, for the case of Roubaix, which we both address, there is evidence against his historical argument. The reader is referred to the study of Robert Pierreuse, "L'Ouvrier roubaisien de 1890 à 1900," *Revue du Nord*, LI (1969), 249–73, wherein he argues that, for at least the last decade of the century, it proved impossible to mobilize the workers of Roubaix around any issues but increased pay and the length of the work day. This reading of the labor history of Roubaix probably goes too far in the other direction. A major theme of my study is that the textile owners themselves, finally, also found the market game destructive to the maintenance of their noneconomic values, both with respect to their families' standing and to their public authority. That is why they wished to thwart the workings of the market by means of tariff protection. Moreover, it is true that the culture of the market is a social artifact that can be made to yield its secrets to the kind of insightful anthropological questioning Reddy undertakes in this book. It is also true that in our culture, the culture of Western capitalism, the enhancement of the economic position of workers has been, and to a large degree still is, seen as the key to bringing about changes in qualitative issues of personal freedom, health, family life, and even an individual's sense of self. Perhaps cultural anthropology, a field suffering its own serious problems of defining its object and its methods, is not the best guide for historians of a modern, urbanized, literate Europe.

Important Sources

What follows are the major archival and published sources upon which this study is based. At the end I will note some of the most valuable secondary treatments. The notes to the various chapters provide more precise guidance on the important literature on individual topics.

Primary Sources. Because of the national focus of the study, the Archives Nationales provided most of the archival material of value. There I consulted the holdings of the Ministry of Commerce and Agriculture, which was divided into two ministries in 1882. The dossiers on industry in these F^{12} series were much more abundant than those on agriculture. The C series, the legislative archives, offered much help too, especially the minutes of the various commissions that deliberated over tariff or banking questions. The dossiers on the Enquête parlementaire sur la crise économique et sur la situation industrielle, commerciale et agricole en France, 1884 (C^{3329}) underpinned much of the argument of Chapter II. The series 27 AS contained the records of the Association de l'Industrie Française; however, their published materials proved both more interesting and more instructive. The Guesde Papers housed in the archives of the Internationaal Instituut voor Sociale Geschiedenis in Amsterdam supplied material on the Parti Ouvrier's search for an agrarian program. Especially useful were the replies from the party's questionnaire discussed in Chapter IV. One can often glean something of the spirit of a past mode of life by visiting former centers of that existence. A visit to Remiremont in the Vosges, Jules Méline's home, not far from the homes of Jules Ferry and Nicolas Claude, gave me a sense of the life of the provincial bourgeoisie of the region. Conversations with members of the Société des Amis de Jules Méline gave me some useful guidance for my research.

In the case of the published primary materials, *Le Travail national* and *La République française*, organs of Méline and the protectionists, were very useful. The *Echo du Nord* sometimes contained material valuable for this study. The *Journal Officiel* was indispensable for studying the interpenetration of ideology and policy. Moreover, the *Bulletin de la Société des agriculteurs de France* provided an entry into the public discourse of the aristocratic growers. Finally, correspondence of important contemporaries illuminated and guided this work. In particular Paul Cambon, *Correspondance, 1870–1924* (3 vols.; Paris, 1940), and Friedrich Engels, Paul and Laura Lafargue, *Correspondance*, ed. Emile Bottigelli (3 vols.; Paris, 1959), supplied valuable insights into the thinking of some of the important actors in the contemporary drama.

Secondary Works. The secondary sources most appropriate to each section are given in the notes. A number of titles deserve special mention. Jean Bouvier has investigated the relation between economic cycles and labor militancy in a pioneering article, "Mouvement ouvrier et conjunctures économiques," *Mouvement social*, XLVIII (1964), 3–28. Pierre Sorlin's masterful study of the life and politics of Waldeck-Rousseau, *Waldeck-Rousseau* (Paris, 1966) deserves careful reading, as does Michelle Perrot, *Les Ouvriers en grève: France 1871-1890* (2 vols.; Paris, 1973). Perrot can make cliometrics passionate. On the Parti Ouvrier, see the comprehensive study by Claude Willard, *Les Guesdistes: les Mouvement socialiste en France, 1893–1905* (Paris, 1965). Of the many studies of the republic a recent one should prove valuable as a starting point both because of its argument and its bibliography: Odile Rudelle, *La République absolue, aux origines de l'instabilité constitutionnelle de la France républicaine, 1870–1889* (Paris, 1982). Finally, see the appropriate volumes of the *Nouvelle histoire de la France contemporaine* put out by the Editions du Seuil. Volume X, Jean-Marie Mayeur, *Les Débuts de la Troisième République, 1871–1898*, is adequate. Volume XI, Madeleine Rebérioux, *La République radicale? 1899–1914* is excellent.

From the point of view of method, I have tried to influence my colleagues in two ways. One contribution of this study, hopefully, shall be to highlight the importance of initiatives that failed, of actions undertaken from misdirected motives, of misunderstood motives, and of misanalyzed situations. Here I have attempted to combat the naïve Hegelianism with its teleological visions of the human enterprise that sometimes influences the work of Marxist and non-Marxist historians alike. I have tried, too, to foster a comparative view of European history. If this study encourages more comparative studies of the late nineteenth century, it will have made what I consider a signal contribution to the study of European, and therefore French, history.

Index

Aclocque, Paul, 90, 125–26, 125*n*
Africa, 150, 151
Ageron, Charles-Robert, 144*n*, 155
Agricultural goods: tariff protection for, 36, 67–68, 82, 85, 85*n*, 121–22, 144, 182; prices of, 39, 43, 84, 167; relationship to manufactured goods, 39–41, 42; value of, 49; sales taxes on, 75; exports to colonial empire, 87
Agricultural workers. *See* Peasants; Syndicats agricoles
Agriculturalists: support for tariffs, 24, 36, 49–50, 70; alliance with industrialists, 41, 49–50, 72–78, 77*n*, 81–82, 85; proponents for, 49; during Great Depression, 52; problems of, 72, 101; loyalty to monarchism, 76; aristocracy as, 78–80; land ownership of, 80; financial ventures of, 101–102; specialization of, 105–106; and woodcutters' strikes, 112; and syndicats agricoles, 115–16; organizations for, 117–19; conservatism of, 172; capitalism of, 173; Méline's reforms for, 180–83
Algeria, 86, 144–45, 150, 153
Allier, 104, 109
Alsace, 11, 14, 14*n*
Amiens, 11, 95
Anarchists, 34–35, 87, 117, 117*n*, 127–28, 162*n*
Aristocracy: 22*n*, 47–48, 78–80, 78–79*n*, 82*n*, 101–102, 141, 141*n*, 190*n*
Association de l'Industrie et de l'Agriculture Française, 120, 124–28, 148*n*, 154, 161*n*, 177, 180*n*, 197–201

Association de l'Industrie Française: political participation of members, 27; analysis of Great Depression, 44; leadership of, 58*n*, 126, 136, 193–97; strikes and, 63, 64; support for tariff, 64–65, 90, 108, 145; founding of, 71; cooperation with agriculturists, 82, 85, 120, 124–28; and colonial empire, 86, 86*n*, 145, 146; support for, 89; membership of, 96, 137; position on working conditions, 125*n*; Catholic membership of, 137
Association pour la Défense du Travail National, 57
Aubry, Emile, 13, 14*n*, 15, 66
Augé-Laribé, Michel, 172*n*, 174
Austria-Hungary, 47*n*, 54, 68, 159, 175

Baker, Robert P., 14*n*
Bank of France, 168–71, 174–75, 179
Banking: relationship with industrialists, 27; profit declines, 51; view on free trade, 54, 179*n*; colonial ventures, 141; Lyon, 153; and rural credit, 165–69, 179; socialists' support for national bank, 171; foreign stocks and bonds, 168–69, 168*n*, 175–80. *See also* Bank of France; Rural credit
Barral, Pierre, 102*n*
Baudin, Eugène, 109
Belgium, 14*n*, 53, 68, 152
Bernstein, Eduard, 43*n*
Béthune, 95, 137
Billot, General, 161*n*, 182
Bismarck, Otto von, 16, 17, 22, 29*n*, 30–31, 45*n*, 48, 60, 131, 175*n*